TRUMPING RELIGION

Trumping Religion

The New Christian Right, the Free Speech Clause, and the Courts

STEVEN P. BROWN

THE UNIVERSITY OF ALABAMA PRESS

Tuscaloosa and London

Typeface is AGaramond

∞

The paper on which this book is printed meets the minimum requirements of
American National Standard for Information Science-Permanence of Paper for
Printed Library Materials, ANSI Z39.48-1984.

Cataloging-in-Publication Data

Brown, Steven Preston.
Trumping religion : the new Christian right, the free speech clause, and the courts /
Steven P. Brown.
p.   cm.
Includes bibliographical references and index.
ISBN 0-8173-1178-5 (cloth : alk. paper)
1. Church and state—United States. 2. Freedom of religion—United States.
3. Christianity and politics—United States. I. Title.
KF4865 .B76 2002
342.73′0852—dc21

2002003838

Contents

Acknowledgments

The subject of this book grew out of a passing remark by David M. O'Brien who stated during my first year of graduate study at the University of Virginia, "Someone ought to write about the Christian Right in the courts." There were many angles to that challenge that I might have pursued but having long been interested in the relationship between church and state, I decided to focus on the religion cases litigated by New Christian Right organizations. I was generally acquainted with the political activities of conservative Christian groups during the 1980s and early 1990s as a result of the ongoing abortion debate, the introduction of "family values" into the American political lexicon, the 1988 and 1992 presidential elections, and the confirmation hearings of Supreme Court Justices David Souter and Clarence Thomas. But I knew nothing of the organized efforts of the New Christian Right in the courts. I was (and continue to be) fascinated by the judicial branch activities of the New Christian Right where religion is concerned and I remain extremely grateful to Professor O'Brien's aside comment. More important, I appreciate the guidance, advice, and friendship he has provided since that time. His influence on me both professionally and personally is incalculable.

I am similarly indebted to Professors Henry J. Abraham, Glenn Beamer, A. E. Dick Howard, and James Sterling Young. Although they each devoted time and effort to the original incarnation of this work, it was their scholarship, enthusiasm, and teaching that had the greatest impact. I long ago relinquished any desire to develop my "own style" in hopes that I might somehow, someday be a composite of each of these men instead.

The research associated with this project afforded me the opportunity to meet with and interview Alan Sears of the Alliance Defense Fund, John Stepanovich of the American Center for Law and Justice, Steven McFarland of the Center for Law and Religious Freedom, and Rita Woltz with the Rutherford Institute. In each instance, they were courteous, forthright, and more than willing to answer my questions. I was impressed by both their professionalism and their dedication and count it my good fortune to have made their acquaintance. I am very grateful to these individuals and others associated with their organizations for their cooperation in granting my interview and research requests.

Of course, while all of the above individuals in some way helped shape this work, I alone am responsible for any errors or shortcomings.

My colleagues at Auburn University have been great from the beginning. While I have always appreciated their friendship, their interest in and support for my work has helped me in ways they will never know. Similarly, I have been rewarded immensely in my association with the students enrolled in my constitutional law classes at Auburn. The transformation from their being rather detached observers to serious students of the legal, social, and political influence of the constitutional law cases we study is something I am privileged to witness every semester.

The University of Alabama Press has not only been supportive but has helped me along every step of the way. I am especially grateful for former press director Nicole Mitchell, who expressed interest in the project when I mentioned it in an aside comment of my own. The suggestions made by the reviewers of the original manuscript contributed significantly to this final product and I appreciate their input. I also appreciate the assistance and advice of Jennifer Backer, who has been an extraordinary copyeditor.

On a personal note, I would like to thank my wife Melanie and my children for their love and support. Life being what it is, other considerations often threaten to bump them from the top of my priority list. Fortunately for me, however, not a day goes by without my being reminded of the truly important things in life. Finally, I would like to express my appreciation for my parents, whose example of service, sacrifice, and commitment from Peoa to Bangalore now spans continents.

TRUMPING RELIGION

1 The Bible and the Bench

An Introduction to New Christian Right Activism in the Courts

Because so many people find the gospel annoying, those in powerful positions have no qualms about making evangelism illegal because it strikes them as rude and obnoxious. Consequently, it's become increasingly difficult for Christians to share that message with the freedom they have traditionally had. . . . [I]t is clear that there is much work to be done in ensuring that the First Amendment rights of Christians are protected at home, at school, in the workplace, and in the public arena.

> Jay Alan Sekulow, chief counsel,
> American Center for Law and Justice, 2000

"1996 will be a pivotal year for your country, your community and your family. Now more than ever Christians need to act out their faith in the public arena."[1] With that call to action, Coral Ridge Ministries summoned concerned Christians to Fort Lauderdale, Florida, to take part in its annual Reclaiming America for Christ conference. The convention promised participants a diverse assortment of workshops, including "What Politicians Really Think about the 'Religious Right,'" "How to Get Involved in Elective Politics and Win," "Why Public Education Threatens Religious Liberty," and "Why Today's Supreme Court Is at Odds with the Founding Fathers."[2] After touting the expected presence of several noted conservative leaders, the 1996 conference brochure concluded with this reflection: "For more than thirty years, America has undergone a sustained and wide-ranging attack on the godly foundation which made our nation a well-ordered bastion of liberty, peace, and prosperity. That attack is finally meeting resistance. More and more Christians are awakening to their duty to defend faith and freedom in an increasingly hostile, secular society. Now more than ever, they have discovered the need to reclaim America."[3]

Although the Coral Ridge convention annually attracts thousands of community and university Christian activists, its "reclaim America" theme has become something of a rallying cry for a much broader social and political movement popularly known as the "Religious Right," "Christian Right," or, as used here, "New Christian Right."[4] Coming to prominence in the late 1970s after decades of largely self-imposed political exile, conservative Christian activism has engendered public controversy like few other special interest movements organized during the past quarter century.

Although a concrete definition of the New Christian Right remains elusive, the movement is strongly rooted in the conservative evangelical Protestant tradition. Evangelical Protestantism is highly decentralized, embracing not only large denominations, such as the Southern Baptist Convention, but also thousands of independent Baptist, Reformed, Pentecostal, Churches of Christ, and nondenominational evangelical churches, among others. Those within this diffuse grouping affirm the inerrancy of the Bible, the divinity of Jesus Christ, the need for personal conversion, and the necessity of religious activism or "witnessing" to bring about the conversion of others.

Geographically, evangelical Protestantism remains strongest in the southeastern United States, but more than one-quarter of all Americans belong to evangelical churches, making that religious tradition the largest in the nation with slightly more adherents than either mainline Protestantism or Roman Catholicism.[5] Perhaps more important, in the last thirty years the number of Americans belonging to evangelical Protestant churches has increased while the membership of most other denominations has declined.[6]

As a whole, evangelical Protestants tend to be much more religiously committed to weekly and daily religious practices than those associated with other religious traditions.[7] By linking their political and social activism to moral values, New Christian Right organizations are able to take advantage of this strong sense of religious commitment among evangelical Protestants to develop and mobilize support for their causes and/or political candidates.

Although evangelical Protestants serve as its primary base, the New Christian Right is also ecumenically fluid, drawing support from Roman Catholics, Mormons, mainline Protestants, and others who, despite considerable theological differences with evangelicals, may at times sustain various aspects of the movement's conservative social and political agenda.[8] It is not surprising then—given the shifting nature of issue-dependent support— that it is virtually impossible to determine the actual size of the New Christian Right constituency.

In fact, because it is far more nebulous than commonly perceived, the New Christian Right cannot rightly claim the status of political monolith so often imputed to it by both critics and supporters. The movement can be more accurately characterized as a vast mosaic of interests dominated by a handful of influential leaders and a growing number of special interest organizations that seek to convert the socially conservative views of their followers into political activism.

The vast array of subunits that make up the New Christian Right rely on the political and financial mobilization of their grassroots constituencies to influence electoral outcomes and public policymaking decisions. Perhaps the best known among these organizations is the Christian Coalition of America, which claims some 1.5 million members. Other politically prominent organizations include the American Family Association, which looks to its 600,000 members to combat sex and violence in the media. Focus on the Family, with its strong stance against homosexual rights and feminist theory, is reportedly backed by a membership of some 2 million Americans. With 250,000 members, the Family Research Council lobbies Congress and executive-branch agencies on behalf of a wide range of conservative themes related to marriage and family. And Concerned Women for America focuses the efforts of its 600,000 members on opposing gay-rights legislation and other issues it believes are detrimental to women and families.

Successful efforts by these and similar groups to mobilize their supporters have contributed to victories at the state and local level where candidates and issues were backed by New Christian Right organizations, provided important early support for a presidential run by one of their own (Pat Robertson in 1988), and led to unprecedented success for conservative Christian candidates in the 1994 congressional races.[9] Now viewed as the Republican Party's most dependable and active constituency, the New Christian Right and its evangelical Protestant base also provided critical support to George W. Bush in both the Republican primaries and general election during the 2000 presidential campaign.[10]

But serious questions linger about the ultimate political relevance of the New Christian Right. Some observers contend that its inability to generate support for its policy preferences outside its core constituency is indicative of the movement's generally limited appeal and uncertain political future.[11] Recent studies now contradict earlier research regarding the impact of religious conservatives on the presidential elections of 1980 and 1984, demonstrating that such influence was considerably less than what was believed at the time.[12] And the marginal success of New Christian Right–supported candidates and issues in the late 1990s appears to underscore the observation that the movement occupies little more than a "small but prominent niche in national politics."[13]

Dissatisfied with both the electoral and policy results of their role in American political life during the past quarter century, even some New Christian Right leaders have begun to voice doubt as to the efficacy of their continued reliance on the political process as a means of implementing the conservative social vision necessary for reclaiming America. Paul Weyrich, a founding member of the Moral Majority (the pioneering organization that linked religious conservatives with Republican political activism in the 1980s) and current president of the conservative Free Congress Foundation, stunned his supporters in February 1999 by announcing, "I no longer believe that there is a moral majority. I believe that we probably have lost the culture war. That doesn't mean the war is not going to continue and that it isn't going to be fought on other fronts. But in terms of society in general, we have lost."[14]

Echoing Weyrich's message just a few months later were conservative syndicated columnist Cal Thomas and Ed Dobson, both former officers in the Moral Majority, who argued that the involvement of religious conservatives in the political arena had had a corruptive influence on the church while accomplishing relatively little in terms of social change. "The history of the past twenty years," they admitted, "shows that while conservative Christian activists were effectively promising to end the moral slide, stop the gay rights agenda, and do other wondrous things, we never did achieve them. We did not achieve them because we lacked the power."[15] Without the power to alter a society they viewed as badly flawed, Thomas and Dobson conceded that they "no longer believe[d] that our individual or collective cultural problems can be altered exclusively, or even mainly, through the political process."[16]

Although the widespread media coverage of these statements was rife with speculation about the political future of Christian conservatives, Weyrich, Thomas, and Dobson were hardly the first to express dissatisfaction with the results of the New Christian Right's efforts to influence policy within the electoral branches of government. In a May 1996 newsletter, the president of the Alliance Defense Fund, an organization that finances conservative legal challenges, described the limitations of the New Christian Right's traditional dependence on electoral politics and elected officials for policy change:

> In this highly charged election year, I hope we all keep one thing in mind. . . . While we can bring about quick fixes in the voting booth, it is in the courts that we will bring about the type of change that transcends all generations. Think about that! Six presidents have come and gone, but *Roe v. Wade* has remained the law of the land. That's why the national legal precedents we can achieve to protect religious freedom, the traditional family, and the sanctity of life are going to touch our lives much longer than any political candidate or office-holder can.[17]

The Alliance Defense Fund is just one of several New Christian Right organizations that have recently come into existence with the intention of using the courts as the next battleground of conservative Christian activism. For these groups, the law represents a new opportunity to spiritually rejuvenate America without screening candidates, canvassing for votes, or lobbying Capitol Hill. With a cadre of well-trained lawyers, the courtroom activism of liberal public interest groups before it, and a remarkably successful legal strategy of its own, the New Christian Right now looks to the courts to recognize and legitimate the ideals and policies its supporters see as essential components of an America "reclaimed."

The New Christian Right's increased emphasis on the judiciary has not gone unnoticed by its critics, but the academic community has given it relatively little attention.[18] Some observers of the movement in the late 1980s noted that the use of the judicial branch as an avenue of political access had not been overlooked by the New Christian Right, but it "was considered more of an adversary than an opportunity."[19] They predicted that the expense of courtroom activism would cause the New Christian Right to redirect its efforts to grassroots political mobilization on state and local issues. Other scholars acknowledged the importance of litigation to the New Christian Right but concluded that the limited success of its agenda in the courts would inevitably lead it back to electoral politics.[20] True to these observations, there are currently several notable organizations within the New Christian Right such as the Family Research Council and American Family

Association whose litigation efforts, either in their own name or through direct affiliates (such as the latter's Center for Law and Policy), do little more than supplement the organizations' primary focus on the executive and legislative branches.

The New Christian Right groups that have been the most active in the courts, however, and that have had the greatest influence on the law generally are not subsidiaries created merely to complement a parent institution's existing political efforts. The sole purpose for which they were founded is litigation. Some have had substantial backing from leading organizations within the New Christian Right; others began as part-time enterprises originating in private commercial law firms. But all were initially founded with the intention of using the courts to create policy change, independent of efforts taking place in the other branches of government. And with increasing budgets and a growing body of legal precedent on their side, there is little evidence to suggest that these New Christian Right lawyers will abandon the courtroom anytime soon.

The New Christian Right's entry into public interest law is of twofold importance. First, because it involves few actors and little in the way of political mobilization, litigation represents a significant change from traditional forms of New Christian Right political activism. While subsequent chapters will address the several motivating factors behind the adoption of a judicial strategy, the formation of New Christian Right public interest law firms can be viewed, in part, as a belated response to the conspicuous absence of religious conservatives from the courtrooms of the past.

In the early 1980s, the evangelical philosopher Francis Schaeffer questioned, "[W]here were the Christian lawyers during the crucial shift from forty years ago to just a few years ago? . . . Within our lifetime the great shifts in law have taken place. Now that this has happened we can say, surely the Christian lawyers should have seen the changes taking place and stood on the wall and blown the trumpets loud and clear."[21] Unwilling to default to their liberal counterparts in the courtroom any longer, New Christian Right public interest law firms came to view litigation as a necessary tool in preventing further encroachment on the values, traditions, and policies they held dear.

Second, the New Christian Right's adoption of a judicial strategy reflects an acknowledgment that judges can rule *for,* as easily as against, religious conservatives. Rather than simply react to cases brought by opposing liberal interest groups, New Christian Right lawyers realized that they too could initiate lawsuits to impel favorable policy change. Thus, in addition to defending its values from further erosion, the New Christian Right came to appreciate the offensive component of its legal activism in the courts as well.

Given the broad spectrum of issues pursued by New Christian Right organizations within the electoral arena, it is not surprising to learn that the movement's public interest law efforts are similarly diverse. Among other things, New Christian Right lawyers have actively litigated on behalf of abortion clinic protestors, antigay policies, homeschooling parents, and a number of "family values" initiatives. In the Supreme Court's 1999–2000 term alone, the New Christian Right firms that make up the focus of this study participated in cases dealing with Nebraska's ban on partial birth abortions (*Stenberg v. Carhart*), the Boy Scouts of America's decision to ban homosexuals from its organization (*BSA and Monmouth Council v. Dale*), the use of student activity fees to fund unpopular campus groups (*Board of Regents of the University of Wisconsin System v. Southworth*), third-party visitation privileges versus parental rights (*Troxel v. Granville*), municipal bans on nude dancing (*City of Erie, et al. v. Pap's A.M., tdba "Kandyland"*), restrictions on abortion clinic protesting (*Hill v. Colorado*), governmental assistance to religious schools (*Mitchell v. Helms*), student-led prayers before high school football games (*Santa Fe Independent School District v. Doe*), as well as a host of criminal procedure cases.

Although such a listing reflects the breadth of issues of concern to these groups, the single greatest component of New Christian Right litigation deals with questions of religious liberty. Itself a broad topic, religious liberty encompasses traditional conceptions of religious expression in the schools and workplace as well as such disparate issues as abortion (should medical personnel be required to assist in abortion procedures if doing so would offend their religious beliefs?); rental housing (must a landlord rent to unmarried couples if his religious beliefs proscribe cohabitation?); and sex education (can students be compelled to take a sex education class that promotes lifestyles contrary to their religious values?).

In addition to these and countless other scenarios in which religious belief and expression might legitimately give rise to litigation, the pursuit of religious liberty claims in the courts is also seen as a way for New Christian Right lawyers to return religion to a position of prestige within society, a view they believe modern America has largely rejected. As Coral Ridge

Ministries' D. James Kennedy, a founding member of the Alliance Defense Fund, writes,

> In the last decade, think of all the times you have heard the phrase "separation of church and state." In almost every case, that phrase is used by secularists and ultra-liberals to tell us Christians what we can and can't do. "Separation of church and state" is used to tell ministers what we can't do. And what churches can't do. That's exactly opposite of what our Founding Fathers were talking about and why they founded America.
>
> America is a nation whose foundations are Christian. That's why as Christians we must try to maintain the legal struggle to preserve our First Amendment freedoms and religious liberties.[22]

Although their embrace of the law is a departure from previous methods of New Christian Right political activism, religious conservatives have not altogether ignored the judiciary in the past. Much of the harshest political rhetoric of New Christian Right commentators, for example, has been leveled at the judiciary for its "utilitarian calculus of convenience, premised on the assumption that neither God nor natural law, neither Bible nor Tradition, may make any claim on Almighty Man."[23]

The prolific New Christian Right author and lecturer David Barton holds judicial decisions responsible for everything from increases in violent crime and sexually transmitted diseases to decreases in SAT scores and family stability.[24] Barton maintains that the "[c]ourts over the past half-century have steadily divorced the Constitution from the transcendent values of the Declaration [of Independence], replacing them instead with their own contrivances. The results have been reprehensible."[25] Pat Robertson himself has opined that judicial decisions bear considerable responsibility for having virtually "guaranteed the moral collapse of this nation."[26]

The federal courts have borne the brunt of such criticism, but they have not been the sole target of New Christian Right ire. The fact that many of the legal decisions most offensive to conservative Christians stem from religion cases brought by the American Civil Liberties Union (ACLU), the American Jewish Congress, and Americans United for the Separation of Church and State has not been lost on the New Christian Right. The pioneering activism of these public interest groups in the courts has been characterized by New Christian Right leaders as a type of "legal engineering" which, "through the strategic use and abuse of the court system, . . . use[s] litigation to turn wrongs into rights."[27] Even worse, writes John Whitehead of the conservative Rutherford Institute, these organizations have used their well-developed resources in open hostility against religion: "Secularizing agents such as the American Civil Liberties Union know very well what they are doing. When ACLU attorneys threaten or sue public school districts in the name of freedom to stop a child from voluntarily praying, they are not standing for freedom. The ACLU is repressing a whole segment of society—religious people—as if it were an appendage of the secular state."[28]

In years past, religious conservatives could do little but express scorn and frustration at such perceived repression. During the 1980s and early 1990s, however, one segment of the New Christian Right transformed itself from a bitter observer of the judicial process into an active courtroom participant.

An important indicator of the extent of New Christian Right activity in the courts is the influence public interest law firms associated with the movement have developed within a relatively short period of time. While the religious beliefs and practices of the Amish, Catholics, Mormons, Quakers, Seventh-Day Adventists, Unitarians, and others have been the subject of many of the Supreme Court's landmark rulings on religion, it was the steady stream of precedent-setting cases brought by Jewish organizations, the Jehovah's Witnesses, and secular separationist groups like the ACLU that fundamentally changed the legal relationship between church and state in America.[29] Reflecting the arguments made by these organizations, the Supreme Court for thirty years interpreted the establishment clause of the First Amendment as erecting a high wall of separation between church and state, an interpretation the Court invoked frequently between the 1940s and 1970s to strike down (primarily state) laws and practices that directly or otherwise promoted religious doctrines, beliefs, or traditions.

The separationist organizations that so completely altered early church-state jurisprudence continue to be active today, but their influence has lessened. Indeed since 1980, and particularly during the last decade, New Christian Right organizations (using litigation strategies perfected by these same separationist groups that now oppose them in the courtroom) have arguably had a greater impact on the nexus of law and religion than any other movement active in the federal courts. The rapidly increasing number of religion cases in both the Supreme Court and lower federal courts in which New Christian Right legal organizations have factored prominently further testifies to the fact that these groups are no longer simply engaged in defensive maneuvers.

Of greater significance than the quantity of New Christian Right participation in the courts, however, is the substance of its legal arguments in religious liberty litigation. Perhaps surprisingly, New Christian Right lawyers neither boldly renounce the Supreme Court's establishment clause rulings of the past nor offer any new interpretation of the free exercise clause to protect religious expression. Instead, they turn to the free speech clause of the First Amendment.

Although this may appear to be an especially odd strategy for New Christian Right lawyers to embrace in religion cases since it essentially abandons traditional legal arguments grounded in the religion clauses of the Constitution, it is consistent with the growing secularization accompanying other types of New Christian Right political activism.[30] And it is just this approach which, after years of frustrating losses in the courts, has provided the movement with a number of significant legal victories in both the Supreme Court and the lower federal courts.

Such victories, however, have not come without a price. Wholly rejecting the notion that free speech protections trump the separationist requirements of the establishment clause, critics of the strategy contend that the free speech approach to religion is little more than an end run around the Supreme Court's decisions mandating a separation of church and state.

Conversely, among those supporting a greater accommodation of religion in the public sphere, there are concerns that in seeking refuge in the free speech clause, New Christian Right lawyers may well have cheapened religion by linking it with pornography, commercial advertising, racial invectives, flag burning, and other forms of "protected" speech.[31] Of perhaps greater concern, however, is the fact that in appealing to the free speech clause for protection of religious speech, New Christian Right attorneys have also necessarily stretched that clause to protect other forms of speech that may in fact be anathema to many of their conservative Christian supporters.

This study explores the goals behind the New Christian Right's judicial agenda, the litigation and nonlitigation strategies utilized to alter both public policy and public perception regarding religious expression, and the religion cases in which the major New Christian Right public interest law organizations have been involved in the federal courts between 1980 and 2000. Throughout, it highlights both the considerable success and irony associated with the New Christian Right's appeal to the free speech clause in the religion cases it litigates.

The 1980–2000 time frame was selected because it was the 1980 presidential election's highlighting of the use of the courts as instruments of public policymaking that led conservatives to turn to the judiciary in earnest. The subsequent increase in the courtroom efforts of the New Christian Right, particularly after 1994, and the landmark rulings the federal courts have rendered governing religion and speech necessitate a careful study of its more recent efforts as well.

Chapter 2 explains why the New Christian Right turned to the courts for assistance in establishing its agenda and how this strategy arose out of a long history of interaction between religion and politics in America. Invoking the two-hundred-year heritage of Protestant hegemony in American life, the efforts of the New Christian Right in and out of the courtroom seek to return the religious ethic to a past position of societal respect and political influence.

Chapter 3 introduces the five major public interest law firms primarily responsible for the New Christian Right's religious liberty litigation: the Alliance Defense Fund, the American Center for Law and Justice, the Christian Legal Society's Center for Law and Religious Freedom, Liberty Counsel, and the Rutherford Institute. Independently founded, there are, nevertheless, substantive areas of agreement among these groups that allow for cooperative efforts in the courts. In addition to examining the goals and strategies common to each of these firms, this chapter also looks at the considerable differences that exist among them.

The legal strategies utilized by New Christian Right lawyers is the subject of chapter 4. Latecomers to the field of interest group litigation, New Christian Right public interest law firms have adopted the procedural litigating strategies perfected by the ACLU, the NAACP Legal Defense Fund, the American Jewish Congress, and others. This chapter also examines the New Christian Right's unique emphasis on the free speech clause in the religious liberty claims it litigates.

Using case study examples, chapters 5 and 6 detail New Christian Right religious liberty litigation from 1980 to 2000 at the Supreme Court and lower levels of the federal judiciary, respectively. These chapters also provide a comprehensive listing of the religion cases in which these firms have participated (where a decision on the merits was rendered) in the Supreme Court, U.S. Courts of Appeal, and U.S. District Courts as well as their successes and failures in each of these judicial venues.

Because lawyers seek more than just favorable judicial rulings in influencing public policy, chapter 7 considers the extra-courtroom efforts (termed public education, prelitigation, and nonlitigation strategies) employed by New Christian Right public interest legal organizations to alter public decision making on religious liberty issues.

The concluding chapter offers an overview of the New Christian Right's presence and influence in the courts as well as a consideration of the costs of its willingness to incorporate greater elasticity into free speech clause jurisprudence.

The entry of the New Christian Right into public interest law is a marked change from the strategy politically active Christians have historically used to gain access to and exert influence on the policymaking process. However different this new form of political activism may be from previous methods, the motivating force remains the same: to protect the religious expression of Christians as well as inject that influence into larger issues of public policy.

Relying on judges and jurisprudence rather than elected politicians and the legislative process, New Christian Right activists regard public interest law as more than just a new twist to the movement's efforts to influence policymaking decisions. As the chances for broad implementation of their agenda in the electoral branches of government become increasingly uncertain, New Christian Right attorneys regard the law, the courts, and the free speech clause as perhaps their last and most enduring allies in their quest to protect faith and reclaim America.

2   A Perfect State of Society

The Emergence of Conservative
Christian Public Interest Law

> Society is perfect where what is right in theory exists in fact; where prac-
> tice coincides with principle, and the Law of God is the Law of the Land.
> Evangelist Jonathan Blanchard, Oberlin College Address, 1839

Although the emergence of New Christian Right public interest law is a
rather new phenomenon, the influence of religion on American politics is
not. Of his visit to America in 1831, Alexis de Tocqueville would later note
that "the religious atmosphere of the country was the first thing that struck
me on arrival in the United States. The longer I stayed in the country, the
more conscious I became of the important political consequences resulting
from this novel situation."[1] What Tocqueville found so fascinating was not
so much religion's direct influence on politics (which he believed to be mini-
mal because he observed church and state functioning in separate spheres)
but its predominance in shaping nearly every other aspect of Jacksonian
America.

Protestant leaders in the early 1800s generally viewed involvement in
politics as inappropriate for the religious. "[There was] a feeling, common
to many reformers, that politics was degraded and disgusting to moral men.
. . . Political action, furthermore, went against the evangelical belief that
true goodness could only flow from a converted heart. People had to *want*
to behave properly, and that came from enlightenment, not force."[2] Although this perspective enjoyed considerable support at the time of Tocqueville's visit, the social and political challenges of the mid–nineteenth
century would see the deliberate extension of "hegemonic Protestantism"
into the political arena it had once so carefully avoided.[3] This historic
Protantism, it should be noted, has a dual legacy. Although contemporary usage of the term "evangelical" generally denotes certain denominations and/or a specific set of beliefs, its nineteenth-century meaning was
much broader, making evangelicalism virtually synonymous with orthodox

Protestantism. Subsequent internal divisions gave rise to the "conservative" and "liberal" wings of Protestantism that today are often categorized as "evangelical and fundamentalist" and "mainline" denominations, respectively.

Part of the motivation behind nineteenth-century Protestant political activism stemmed from the religious doctrine of postmillennialism. Millennialism refers to beliefs about the biblically prophesied return of Jesus Christ and the establishment of his one-thousand-year reign of peace on this earth. The postmillennial precept declared the necessity of cleansing the world of evil and corrupting influences to prepare for as well as hasten the second coming of Christ. The secular manifestation of this spiritual principle was social and political reform. Religious revivals that served the spiritual needs of believers also called attention to the condition of the temporal world in which they lived. As a result of the revivals and the reform impulse that accompanied them, "every aspect of society began to be subjected to eager scrutiny in order to scour and purify the earth in preparation for God's final act of redemption."[4]

Until the all-encompassing debate over slavery engulfed religious groups along with the rest of the country, Protestant leaders had focused their society-cleansing efforts on ridding the nation of the debilitating spiritual and social consequences of alcohol. Founded in 1826 by a group of evangelical ministers, the American Temperance Society embarked on a national campaign, taking its message directly to the churches. Within eight years of the society's founding, there were state affiliates of the society in all but three of the union's nineteen states and an estimated six thousand local organizations devoted to the temperance cause. With a membership of well over one million, it was the most significant voluntary organization of its time.[5]

The American Temperance Society and its successor, the American Temperance Union, initially concentrated their efforts on persuading individuals to abandon liquor. However, with the 1838 passage of a Massachusetts law banning the retail sale of distilled liquor in less than fifteen-gallon amounts, many of those same Protestant leaders who had formerly avoided the dirty world of politics embraced the idea of utilizing the law to enforce their temperance views.

Using its grassroots network of support to vote for increased restrictions on local liquor retail licensing, the American Temperance Union was instrumental in the creation of whole blocs of dry communities en route to lobbying for outright state prohibitions. By 1855, New England, New York, and large parts of the Midwest were dry. Although nearly all of the statewide prohibitions were repealed by the end of the Civil War, the legislative success of anti-alcohol evangelical activism was "proof that vices might be legislated away more easily than sinners could be converted."[6] The early success of such activism would also serve to guide subsequent evangelical efforts (most notably the Anti-Saloon League) to regulate alcohol, culminating in the ratification of the Eighteenth Amendment in 1919.

Although alcohol was the focus of early reform efforts, there was no greater barrier to the purified world these early Protestants sought to create than slavery. Northern evangelicals were active in spreading the gospel of abolitionism using methods that wedded familiar revivalist techniques with the antislavery cause: "Revivalist lectures were a popular form of winning followers and made much more forceful impressions than pamphlets. Personal persuasion, which the evangelist had utilized in reaping souls, was taken over by antislavery reformers. Indeed, even hymns had their part to play in the conversion to abolitionism."[7]

Not only were evangelical methods utilized in the fight against slavery, but the churches themselves were enlisted in the cause. One of the most prominent antislavery organizations in the North, the American Anti-Slavery Society, was created specifically to win over the membership of Protestant churches to the abolitionist cause. The reason for focusing the abolitionist strategy on churches was simple: for excluding "the political parties and the government itself, the Protestant denominations were practically the only institutions that functioned in every part of the nation."[8] Although political authority and the misery of civil war would ultimately be necessary to eradicate slavery from the United States, it was Protestant fervor, driven by a spiritual call for reform and capitalizing on existing and effective methods of proselytizing, which helped legitimize the abolition movement.

The reform ethic that guided the significant efforts of Protestants to abolish slavery and promote temperance led to political activism in other areas. As political scientist Kenneth Wald has noted, Protestantism also acted as "a driving force behind such disparate movements as currency reform, woman's suffrage, regulation of corporate abuses, arbitration of international conflicts, and adoption of 'direct democracy' through the initiative, referendum, and recall election. These reforms of the Progressive Era were advanced as a means to defend the economic interests and social values of traditional Protestantism. Their widespread adoption before World War I attests to the central place of evangelicalism in American culture."[9]

These reforms resulted from efforts by independent organizations to mobilize support within the legislative and (to a lesser extent) executive branches of government, but they were also guided by the Protestant influence in party politics. Historian Paul Kleppner has described the intertwining of the Protestant religion with both the Democratic and Republican Parties during the late nineteenth and early twentieth centuries as a "political church" where the religious and the political "unambiguously reinforced each other."[10]

The judiciary also saw the influence of Christian activism. At the state level, this took the form of rulings that "were affected, and sometimes controlled, by the thesis that Christianity is a part of the common law."[11] At the federal level, this view was famously championed by Supreme Court Justice Joseph Story, whose rulings for the Court and influential *Commentaries on the Constitution of the United States* (1833) confirmed his belief that

> [t]he promulgation of the great doctrines of religion, the being, and attributes, and providence of one Almighty God; the responsibility to him for all our actions, founded upon moral freedom and accountability; a future state of rewards and punishments; the cultivation of all the personal, social, and benevolent virtues, —these never can be a matter of indifference in any well-ordered community. It is, indeed, difficult to conceive how any civilized society can well exist without them. And at all events, it is impossible for those who believe in the truth of Christianity as a divine revelation to doubt that it is the especial duty of government to foster and encourage it among all the citizens and subjects.[12]

The last decade of the nineteenth century saw Associate Justice David Brewer proclaim a similar view. In November 1890, one month into his first full term on the Supreme Court, he announced to his fellow Congregationalists that "the law and the gospel ought always to go together."[13] Two years later, Brewer, the son of a Christian missionary, a lifelong member of the American Bible Society, and a regular Sunday school teacher at the First

Congregational Church in Washington, D.C., would famously declare for a unanimous Court "that this is a Christian nation."[14]

It is this legacy of activism and influence on a broad spectrum of issues across the institutions of government that contemporary New Christian Right leaders refer to when they sound the call to "reclaim America." Leaders of the New Christian Right would like more than to simply restore the faith and virtue of which they believe modern America is bereft. They also want to reclaim the political heritage that saw Protestant participation and influence in some of the most pressing and progressive social and political issues of the nineteenth and early twentieth centuries. Admittedly, there is no direct political pedigree between these earlier movements and the contemporary New Christian Right, but the hegemonic force of Protestantism over American life during this time represents an ideal whose return is sought by religious conservatives.

With the dawning of the twentieth century, however, Protestantism, despite having long been recognized as a social and political force in America, would lose its status as a leading mainstream influence with astonishing rapidity and seeming finality. Initially rupturing from within, doctrinal strife began to divide believers and the churches to which they belonged.

Protestantism found itself increasingly split between those maintaining the traditional orthodoxy and a growing number of "modernist" believers who either compromised or abandoned outright such core beliefs as the infallibility of the Bible, the literal creation of the earth, and the divinity of Jesus Christ.[15] The modernist theology found its greatest support in the North, where there were large non-Protestant immigrant populations as well as America's premier colleges and universities, many of which had gradually abandoned their Protestant roots to embrace European intellectualism.[16]

In an attempt to combat the increasingly popular modernist or liberal view of Protestantism, a series of pamphlets called *The Fundamentals: A Testimony to the Truth* was published by conservative Protestants between 1910 and 1915. The twelve pamphlets making up *The Fundamentals* not only reiterated the core beliefs of conservatives, they also took strong positions against evolution and higher criticism, as well as Catholicism and other religions.[17] *The Fundamentals* were widely circulated (and led to the coining of the term "fundamentalist"), but as sociologist James Davison Hunter notes, their "net accomplishment was dubious; at best, [they] provided only a pause in the decline of conservative power in the Protestant denominations."[18]

The societal reform impulse that arose out of the spiritual revivals also began to divide the Protestant community. By the end of the first decade of the twentieth century, Protestants found themselves debating the temporal application of their millennialist views. Earlier battles on behalf of abolition, temperance, and other issues were outward looking, having been waged, in part, on the *post*millennial belief that the eradication of society's ills and injustices through social and political reform would hasten the second coming of Jesus Christ. Although many evangelicals still believed that political activism was an appropriate vehicle for social reform, others increasingly embraced the *pre*millennial belief that such efforts could do little to stop the world from getting worse. Looking inward, the role of the premillennialist was to reform and perfect himself first and then try to help others do the same, even as the world around them continued to degenerate. For premillennialists, it was not the cleansing of the earth of its ills that would bring Christ back but the downward spiral of societal and moral decay which, at its nadir, would see Christ return and reign for one thousand years with those who had prepared themselves.

Where reform continued, as many churches struggled to bring about progressive societal change, particularly in the urban areas of the North, their efforts were called into question by conservatives who believed that their liberal counterparts were subordinating the "gospel" to the "social" in Social Gospel reform initiatives.[19] The successful effort of the liberal mainline wing of Protestantism to create an ecumenical organization devoted to the realization of the Social Gospel only further alienated conservative evangelicals and fundamentalists who viewed interfaith organizations as a threat to traditional orthodoxy.[20]

As the Northern Protestant ethic began to focus more on modernity and the Social Gospel, "the center of gravity in evangelicalism shifted to the rural South."[21] Unlike the North, the rural surroundings of Southern evangelicals produced very little in the way of either societal reform or application of intellectual rigor to theology. There were political consequences to this religious shift as well: "The social and economic deprivation that typified [Southern] evangelicals denied them the time, energy, and skill to carry on sustained political participation and isolated them from experiences that would have promoted tolerance, compromise, and other democratic values. . . . Furthermore, the other-worldly orientation of southern religion, the divorce of religion from social conditions, discouraged participation in the earthly process of political action."[22] Conservative evangelicals were increasingly perceived as lacking in "tolerance, compromise, and other democratic values," a view that was only further underscored by the 1925 Scopes trial.

In the courtroom, William Jennings Bryan, a three-time Democratic Party presidential nominee and former secretary of state, was victorious in defending Tennessee's anti-evolution statute. However, neither he nor the conservative evangelical beliefs he championed were spared Clarence Darrow's critical line of questioning. Witnessing the whole affair was an amused and often hostile press that ridiculed Bryan, his fellow believers, and the outcome of the trial in papers nationwide. Bryan died just days after the trial but had lived long enough to see the beginning of the end of evangelical Christianity's political relevance.[23]

The Scopes trial and other battles over evolution in the 1920s highlighted the interplay between religion and politics in America. However, there were other issues that received evangelical attention during this decade as well, including communism. Conservatives, whose antagonism toward German intellectualism and other European social and political ideals had been criticized as narrow-minded and nativistic, were especially concerned about the new political regime in Russia. Communism was a natural target for conservative evangelicals who saw in its atheistic order a complete repudiation of all things eternal.

Notwithstanding the vocal concerns of evangelicals on these and other issues, there were few who believed that religion alone could provide answers to the increasingly complex political, social, and economic questions confronting pre-Depression America. Due in part to the Scopes trial but to a greater degree the intellectual, demographic, and spiritual changes taking place in America, evangelical Christianity was reduced to a position of "cognitive marginality and political impotence."[24]

For the next sixty years, evangelicals largely adopted a position of political retrenchment. Sporadic attempts to reassert the evangelical influence over America's political conscience met with little success and were separated by long periods of dormancy. When such activism did occur, as when the American Council of Christian Churches issued warnings on the dangers of both domestic and international communism, it was largely conducted by specific organizations or denominations that enjoyed neither the widespread support of conservative Christians specifically nor other Americans in general.

And yet, however little evangelicals were actively engaged in the political process after the 1920s, they were not, as church-state scholar Clyde Wilcox puts it, "passively waiting for the second coming."[25] Of both practical and ultimately political significance during this period was the development of a conservative evangelical information infrastructure. Unable to influence mainstream America, the conservative Christian worldview was propagated to believers through a dramatic increase in the number of Christian bookstores, seminaries, Bible institutes, and evangelical liberal arts colleges. Taking advantage of a Federal Communications Commission mandate requiring television stations to air some degree of religious programming, evangelical preachers took to the airwaves (a practice most mainline Protestant denominations avoided) to express both their spiritual and secular concerns before widespread audiences.[26] Technological advances and a growing number of Christian radio and television stations took these evangelical messengers into more American homes than ever before.

The placement of contemporary social and political issues before these audiences was a key factor in the reawakening of Christian political activism from its political lethargy. Of at least equal importance was the timing of the information infrastructure's emergence. As social critic Nathan Glazer recalls, conservative Christians "had been reduced to irrelevance in the Depression of the 1930s and the war against Nazism in the 1940s. In the family-building period of the 1950s, there had been little to arouse them. But the cultural revolution of the 1960s and 1970s did."[27]

Heeding their leaders' broadcast warnings in the wake of the widespread social and cultural changes taking place in America, conservative Christians began to reconsider the necessity of making their political voice heard. The result was a gradual realization on their part that political expression could be used as both a sword and shield against those influences bent on destroying the "God, Family, Country" creed of evangelicals. Thus, just as the rise of intellectual and humanistic theories coupled with social and demographic changes had driven evangelical Christians out of the public world of politics, the onward roll of these same forces summoned them back from political exile.

Contrary to previous political efforts that were characterized by their almost exclusive focus on single-issue campaigns such as abolition, temperance, and communism, the new generation of Christian activists in the early 1970s galvanized support for a return to the political arena by adopting a scattershot style of activism that concentrated on several different issues at once. The ideological tie that bound these various issues together was their "almost exclusive . . . orient[ation] toward stemming the tide of moral decline in American culture."[28]

Concerned not only about value-laden issues at the local level such as textbook and curriculum decisions made by school boards, this emerging movement of socially conservative Christians was also troubled by the increasing absence of virtue in the "public square." Watergate and other scandals involving public officials "dramatized the connection between private morality and the public good and demonstrated that personal immorality could threaten the whole of society."[29] Of particular concern was the Supreme Court's decision in *Roe v. Wade*.[30]

By the time the *Roe* decision was handed down in 1973, Christian conservatives had been paying close attention to the Court for over a decade. The impact of *Engel v. Vitale*[31] and *School District of Abington Township v. Schempp*,[32] can still be seen some four decades later in the New Christian Right's persistent condemnation of these Warren Court rulings banning mandated prayers and Bible verse readings in public schools.[33] To critics, these decisions did not reflect constitutional concerns about the First Amendment's establishment clause. Rather, they demonstrated a deliberate hostility on the part of the Warren Court toward the religious ethic that conservative Christians believed had existed in America since its founding.[34]

Increasingly alarmed by what they perceived as rampant judicial activism, particularly in such areas as obscenity and privacy, many conservative Christians came to view the Court as a promoter of moral decadence that permitted almost any form of expression except for the religious. The *Roe* decision on abortion, however, was particularly offensive. For Christian conservatives, no other previous ruling of the Court so exemplified the almost complete triumph of secular humanism in America. Indeed, to them it was unthinkable that the question of God-given life would even come before a panel of human judges, much less lose out.[35]

In spite of a decade of Court-watching, however, religious conservatives were not prepared to contest the *Roe* decision when it was first handed down. Opposed but without organization, frustrated but still fragmented, the growing number of politically conscious conservative Protestants looked to Roman Catholics to lead the anti-abortion effort for the first several years after *Roe*.[36]

Nevertheless, the impact of the Supreme Court's abortion decision on the organization and mobilization of the New Christian Right cannot be overemphasized. Conservative Christians had long been alarmed at the declining state of the nation's moral health, but however often these early concerns may have been addressed in denominational services or on evangelical radio and television programs, there was little political mobilization on these issues. What did arise out of the political and cultural climate of the 1960s and early 1970s, however, was a feeling among conservative Christians that they could no longer sit on the political sidelines and watch the unobstructed march of secular humanism. With the Supreme Court's abortion ruling as the catalyst, the "diffused cultural discontent [of the 1960s and 1970s] . . . became congealed into a full-fledged political movement."[37]

In addition to the *Roe* decision, there were several other events in the mid-1970s credited with the political mobilization of the movement. The first of these was a 1974 petition to the Federal Communication Commission (FCC) calling for an investigation into noncommercial television and radio broadcasts, including religious programming. The petition also requested that licenses for additional religious programming be frozen until the investigation was completed. Evangelical broadcasters saw the petition as a threat to their ability to continue their ministry on the airwaves, a view apparently shared by many in their radio and television audience. Although the FCC denied the petition in 1975, letters from concerned citizens regarding the issue poured into the FCC at the rate of 130,000 a month for the next decade.[38]

In addition, just months after Jimmy Carter's inauguration the Internal Revenue Service (IRS) began to revoke the tax-exempt status of private schools that it believed were practicing racial discrimination. Conservative Christians thought this action smacked of religious harassment since a large portion of the private schools affected were religious schools and colleges. As part of the developing evangelical information infrastructure, the number of these schools had proliferated during the 1960s and 1970s "in response to the secularization of the public schools caused by evolution, school-prayer, and the school-busing court decisions, as well as the professionalization of the National Education Association and its concomitant hostility to forms of religious expression in the public schools."[39]

The Supreme Court would ultimately adjudicate the issue in favor of the IRS but the issue had already contributed to the growing political mobilization of the New Christian Right.[40] As Jerry Falwell later recalled, "It was the IRS trying to take away our tax exemptions that made us realize that we had to fight for our lives."[41]

Elected as the first publicly professing evangelical Christian since Woodrow Wilson, Jimmy Carter himself contributed to the rise of the New Christian Right. Carter's stance against school prayer, anti-abortion legislation, and other issues infuriated many of his fellow evangelicals. The emerging New Christian Right lambasted both Carter and the Democratic Party policies he advocated and in the process helped cultivate widespread evangelical support for the Republican Party's presidential nominee in 1980, Ronald Reagan.

The incorporation of conservative Christians into the larger New Right movement, the efforts of the New Christian Right to elect Ronald Reagan in 1980, and the success of its social and political agenda have been the focus of numerous retellings in both the popular media and the academic community.[42] What bears noting here, however, is the manner in which the judicial branch served as one point of convergence for the New Christian Right and the Reagan administration.

Due to the Court's rulings on school prayer and abortion as well as the efforts of President Reagan's Department of Justice, the New Christian Right came to appreciate that the judiciary mattered politically. Although New Christian Right leaders had frequently voiced their disgust for "liberal" judicial rulings, the political efforts of the movement largely ignored the courts. Part of the reason for this was a conspicuous lack of both funding and political sophistication, which precluded the New Christian Right from seriously pursuing the judiciary as an avenue of political access.[43]

Reagan's election, however, created the opportunity on the part of his administration to reconsider the judiciary's role in the political process. What appealed to both the Reagan administration and the emerging leaders of the New Christian Right movement was the potential of the law, as interpreted by judges, to promote a political and moral vision for America that would persist long after the elected officials who championed those same views left office.[44]

Appointing nearly one-half of all lower federal court judges as well as three new Supreme Court associate justices and a chief justice, Ronald Reagan transformed the federal judiciary unlike any president since Franklin Roosevelt. The Justice Department underwent a number of reorganizational facelifts to enable it to cope with its expanded role in the judicial selection process, but it was guided by a single, simple principle: appoint to the federal bench only those who possessed a conservative judicial philosophy.[45]

Believing that the expansive judicial rulings of the past would be displaced by a greater fidelity to constitutional and statutory texts, religious conservatives hoped that the Reagan administration's desire to place the "right people" on the federal bench would bring about a judicial repudiation of such constitutional controversies as the right of privacy and its abortion progeny as well as the Supreme Court–mandated wall separating church and state.

Consequently, supporters of the New Christian Right were predictably disappointed when they discovered that the legal philosophy of many of these judges trumped the conservative ideology they were appointed to maintain. That is, the philosophy of judicial restraint that religious conservatives endorsed and Ronald Reagan promised to inject into the federal courts actually took root. Refusing to "legislate" even the conservative agenda from the bench, some judicial appointees of both Reagan and Bush were much more deferential to the legislative and executive branches of government on questions of civil rights and civil liberties than were their more liberal predecessors.[46]

This is not to infer, of course, that these appointees were idle in their judicial efforts to foster conservative principles. In both the Supreme Court and lower federal courts, judicial retrenchment in such areas as criminal justice, privacy, and equal protection has been and continues to be a hallmark of the Reagan/Bush appointees. Although retrenchment is admittedly a form of judicial activism in its own right, it is nevertheless a far cry from the sweeping judicial embrace of conservative moral values that some within the New Christian Right were perhaps expecting.

Unable to depend on Republican appointees to the federal bench to actively promote the conservative Christian agenda, a number of New Christian Right lawyers began to focus their legal efforts on a few issues of general concern to conservative Christians, but religion's role in the public square was of primary importance.[47] Given the well-documented presence and growth of interest group activity in the courts, the only thing surprising about the New Christian Right's adoption of this strategy is how long it took.[48] This is all the more curious because of the increasing pace of interest group litigation during the 1950s and 1960s focusing on the separation of church and state, an issue of particular concern to religious conservatives.

Organizations such as the American Jewish Congress, Americans United for Separation of Church and State, and the ACLU actively challenged local, state, and federal governmental policies and programs that either aided Christianity specifically over other religions or generally favored the religious over the nonreligious. Having decided only a handful of religion cases since 1789, the Supreme Court's 1940 ruling that the free exercise clause applies against state as well as federal government action, to be followed by the similar incorporation of the establishment clause in 1947, resulted in an amazing array of litigation brought by groups advocating a high wall of separation between church and state.[49]

New Christian Right rhetoric had long laid the unraveling of America's moral fabric at the feet of a judiciary dominated by liberal judges and public interest groups hostile to religion.[50] Other voices within the movement, however, conceded that the separationist legal victories so often condemned by the New Christian Right had occurred as much by default as by design.[51] Indeed, while the primary separationist groups of that era, the ACLU, American Jewish Congress, and Americans United, were increasing the pace of their litigation efforts in bringing a host of church-state cases, there was little organized opposition in the courtroom. Several Roman Catholic organizations whose interests were tied to the parochial school aid often challenged by separationist groups responded in kind, but there was no coordinated defense, consistent presence, or counteroffensive strategy to speak of.[52] In short, as Frank Sorauf notes in his classic *Wall of Separation,* among the accommodationists, "there was nothing approaching the interest group division of effort—the 'system'—one could find in the separationist camp. As a result of all of this, the battle over church-state issues in American courts was a very unequal one."[53]

The proliferation of New Christian Right public interest law firms suggests that these organizations are now ready to fill the courtroom void of years past. With a litigating agenda, ready access to funding, and a vast network of affiliated lawyers, the New Christian Right, particularly within the last decade, has successfully challenged the pioneering separationist organizations (most of which are still active in church-state litigation) within the judicial arena that they historically dominated. Clearly not content to engage in defensive maneuvers alone, the litigating firms associated with the New Christian Right have gone on the offensive, seeking judicial affirmation of policy preferences of their own. In so doing, two conclusions seem clear. First, the New Christian Right has embraced what it once despised—the use of public interest litigation to effect policy change. Having long bemoaned interest group activism in the courts on issues relating to religion, the legal efforts of New Christian Right law firms clearly acknowledge and imitate the pathbreaking efforts of liberal interest group activity in this area.

Second, the adoption of a judicial strategy by these groups reflects a pessimism with the further reliance on the efforts of their ideological counterparts in the electoral branches of government. As noted earlier, among the organizations that make up the New Christian Right are many that see promise in continued political mobilization within the executive and legislative branches. But given the repudiation of Protestantism's historic mainstream impact on society in the early twentieth century, the reluctance of conservative Christian activists to reenter the political arena, and their subsequent disappointment with the political gains of the Reagan/Bush era, the judiciary may be the last hope for New Christian Right influence. As New Christian Right attorney Mathew Staver noted of his own entry into public interest law, "Once conservatives and Christians began to see that the political arena was not addressing their concerns . . . it was time to get involved."[54]

3   One in Purpose

The Firms That Litigate the New Christian Right Agenda

[It is] an idea whose time has come. It is the concept that by pooling resources, substantial amounts of money can be channeled into a critical aspect [of] the civil war for values, namely, the legal battle in our nation's courts.

Dr. James Dobson, founding member of the Alliance Defense Fund

Within the growing body of organizations litigating the New Christian Right agenda in the courts are such groups as the American Family Association, Concerned Women for America, Focus on the Family, and the Family Research Council. Focusing primarily on the development of grassroots support for public policies that reflect their views on abortion, gay rights, homeschooling, pornography, and other issues, each has adopted litigation in recent years to complement traditional methods of political activism.

In addition to these organizations for which public interest litigation is a supplemental strategy, there are several other New Christian Right groups whose main focus is the law. Where issues of religion are concerned, there are three categories of conservative courtroom activists. The first consists of private law firms that litigate constitutional issues as part of their overall general practice. Large firms such as Chicago-based Mayer, Brown and Platt (which has participated extensively in both Supreme Court and lower federal court religion cases through its lead counsel, Michael McConnell) have specialty areas devoted to religious litigation and appellate practice. Smaller firms and solo practitioners obviously have far fewer resources available for specialized constitutional litigation, making religious liberty disputes little more than an interesting side practice in which they participate only occasionally.

These firms may have practice areas devoted to specific areas of constitutional law such as religious expression and may even employ attorneys who moonlight as constitutional lawyers. But their legal interests are broad;

they do not exist to litigate constitutional issues alone. And because the litigation in this first category is usually carried out under the name of the private law firm itself, even when an organized New Christian Right presence oversees the litigation, it is virtually impossible to determine the actual number of lawyers who litigate the New Christian Right agenda in the federal courts.

A second and somewhat more distinct group consists of small nonprofit public interest law firms. While some of these firms apply their resources solely to issues of church and state, others litigate religion cases as part of a larger constitutional agenda in the courts. There are many such organizations within the New Christian Right mosaic ranging from the mom-and-pop groups that litigate a single case or two in federal court and are never heard from again to such small but enduring organizations as the Center for Faith and Freedom, Christian Law Association, Liberty Legal Institute, and Pacific Justice Institute. The public interest legal organizations that fall within this category are characterized by their relative anonymity, infrequent presence in the courts, and chronic lack of adequate funding. A circular challenge confronts each of them: poor funding limits their ability to take cases that might enhance their reputation, the lack of which makes it difficult to secure funding. Such obstacles severely hamper the efforts of these groups to either expand their influence or substantially advance their interests in the courts.

The third group consists of larger nonprofit organizations that have an established presence in the federal courts, a regional or national network of affiliated lawyers, and generally ready access to funding. There is a core group of New Christian Right public interest legal organizations whose experience, financial strength, national reputation, and success in and out of the courtroom clearly put them above all other conservative organizations that litigate issues of religion and religious expression.

The firms that make up this nucleus are the Christian Legal Society's Center for Law and Religious Freedom, the Rutherford Institute, the American Center for Law and Justice, Liberty Counsel, and the Alliance Defense Fund (see table 1). Each of these organizations works in concert with law firms in the first and second categories of conservative courtroom activists, but their individual efforts are particularly important, having set the standard for New Christian Right litigation in religion cases. Establishing solid legal precedents, providing training to an increasing number of affiliated

Table 1. Major New Christian Right public interest law firms involved in religious liberty litigation

Firm, Year Founded, and Key Personnel	1999 Budget	Staff Attorneys	Characteristics of Group
Center for Law and Religious Freedom Annandale, VA (1975) Director: Gregory S. Baylor	$1.5 million	3 staff attorneys and 4,500 members of CLS	Affiliated with the CLS, the center is known for its ability to work with its ideological opponents as well as litigate.
Rutherford Institute Charlottesville, VA (1982) President: John W. Whitehead	$4.5 million	3 staff attorneys and 1,000 affiliated volunteer lawyers	Rutherford pursues claims of religious liberty infringement worldwide. Steadfastly refuses alliances with other New Christian Right legal groups.
American Center for Law and Justice Virginia Beach, VA (1990) CEO and Chief Counsel: Jay Sekulow	$9 million	25 staff attorneys and 330 affiliated volunteer lawyers	Founded by Pat Robertson, the ACLJ benefits from extensive media exposure, a huge budget, and Sekulow, a frequent advocate before the Supreme Court.
Liberty Counsel Orlando, FL (1990) President: Mathew Staver	$500,000	6 staff attorneys	Typical of many small firms engaged in public interest law, Liberty Counsel maintains a strong regional presence but has recently increased its national efforts.
Alliance Defense Fund Scottsdale, AZ (1994) President: Alan Sears	$9 million	No staff attorneys since it does not actually litigate cases	ADF provides funding for the legal defense of religious liberty and other issues. Helps coordinate the litigation efforts of other New Christian Right law firms.

Note: Data assembled by author from interviews and tax documents provided by New Christian Right organizations.

lawyers, and relying on their access to financial resources, these New Christian Right public interest legal organizations have altered the intersection of church and state unlike any other groups active in federal court religion cases during the 1990s.

Although the similarities among these New Christian Right groups may appear obvious, there are considerable philosophical and practical differences. This is a reflection of the New Christian Right movement as a whole as well as the evangelical Christian base upon which it relies. Both see extensive organizational creation and development, but neither has a single guiding figure, institution, or philosophy to fully coordinate the independent actions of their subunits.

Similarly, New Christian Right activity in the courts has largely been without direction or coordination. For example, the smallest of the groups in this study, Liberty Counsel, was initially formed as a small nonprofit appendage to founder Mathew Staver's successful commercial law practice. Others such as the Rutherford Institute and CLS Center were created to focus on constitutional issues alone, the former as a totally independent organization and the latter as the litigating arm of a membership society made up of Christian judges, lawyers, and law students. Both struggled for years to make their name in the courts. Still others, like the Alliance Defense Fund and American Center for Law and Justice, were founded and funded by prominent New Christian Right leaders with the intention of making an immediate impact on the law.

While the Rutherford Institute vigorously asserts its independence from all other New Christian Right organizations, the Alliance Defense Fund proudly notes the support of its founding ministries and its interaction with other conservative organizations in the courts. The advantages of being a formal affiliate of a larger organization are most clearly seen in the rise and development of the American Center for Law and Justice, which burst into public interest litigation in 1990 backed by the already tested organizational and fund-raising skills of Pat Robertson's Christian Coalition. Even Liberty Counsel has evidently seen the need to combine its resources by recently becoming a formal affiliate of Jerry Falwell's ministry. In financing, reputation, access to affiliated lawyers, courtroom success, and many other ways, these groups demonstrate that, their common ideological front notwithstanding, considerable differences remain.

Each of the organizations in this study pursues cases in several key areas, including abortion, parental rights, obscenity, and "family values." The greatest proportion of their litigation activity, however, has been devoted to claims of religious discrimination. Focusing on religious liberty cases has earned New Christian Right attorneys a predictable mix of praise and scorn. Their supporters welcome any attempt to challenge previous judicial rulings viewed as hostile to religious expression. Their courtroom rivals, on the other hand, are deeply opposed to any lowering of the historic legal wall separating church and state, a concern shared by both secular separationist groups that are apprehensive about religion's role in governmental decision making as well as religious separationists who fear the governmental influence a lowered wall would permit into the religious sphere.

Equally controversial is the manner in which New Christian Right public interest law firms now argue their religion claims in the courts. What at one time were questions clearly framed by the free exercise and establishment clauses of the First Amendment are now often presented as matters of free speech. Secular critics view this admittedly successful tactic as an end run around the wall of separation while others, even some who are ideologically sympathetic, question the wisdom of equating religious belief and expression with mere speech.

A detailed look at each of the major New Christian Right groups litigating religion in the federal courts helps explain their origins, the depth of their commitment to maintaining a long-term courtroom presence, and their reliance on the free speech clause to fundamentally alter the legal relationship between church and state in America.

Center for Law and Religious Freedom

The Center for Law and Religious Freedom is the formal advocacy arm of the Christian Legal Society (CLS), a group founded in 1961 with a current membership of 4,500 Christian law students, lawyers, and judges. Formed in 1975 to advocate the right of student religious clubs to function within public high schools as any other student organization would, the CLS Center is now the oldest and most experienced of the New Christian Right organizations litigating religion cases. With a $1.5 million budget and just three staff attorneys, the center is obviously limited in its ability to bring about policy change. However, the assistance of the CLS attorney network coupled with the center's own efforts to influence policymaking through political avenues other than the judiciary gives it a surprisingly greater influence than what might be expected from such a small organization.

The CLS Center's ability to utilize its sparse resources on a number of political fronts is just one aspect that distinguishes it from other New Christian Right public interest law firms. While it has been active in the courts, it has also devoted considerable effort to lobbying Congress and executive branch agencies from its Annandale, Virginia, office on issues of concern to religious conservatives.[1]

During its twenty-five years of existence the center has also worked to develop professional relationships with a number of seemingly incompatible organizations such as the ACLU, American Jewish Committee, Americans United for Separation of Church and State, and People for the American Way. In addition to uniting with these and other ideologically dissimilar groups in promoting a variety of religion-related initiatives before Congress, the CLS Center has joined with them to draft and promulgate several broad statements of consensus regarding religious expression in the public schools. The broad range of views incorporated into such documents as "Religion in the Public Schools: A Joint Statement of Current Law," "Religion in the Public School Curriculum: Questions and Answers," and "Public Schools and Religious Communities: A First Amendment Guide" led to their formal endorsement by the Clinton administration in 1995. Secretary of Education Richard Riley subsequently sent out a packet of information containing these and other guidelines on religious expression to the nation's fifteen thousand school districts.[2]

The CLS Center's bridging strategy with its ideological rivals has come under the reproachful eye of some within the New Christian Right who view this aspect of the center's work as a form of consorting with the enemy. There have been additional charges that the center's efforts lack the intensity necessary to bring about substantive policy change where religion and the public square are concerned. The center has not let charges of being soft go unanswered. As former director Steven McFarland indicated in a 1994 interview, "There are some folks who are going to think that . . . because we don't take a tactical hardball approach, [we] are wimps. And there are those who find those tactics unacceptable and un-Christian."[3] In truth, however, the center's courtroom efforts have historically been "soft," consisting almost solely of writing third-party amicus curiae briefs for the

Supreme Court, mediating disputes out of court, and providing legal assistance to CLS member attorneys in some three hundred cases annually.[4]

As the oldest New Christian Right legal advocacy group, the CLS Center has a unique vantage point from which to view the efforts of more recent entrants into conservative religious liberty litigation. McFarland openly acknowledges that "there is not harmony among all of the groups. There's only so much funding out there, and each group is trying to get its share."[5] The CLS Center would particularly like to see its one-time associate John Whitehead, who wrote the center's first brief, and his Rutherford Institute become more involved in a collaborative New Christian Right legal effort, but that is an appeal Whitehead has repeatedly rejected.[6]

Although the center admittedly remains more reluctant than other New Christian Right public interest law firms to get involved in direct litigation, it has attempted to become somewhat more aggressive during the last few years. With the founding of the Alliance Defense Fund (ADF), a new source of funding was created for the type of expensive direct legal participation that the center had largely avoided. During 1998, the ADF gave nearly $200,000 to the CLS Center and its then affiliated organization, the Western Center for Law and Religious Freedom.[7] And despite the ADF's purported selectivity in its disbursal of funds, it rarely rejects a CLS Center request for financial assistance.[8]

One indication of the CLS Center's increasing level of participation in religious liberty disputes was its creation of the National Legal Resource Center (NLRC). Financed by the ADF, this online service offers both affiliated lawyers and other like-minded legal advocacy groups access to scholarly material on religious liberty as well as legal briefs, memos, and other information to assist them in their courtroom efforts. With this clearinghouse of information, the center hopes to improve both the quality and the success rate of the religious liberty litigation pursued by its affiliated lawyers. The NLRC also serves as a Christian attorney referral service for individuals in need of legal assistance.

Unlike other New Christian Right organizations active in the courts, there are no plans to either expand the CLS Center's operations or dramatically depart from its essentially "soft" approach to litigation. While its ability to litigate more cases has been enhanced by the funding opportunities presented by the ADF, there is no indication that the CLS Center will abandon either its preference for third-party amicus participation within the courts or its legislative and executive branch activism without.

Rutherford Institute

The concept behind the Rutherford Institute originated in the mid-1970s on the West Coast where attorney John W. Whitehead had moved with his family after leaving his private law practice in Arkansas to enroll in a California seminary program. Shortly after beginning his religious studies, Whitehead was asked to assist a public school teacher who had been reprimanded for explaining to her students her reasons for wearing a crucifix. Successful in this initial dispute, Whitehead subsequently moved to Virginia and took the first steps toward creating an organization that, as he envisioned it, would pursue claims of religious discrimination and infringement through the courts and without cost. The result was the 1982 founding of the Rutherford Institute. Like most of the other organizations in this study, Rutherford litigates in several areas but religion remains a central focus of its efforts. Rutherford has long claimed to handle over 80 percent of all religious liberty litigation. Although such a declaration is difficult to quantify, it very well could have been true prior to the 1990s and the rise of other New Christian Right public interest law firms. Headquartered in Charlottesville, Virginia, the Rutherford Institute currently has three staff attorneys, one thousand affiliated lawyers nationwide who provided $925,000 in donated services in 1999, and an international office in Hungary.[9] Its domestic and international efforts on behalf of religious liberty and other issues operate on a $4.5 million budget, a figure significantly less than in previous years.[10]

Named for Samuel Rutherford, the seventeenth-century Scottish minister who disputed the divine right of kings, the Rutherford Institute reflects Whitehead's no-nonsense approach to litigation. The brooding photograph of Whitehead on nearly every piece of Rutherford Institute literature reinforces his image as an aggressive Christian lawyer. Whitehead believes that the combination of Christian beliefs with legal training should yield nothing less than a forceful and determined defense of religious liberty. In his 1982 book *The Second American Revolution,* Whitehead details his combative approach to litigation: "There is an advantage to suing before being sued. The principal advantage is that the entity doing the suing chooses the court in which the case will be heard, and, by suing, frames the issues and arguments from his point of view. There are other advantages, but they can be summed up by saying that the first man out of the chute has the jump on the others involved in the race. It is a matter of strategy and planning."[11] Other New Christian Right public interest law firms have since adopted a similarly assertive stance, but it was Whitehead who pioneered the religious conservatives' proactive approach to law.

Whitehead's Rutherford Institute can also claim credit as an early advocate of the free speech clause as a protector of religious expression. In a rare instance in which it joined with the ACLU, the Rutherford Institute defended a Virginia man's free speech right to put "ATH-EST" on his vanity license plate. The unlikely union between the Rutherford Institute and the ACLU in this case occurred because, as Whitehead put it, "If you can't put ATHEIST on a license plate, you can't put THEIST."[12]

Despite its groundbreaking contributions as an early courtroom proponent of aggressive Christian litigation and the use of the free speech clause in religion cases, Rutherford is not particularly warmed by those that have since joined it in the religious liberty fray. Whitehead himself tries to draw distinctions between his group and other New Christian Right legal organizations and is especially blunt about those that would use the law to "Christianize" America: "If you don't want others ramming their views down your throat, you can't ram your views down theirs. . . . Our agenda is not to have a Christian nation, but to enable religious people to survive."[13]

The Rutherford Institute does indeed litigate a much broader variety of cases than any of the other organizations in this study, including those involving claims of sexual harassment and the rights of the criminally accused. For that reason alone some observers question its New Christian Right credentials. But Rutherford has not strayed far from its founding mission: to educate others in the law and to use the courts to protect religious, usually Christian, expression. To that end, Rutherford provides supporters with a variety of Whitehead's books and pamphlets including "Censored on the Job: Your Religious Rights," "Christians Involved in the Political Process," and "Women's Rights and the Law," the last one offering a biblical perspective on the rights of women.

Despite its pioneering efforts, the Rutherford Institute has long been viewed as the black sheep of the New Christian Right legal family. Both the ADF and the CLS Center have made overtures to Whitehead to coordinate strategy only to be flatly rejected. Rutherford officials are neither comfortable with the strings they believe are attached to ADF funding nor pleased with some of the nonlitigation efforts of the CLS Center. In short, the Rutherford Institute sees little benefit in combining its efforts with other New Christian Right groups. As John Whitehead himself succinctly puts it, "We don't like holding hands. It gets all sweaty."[14]

Rutherford's refusal to cooperate with other New Christian Right organizations may be due to the fact that it views these groups as competitors. Rutherford has been overshadowed by the media (and frequent Supreme Court) presence of the American Center for Law and Justice (ACLJ) and its chief counsel, Jay Sekulow; it lacks the nonlitigation expertise and team-player image of the CLS Center; it enjoys no formal affiliation with parent organizations or ministries like the ADF, the ACLJ, and Liberty Counsel; and it has seen its annual budget cut in half since the ADF was organized in 1994. In part because of its decreasing budget, Rutherford centralized its operations in Charlottesville between 1996 and 1998 by closing its southwestern, western, and Washington, D.C., branch offices, the last of several regional sites in the United States that it once operated. During the same period Rutherford also closed its international offices in Bolivia, England, and France.[15]

In October 1997 the Rutherford Institute took a major step toward increasing its visibility by agreeing to help defray the legal expenses of Paula Jones in her sexual harassment suit against President Clinton. Although Rutherford had never been active in sexual harassment cases prior to this time, Whitehead viewed its newly acquired financier role as consistent with his organization's creed: no one is above the law.[16]

Predictably, national media attention fell upon both Whitehead and the Rutherford Institute, as it did with practically everything else associated with the Paula Jones case. But once the issue was settled out of court the following year, the spotlight on Rutherford quickly faded. It is questionable whether that brief, heightened notoriety will yield the long-term financial support the institute needs to perpetuate itself successfully against its courtroom foes on the one hand and its own theological allies on the other.

American Center for Law and Justice

Founded in 1990 by one of America's most visible New Christian Right leaders, Marion G. (Pat) Robertson, the ACLJ was specifically organized to provide a "Christian counterpart to the ACLU." The ACLJ's first executive director, Keith Fournier, was a Roman Catholic who was sympathetic to Robertson's concerns regarding the lack of an adequate conservative response to liberal interest group efforts in the courts. Fournier later wrote that these organizations "had opened the doors to the legalization of abortion on demand, sanctioning it as a 'reproductive right.' They were assaulting the family from every front and, in a perverse way, they were using the First Amendment to increasingly censor the free-speech activities of people of faith. In the world of these public-interest practitioners, anything they perceived as religious, and particularly Christian, was deemed politically incorrect."[17]

Fournier drafted a series of ambitious objectives, which included making the organization the undisputed leader of Christian public interest advocacy. A decade later, the ACLJ's $9 million budget, twenty-five-lawyer staff, and network of some 330 volunteer attorneys across the country have indeed made it the most prominent of all New Christian Right public interest law firms.[18]

Assisting Robertson in developing a legal counteroffensive to the perceived liberal element in the courts is a flamboyant young lawyer named Jay Sekulow who was once characterized by Fournier as the "Thurgood Marshall of our work."[19] A Messianic Jew, self-avowed liberal, and until recently a registered Democrat, Sekulow appears to be an odd choice for the ACLJ and the New Christian Right agenda it represents.[20] No less strange is the manner in which Sekulow became, arguably, the New Christian Right's most prominent figure in religious liberty litigation today.

After graduating from Mercer Law School in 1980, Sekulow began his legal career prosecuting tax fraud cases for the IRS. He subsequently started his own practice in Atlanta, where the land development corporation owned by his firm was able to take advantage of a booming real estate market. By the mid-1980s, Sekulow was making $250,000 annually, but his professional success was short-lived. A downturn in Atlanta's real estate market coupled with the Tax Reform Act of 1986 and a bitter lawsuit against his firm by a group of project investors caused Sekulow's firm to collapse. In 1987, he was forced into personal bankruptcy with debts of over $13 million.[21]

Sekulow often credits the group Jews for Jesus for his spiritual conversion to Christianity as an eighteen-year-old college student. Twelve years later, with his legal career in shambles, Sekulow saw Jews for Jesus step in and save him professionally as well. Having served as outside counsel to the organization's board of directors in the months prior to the collapse of his firm, Sekulow argued his first case before the U.S. Supreme Court on behalf of the group in March 1987. In its unanimous decision in *Board of Airport Commissioners of Los Angeles v. Jews for Jesus,* the Supreme Court agreed with Sekulow that a Los Angeles ordinance banning all "First Amendment activity" from Los Angeles International Airport, including the distribution of religious pamphlets, was unconstitutional.[22]

Sekulow subsequently founded his own public interest law firm, Christian Advocates Serving Evangelism, to litigate religion cases as well as defend anti-abortion protestors. Here he honed the free speech philosophy that has become a hallmark of his work as the ACLJ's chief counsel. Sekulow has now argued nine cases before the Supreme Court and served as co-counsel in a tenth, using the free speech clause as a basis for his arguments in nearly every one.[23]

The ACLJ occupies a unique position among New Christian Right legal organizations for a number of reasons. To begin with, it is Pat Robertson's second attempt at public interest litigation. In 1985 he founded the National Legal Foundation, which was underwritten almost exclusively by his Christian Broadcasting Network. Although no longer formally affiliated with Robertson, the National Legal Foundation's Supreme Court victory in *Board of Education of Westside Community Schools v. Mergens* (1990), which Sekulow argued, continues to guide the religious liberty efforts of the ACLJ and other New Christian Right public interest legal organizations.

The ACLJ also enjoys far greater financial security than the other conservative groups that litigate religious liberty cases. Located in a large suite of beautifully decorated offices on the grounds of Robertson's Regent University in Virginia Beach, the ACLJ's physical surroundings alone testify to a wealth not enjoyed by other New Christian Right groups active in the courts. The $9 million budget of the ACLJ comes mostly from private donations, which is indicative of another unique aspect of the ACLJ.

While nearly all of the groups in this study utilize television or radio to some extent (see chapter 7), none enjoys the media access and exposure of the ACLJ. The repeated presence of the ACLJ, and particularly Jay Sekulow, on Christian television and radio stations has helped the organization develop a direct mailing list of over 450,000 names to which it can appeal for funding, receive case referrals from those viewing or listening to its programs, and enjoy a reputation as the preeminent New Christian Right public interest law firm engaged in religious liberty litigation.

Like the Rutherford Institute, the ACLJ has never been content with the mere defense of religious expression. At the outset Keith Fournier envisioned an aggressive role for the ACLJ: "I see the litigation efforts of groups like the ACLJ as the sword. They help us fend off the social marauders, those who are stripping away the remnants of civilization, suppressing people of faith, and substituting a new culture in the United States."[24] Perhaps because of its aggressive style, the ACLJ has come under fire for the manner in which it utilizes litigation to defend religious interests. As journalist Tim Stafford wryly noted, "[It] is hard to build the kingdom of God by suing people."[25] To such charges Sekulow counters, "The Apostle Paul himself utilized the courts when his rights were denied. This can be seen in the Book of Acts. The Bible says [that] Christians should not take other Christians to court. It does not say that Christians cannot use the courts to obtain justice when the government attempts to deny it fundamental rights."[26]

Of all the major New Christian Right public interest law firms active in the courts, the ACLJ appears to be making the greatest effort to expand its influence. Currently it depends on the volunteer attorneys affiliated with the organization to give it an extended reach into state and local religious liberty disputes. Although it will no doubt continue to rely on these affiliated lawyers, the ACLJ is also undertaking a massive expansion of its operations.

Before an audience at the Christian Coalition's 1996 annual meeting, Sekulow announced that at least one ACLJ office would be opened in every state of the union in order to address religious discrimination at the local level. By January 2000, fourteen such offices had been organized. The ACLJ has also opened up two international offices: the European Centre for Law and Justice in France and the Slavic Centre for Law and Justice in Russia.[27] The expansion of the organization will remain a central component of the ACLJ's ongoing efforts to entrench its presence in the courts.

Liberty Counsel

Although religious and legal concerns are at the heart of each of the public interest law firms examined here, none of the key individuals in these organizations has a background quite like Mathew Staver, a minister-turned-lawyer and founder of Liberty Counsel. The improbable journey from the pulpit to the courtroom started in Kentucky, where Staver served as a minister. Frustrated by what he viewed as ongoing discrimination against Christians and Christian expression, he left the ministry to enroll in the University of Kentucky College of Law.

By the time he graduated in 1987, Staver had already envisioned an organization that would utilize the law to protect the principles of religious freedom, an idea that came to fruition with his founding of Liberty Counsel three years later. For nearly a decade, Liberty Counsel operated out of Staver's highly successful commercial law firm in Orlando, Florida. In January 2000, however, he abandoned his legal practice to devote his attention full time to constitutional issues. With its handful of staff and modest budget (approximately $500,000), Liberty Counsel typifies the many other small, often part-time legal organizations that litigate New Christian Right causes.

Unlike the other groups in this study that litigate across several areas of concern, Liberty Counsel focuses almost solely on issues of free speech. From student religious expression in schools, to abortion clinic protesting, and the displaying of a Ku Klux Klan cross in a public square, Liberty Counsel's efforts reflect Staver's own personal conversion to the free speech clause.

As a minister in Kentucky Staver fought to have the film *The Last Temptation of Christ* banned from local theaters because he considered it blasphemous. Staver's views reportedly changed during law school, however, leading him to embrace a more liberal view of free speech. This new philosophy (which he acknowledges is not shared by many of his supporters) is simple: "If a Christian has a right to pray, so does a Satanist."[28]

In addition to its small size and almost sole focus on the free speech clause, Liberty Counsel further differs from the other New Christian Right organizations in this study because of its strong regional presence. Without the large affiliated lawyer network of a CLS Center or Rutherford Institute or the financial resources of the ACLJ, it has focused its work primarily on religious and free speech issues in Florida. However, its ability to participate in other cases across the nation has been heightened by its access to money and training provided by the ADF. It was the ADF, for example, that provided funding for the landmark abortion clinic "buffer-zone" case, *Madsen v. Women's Health Center, Inc.,* that Staver argued before the Supreme Court in 1994.[29] A frequent recipient of ADF funds, Liberty Counsel was awarded over $93,000 in 1998 alone to use in various case preparations.[30] In addition, ADF-trained attorneys are assisting Staver with litigation as part of their commitment to the ADF's National Litigation Academy.

After a decade of independent work focusing primarily on central Florida, Liberty Counsel recently took two important steps to expand its influence further. In June 2000 the organization announced that it was opening its first branch office in Kansas City to focus on free speech disputes in the Midwest. A month later Staver announced that Liberty Counsel had formally allied itself with Jerry Falwell Ministries and would be opening a branch office in Lynchburg, Virginia.[31] This association will undoubtedly benefit Liberty Counsel (in much the same way as the ACLJ's relationship with Pat Robertson) as it turns to Falwell's supporters for both financial assistance and additional cases to litigate.

Alliance Defense Fund

Based in Scottsdale, Arizona, the ADF describes itself as "a national Alliance funding the legal defense and advocacy of religious freedom, the sanctity of human life, and family values."[32] The ADF neither retains staff attorneys nor directly takes cases to court, but its unique role as an umbrella organization that provides funding to both individual lawyers and public interest law firms unites it with the other New Christian Right organizations considered here.

The ADF was founded in 1994 by a veritable who's who of New Christian Right leaders in response to the lack of coordination among existing conservative Christian public interest law firms.[33] An additional impetus behind the creation of the ADF was the impression that conservatives were largely ineffective for reasons that had little to do with inexperience, unfavorable legal precedents, or unsympathetic judges. Rather, as an ADF fund-raising letter later recounted, it was a matter of money: "When Christians get defeated in court, it's usually because the opponents' pockets are so deep that they are able to see each case through to the finish—no matter the cost—and they are relentless in sustaining the battle. We must be able to do the same."[34]

Accordingly, with seed money donated by the ministries of its founding members, the ADF was created with the lofty objective of someday establishing a permanent annual fund of at least $25 million to be used to finance conservative legal challenges. By 1999, the organization's budget had already surpassed $9 million.[35] The ADF continues to have a small part of its budget underwritten by its sponsoring ministries but now relies almost exclusively on private donations.

Heading the ADF's twelve-member staff is Alan Sears, who serves as both president and general counsel. Best known for his Department of Justice work as executive director of the Attorney General's Commission on Pornography during the Reagan administration, Sears also has an extensive background in public interest advocacy having previously served as executive director of both the Children's Legal Foundation and National Family Legal Foundation. At the ADF, Sears oversees the organization's threefold mission of funding, strategic planning, and training.

From a universe of complaints, the ADF selects only a few to which it will devote funding and other resources. ADF funding criteria requires its cases to have merit, have the potential to be precedent-setting in their impact, and involve one of the three primary areas of ADF emphasis—religious freedom, sanctity of human life, or family values. Since 1994, the ADF has awarded over five hundred grants to cases and projects meeting these standards. Grants for cases involving religious liberty issues have always made up the greatest proportion of ADF-funded projects, and in 1998 they accounted for approximately 43 percent—over $500,000 worth—of total awards granted.[36]

Although individual lawyers who volunteer their time to provide legal services to the ADF can receive grants to help cover the costs of litigation, more than half of the organization's funding is channeled to the groups considered in this study. Admittedly, these groups pursue legal objectives that largely mirror the ADF's goals and thus qualify as legitimate candidates for grant awards. However, there is an additional explanation for this directed funding.

Since its inception, the ADF has stressed the importance of developing a coordinated New Christian Right legal strategy. One way it has sought to achieve this goal is by developing an interlocking relationship with other leaders of the New Christian Right's judicial efforts. This was most clearly evidenced by the composition of the ADF's Grant Review Committee, which awards funding to the most promising applicants. Selected from the ADF's larger Legal Advisory Group, the committee consists of seven members. In 1994 three of the seven members of the committee were directly affiliated with either the ACLJ (Jay Sekulow, chief counsel) or the CLS (Kimberlee Colby, special counsel, and Steve McFarland, director of the CLS Center). Although the ADF no longer makes public the names of its Grant Review Committee members, the public interest law firms in this study continue to benefit greatly from their association with the ADF.

During 1998, for example, the ADF provided a total of $1.1 million for various cases and projects. Over $600,000 of this amount was awarded to the ACLJ, Liberty Counsel, and the CLS Center.[37] Noticeably absent from this list, of course, is the Rutherford Institute.

There is a pronounced coolness between the ADF and the Rutherford Institute, a situation that appears to be motivated more by economics than ideology. While it has expressed serious reservations about the ADF's ability to guide the legal strategy of the cases it funds (and thus deprive grantee organizations of control over their cases), the Rutherford Institute has also seen its budget cut in half since the ADF was founded.[38] Rutherford officials believe that the presence of the ADF has negatively impacted their ability to reach the funding levels of previous years.

In addition to its coordinated strategy formulation and grant-awarding purposes, the ADF is also active in training a network of attorneys through whom it can pursue its mission in the courts. To the extent that the ADF must rely on volunteer attorneys to litigate religious liberty claims, it also attempts to provide them with the skills and information they need to be successful. To this end, the ADF offers affiliated attorneys the opportunity to rent (or own if pro bono work is provided on behalf of ADF causes) a series of training videos outlining strategies for religious liberty litigation.

A more ambitious approach to the ADF's training mission was realized through the creation of its National Litigation Academy in June 1997. The academy consists of four days of intensive training designed to equip volunteer attorneys with the skills and trial techniques they need to effectively litigate issues of concern to the ADF. Participants in the academy are drilled in both the substantive and technical aspects of successful religious liberty litigation by law professors and lawyers associated with conservative causes, including many of those affiliated with the public interest organizations in this study. Currently thirty-eight states recognize the ADF's training school, allowing attorneys to earn Continuing Legal Education credits there.

For its part, the ADF receives a commitment from each graduate (250 through March 2000) to volunteer at least 450 hours to litigate ADF-backed issues. Ultimately it hopes to have over 900 academy-trained lawyers by 2004, many of whom will be strategically located in parts of the country where religious liberty disputes have been a recurring problem.[39] In addition, the ADF's newest program, the Blackstone Legal Fellowship, provides first-year law students with training and summer internship opportunities with public interest law firms allied with the ADF.

As a source of funding, the ADF has filled a noticeable void in New Christian Right public interest law. With the ongoing support of its founding ministries, a growing budget, and a well-developed relationship with most of the other major New Christian Right groups active in the courts, it is already well placed to maintain an extended judicial presence. In addition, the growing network of ADF-trained attorneys and the pro bono work they have agreed to provide for ADF-directed legal challenges suggest that it may have a much more direct role in future litigation than its capacity as financier has allowed for up to this point.

The New Christian Right in the Courts

Given the long history of interest group activity in the courts, it is not particularly surprising that the New Christian Right would embrace a judicial strategy. What is remarkable, however, given the manner in which the political mobilization of the New Christian Right has been intertwined with judicial decisions on school prayer and abortion (as well as its ongoing perception of liberal bias in the courts), is the length of time it took the movement to commit to maintaining a courtroom presence. Conservative organizations have sporadically participated in religious liberty litigation in the past, but only within the last twenty years, and particularly the last decade, has there been a consistent conservative presence in the courts where issues of religion are concerned. The financing provided by the ADF has been a critical factor in this growth.

At the most basic level, these groups are one in purpose, having enlisted themselves in the battle to protect primarily Christian expression against what they believe are overtly hostile forces both in and out of the courtroom. There are also important institutional, financial, and philosophical differences among them, however, which reflect the considerable competition for funding, cases, and recognition. What remains to be seen is whether the commitment to similar causes, occasional courtroom alliances, and common strategies that motivate and guide the religious liberty litigation efforts of these firms assert any real influence.

4 "Incremental Pragmatism"

Legal Strategies of the New Christian Right

> I learned a great deal studying the strategies of the legal activists of the last thirty years, among which was how to begin to undo the damage they've caused and restore some sanity to our jurisprudence. We needed a form of what I called "incremental pragmatism" in our legal strategy. I knew we could not change things quickly; getting from A to Z would not occur overnight. It had taken years to institutionalize murky relativism and judicial insanity. It would take years to undo it and restore sanity. We needed to be prepared to struggle from A to B, then from B to C . . . all the way to Z.
>
> Keith Fournier, former ACLJ executive director, 1994

When questioned about their use of the law to protect religious liberty, New Christian Right lawyers often make reference to a biblical model of legal resistance by citing the example of the Apostle Paul invoking his rights as a Roman citizen when his preaching caused him to be arrested for sedition.[1] New Christian Right attorneys who litigate religious liberty claims see themselves fulfilling a similar role: seeking legal redress for individuals who have been discriminated against because of their religious beliefs, expression, or speech. However, they also envision a much larger purpose to their legal efforts than merely ensuring that a person has his or her day in court.

When asked why his group stressed litigation, ADF president Alan Sears responded by drawing a picture of a three-legged stool. The seat of the stool, he said, represented American culture, which stood on three legs of support: the Great Commission, which creates spiritual change; governmental access by which political changes are brought about; and litigation, which produces legal change. All three legs, Sears explained, including the courtroom presence of religious conservatives, are necessary to support and strengthen this vision of American culture.[2] The fulfillment of such a vision, however, cannot be accomplished by simply reacting to perceived infringements on religious liberty. As the ADF acknowledges, "Many cases are defensive in nature. But increasingly, ADF is funding litigation that is going on the offensive to . . . reclaim the Constitution's guarantee of free exercise of religion."[3]

The ADF is not alone in its proactive approach to law. In fact, each of the New Christian Right organizations in this study actively seeks opportunities to secure religious rights through law. When such claims require litigation, these groups use well-documented legal strategies that have long served other interest groups in the courts (see table 2). As circumstances require, they also use several extra-courtroom strategies to achieve policy change where religious expression is concerned. Termed public education, prelitigation, and nonlitigation, these out-of-court tactics are important tools in and of themselves (see chapter 7).

These groups exist to litigate, however, and thus use familiar judicial branch strategies such as case selection and/or sponsorship and the filing of amicus curiae briefs. Well utilized by courtroom activists from across the political spectrum, these procedures have been the focus of considerable scholarship on interest group litigation, in part because they are generally easy to document.[4]

Of equally strategic importance is the role that some New Christian Right groups play as legal overseers in providing funding and legal expertise to the lawyers and organizations named in the briefs. In most cases the amount of financial or technical assistance given by the legal overseer, or the degree to which it navigates the course of the litigation itself, is virtually unknown except to the parties directly involved.

The last important legal strategy of New Christian Right public interest lawyers involves their focus on the free speech clause instead of the Constitution's religion clauses. Although clearly not a procedural strategy like those listed above, the free speech emphasis so permeates the litigating strategies of New Christian Right lawyers that a separate consideration of the principles guiding its use in religion cases is necessary. In general, the New Christian Right has contributed little to the process-oriented strategies pioneered by the ACLU, American Jewish Congress, NAACP, and other litigating interest groups. But its forging of a new jurisprudential relationship between the free speech clause and religion is a legal contribution that has left a distinct impression on contemporary church-state litigation.

Table 2. Litigating strategies of the New Christian Right

Type of litigating strategy	Who uses this strategy	Advantages of strategy	Disadvantages of strategy
Case selection and sponsorship	ACLJ, CLS, LC, RI (ADF provides funding)	Gives firms complete control over the course of the litigation.	Lie in the financial and legal realities of law: it is expensive to engage in direct litigation, and there are no guarantees of success in the courts.
Amicus curiae briefs	ACLJ, CLS, LC, RI (ADF provides funding)	Allows firms to participate practically at will. Not only is it less expensive than direct sponsorship, but it plays well with supporters.	Amici are not awarded attorney's fees. Also considerable debate as to the actual impact of such briefs on judicial decision making.
Legal overseer	ACLJ, ADF, CLS, RI	Varying levels of control: can sponsor; fund; or provide technical expertise, anony-mously building quiet victories.	For overseer, lack of credit and attorney's fees. For counsel, utilizing overseer's services means playing by overseer's rules.
Appeal to free speech clause	ACLJ, ADF, CLS, LC, RI	Has provided consistent religious liberty victories for New Christian Right firms.	Cannot be utilized in all circumstances. Necessarily protects the views of non-Christians, the nonreligious, and even those whose views are diametrically opposed to those of Christians'.

Test Case Selection Strategy

The test case strategy is the most direct method by which interest groups can access and possibly influence the judiciary. To a greater degree than other courtroom strategies, it also provides such organizations with control over the legal and intellectual flow of the litigation. Theoretically, the use of test cases or planned litigation allows an organization to handpick a case or series of cases whose factual circumstances are particularly well suited to obtaining a desired policy change by judicial mandate. Citing its careful efforts to end the practice of racially restrictive housing covenants and segregation in the public schools, scholars often invoke the NAACP Legal Defense Fund and its use of the test case strategy as a prototype.[5]

However, unlike the NAACP's efforts to end racial discrimination by challenging the explicit, clearly observable practice of segregation, New Christian Right lawyers find themselves fighting legal battles on behalf of causes that often lack precise definition. The ADF, for example, funds cases devoted to "religious freedom, the sanctity of human life, and family values."[6] The ACLJ focuses its legal efforts on "pro-[religious] liberty, pro-life, and pro-family causes."[7] The CLS Center assists member attorneys in "defending religious freedom and the sanctity of human life."[8] Liberty Counsel was created to "preserve religious freedom."[9] The Rutherford Institute provides services in disputes involving "First Amendment rights [and] religious and civil liberties."[10]

The broad nature of these stated purposes notwithstanding, most of these groups have adopted specific criteria to guide them in the case selection process. In financing legal challenges, for example, the ADF is extremely selective in the cases it funds. According to recent tax documents, the five hundred grants the ADF has awarded since its founding in 1994 represents only a quarter of all funding requests it has received.[11] One limiting factor, obviously, is the financial reality that prevents the ADF from meeting every request. However, as mentioned in the previous chapter, the ADF's strict requirement that cases have precedent-setting potential also limits the number of grants it extends.

The ACLJ and Liberty Counsel have case selection criteria similar to that of the ADF. The ACLJ's cases must not only be in accordance with the organization's prorelingion, prolife, and profamily objectives, they must also "affect the public at large."[12] Of his organization's case selection strategy,

Liberty Counsel founder and president Mat Staver notes, "We're not going to defend everyone, we're interested in setting good precedents."[13]

While the ADF, the ACLJ, and Liberty Counsel pursue a case selection formula that focuses on both the potential case's fit with an internal set of criteria as well as its promise for setting precedent, the CLS Center has generally held to a narrower standard. Focusing almost exclusively on religious liberty–related issues, CLS Center staff meet once a year to assess the legal climate of religious freedom generally.[14] Because it reformulates its litigating strategy annually, the CLS Center tends to be much more reactive than other New Christian Right legal organizations.

The least strategic of these groups in terms of case selection is the Rutherford Institute. Although like the others it has priority areas into which its litigation is categorized, it does not require that a case have precedent-setting potential. And though Rutherford's claim that it handles over 80 percent of all religious liberty litigation is impossible to quantify, the fact that the organization's case selection policies are less strategic than those of other New Christian Right firms could understandably have led Rutherford into more potential litigation situations. By its own count, Rutherford answered nearly 9,800 requests for assistance, including prelitigation services, during fiscal year 1997.[15]

Because no public interest law firm can possibly entertain all claims of religious liberty infringement, even Rutherford has had to turn away some requests. Rita Woltz, former legal coordinator for the Rutherford Institute, acknowledged, "We can't do all [meet all requests for assistance], but we tried to for some time."[16] Like the Rutherford Institute, other New Christian Right public interest law firms clearly realize that their ability to pursue religious liberty claims to fulfill broad mission statements or to set far-reaching precedents can be exercised only to the degree that the money is available to take up these challenges.

The case selection strategies pursued by New Christian Right public interest law firms are important for a number of reasons. First and foremost, it is the case itself that has the potential to ultimately transform the legal universe surrounding a particular issue or policy. The relationship between religious expression and the state is considerably different now than it was prior to the CLS Center's *Widmar v. Vincent* case in 1981 that saw a nearly unanimous Supreme Court declare that public universities could not deny religious groups use of school facilities if such were made available to secular groups.[17] The ripple effect of that case continues to be felt as its central holding has been upheld and expanded in both the Supreme Court and the lower federal courts.

Second, the case selection process gives firms an ownership right that they use in soliciting additional support. New Christian Right legal organizations, for example, use claims of religious liberty infringement (especially those that are particularly atrocious) in promotional material to demonstrate the importance of their legal work. This in turn invites the attention and financial support of sympathizers. It may also lead to additional case referrals as these groups, the services they offer, and the issues they litigate become better known. The more direct the participation, the greater the ownership right that can be claimed.

When attorney's fees were awarded to Ronald Rosenberger's legal team in 1996 after his successful Supreme Court bid to gain university funding for his Christian magazine in *Rosenberger v. Rector and Visitors of the University of Virginia* (1995), it was discovered that the Rutherford Institute had declined Rosenberger's initial appeal for assistance.[18] That organization thus deprived itself of important public visibility, an enhanced reputation among its supporters, and overall bragging rights associated with direct participation in one of the most significant religion cases of the 1990s.[19] In contrast, the ADF, having been organized just months before the U.S. Court of Appeals for the Fourth Circuit handed down its decision in *Rosenberger,* quickly recognized the significance of the legal questions involved and helped finance that case to the Supreme Court. The ADF continues to showpiece *Rosenberger* in its fund-raising and public education efforts.

Third, although a selected case may indeed bring about desired legal change and/or ownership right to an organization, the case selection process poses an inherent dilemma for New Christian Right public interest law groups. Organizations that are especially selective invariably face a trade-off between seeking relief for many bona fide instances of religious discrimination on the one hand and the opportunity to utilize a select few cases to bring about larger-scale public policy changes on the other. This dilemma is exacerbated when case selection is coupled with the financial challenges of public interest law.

The precedent-setting criterion for case selection required by many New Christian Right firms assumes that a given case will find its way to the upper levels of the federal judiciary where a favorable decision will have the greatest impact. Not only does it normally require considerable financial backing to shepherd a case through the federal court system (not to mention a bit of luck to obtain plenary consideration by the Supreme Court), but success there is anything but guaranteed. Thus, like other litigating public interest groups, New Christian Right legal organizations are continually confronted with the question of whether to focus their efforts on numerous individual cases at the lower levels of the judiciary or litigate a select handful of claims as far as their financial resources and good fortune will allow.

Amicus Curiae Strategy

New Christian Right groups active in the courts frequently engage in a much less direct method of participation by filing amicus curiae briefs on the merits of a case.[20] Literally meaning "friend of the court," the modern amicus brief has taken on a less objective role than its name implies by generally favoring the position taken by one of the parties involved in the litigation. In amicus briefs filed in cases dealing with religious issues, lawyers frame the central legal questions of the dispute against a backdrop of sympathetic case law, seeking to persuade the court to render a decision favorable to the party they support.[21] It is a participatory strategy that has been adopted by organizations from across the political spectrum that litigate in the federal courts. Its use has increased substantially at all levels of the judiciary in recent years, particularly within the Supreme Court. While less than 30 percent of the Warren Court's (1953–69) cases contained at least one amicus brief, amici supported over 84 percent of cases decided by the current Rehnquist Court through its 1991 term.[22] By the 1995–96 term, nearly 90 percent of the cases decided by the Court were accompanied by at least one amicus brief.[23]

Reflective of both the heightened value of filing amicus briefs as well as the increasing number and participation of New Christian Right organizations in the courts is the fact that since 1990 no Supreme Court religion case has lacked New Christian Right participation as amici. In fact, most of these cases have seen multiple amicus briefs filed by religious conservatives. The presence of several amici does not necessarily mean that the impact of such briefs is multiplied. In fact, the actual influence of either single or multiple amicus curiae briefs on judicial decision making is the subject of ongoing debate.[24] The increased use of amici in Supreme Court cases, however, suggests that considerable value is still placed on their filing and attorneys who argue before the High Court welcome and even seek out amicus participation on behalf of the parties they represent.

A good example of both the opportunities and challenges arising out of the interaction between amici and the lawyers litigating a particular case before the Supreme Court was given by church-state scholar and University of Texas law professor Douglas Laycock, who represented a Florida church whose members practiced animal sacrifice.[25] Laycock noted that in *Church of the Lukumi Babalu Aye v. City of Hialeah* he was compelled to focus the arguments in his brief on the constitutionality of the four city ordinances that targeted the church's sacrificial activities. "You get only fifty pages," he said. "You can only argue so many things. . . . There was no space left to tell [the justices] what was wrong with *Smith*. We left all that to the *amici*."[26] Although united in their condemnation of the Court's 1990 *Smith* decision,[27] the amici (which included the CLS and Rutherford Institute) were not coordinated in relation to each other, as Laycock recalls:

> We had five briefs, twenty-some organizations all together. . . . We had what we called the "mainstream brief," by Michael McConnell at Chicago and Ed Gaffney at Valparaiso. We tried to get all the mainstream churches and civil liberties organizations united on that brief.
>
> And then, there were other people with special concerns of their own who, for whatever reason, wanted to say their own thing and didn't want to join the main brief. The Catholic Bishops filed a brief of neither side but saying *Smith* was bad. The Orthodox Jewish organizations, not surprisingly, filed a brief that said this is a real threat to kosher slaughter, and besides that *Smith* is bad. The Rutherford Institute nearly always files on its own. . . . It's not that they were uncooperative, but they were going to do their own thing, and that was pretty clear from the beginning.[28]

Despite the lack of empirical support for the claim that amicus curiae briefs in general exert influence on Supreme Court decision making, third-party participation as amici remains the legal strategy of choice for religious conservatives in the Supreme Court.[29] Part of the appeal of an amicus brief lies in the flexibility with which it permits public interest organizations and other groups to participate almost at will in cases of importance to them.

No less important is the manner in which amicus briefs encourage political expression. As undemocratic as the judicial branch is by nature, it nevertheless allows for third-party participation by almost any interested party via the amicus brief. As Caldiera and Wright explain, "Participation is not restricted to prestigious individuals, public or private law firms, corporations, or units of federal and state government. . . . The Court's receptivity to brief's *amicus curiae* strongly encourages the aggregation and articulation of interests through general membership organizations. In this sense, the Court is very much a representative institution."[30]

Perhaps what is most significant is the fact that regardless of who is actually sponsoring the litigation, the filing of amicus briefs allows participating parties to claim some ownership right to a case, which again plays well to both interest group members and potential supporters.[31] Literature distributed by New Christian Right public interest organizations, for example, heralds "their" victories and laments "their" losses when describing their amicus participation in the Supreme Court. If nothing else, the amicus strategy allows these organizations to proclaim to their supporters, in essence, "We're important, we're players in the big league of the Supreme Court."[32]

A final advantage to the filing of amicus briefs is that it does not carry the type of financial burden associated with direct sponsorship of a case. This is not to say, of course, that the expense involved in the filing of amicus briefs is inconsequential. Indeed, anecdotal evidence suggests that the costs of these briefs are substantial enough to prevent interest groups from "fil[ing] *amicus curiae* briefs with reckless abandon."[33]

Debate continues among New Christian Right public interest organizations as to how to improve their amicus participation in the courts. Some, like Alan Sears of the ADF, would like to see better coordination among amici so that each brief neither strikes out on its own agenda nor repeats arguments presented in other briefs.[34] Conversely, the Rutherford Institute believes that coordinated amicus brief efforts dilute the participation benefits sought by individual legal organizations.[35]

Although there are a number of reasons for adopting the amicus strategy, there are also fundamental disadvantages to this legal tool that influence the participation decisions of New Christian Right groups in the courts. Although amicus participation may give organizations a judicial voice, permit some claim to ownership over a case, and at a minimum allow litigating groups to "fight the good fight" for their supporters, the questionable influence of amici on judicial decision making largely neutralizes these positives. There are more practical reasons as well for abandoning the amicus brief for more direct participatory strategies. As a CLS Center attorney candidly put it, "[A]micus don't get attorney's fee[s] when their side wins."[36]

Legal Overseer Strategy

Most of the literature on interest group strategies in the courts tends to focus on the test case and amicus brief strategies, in part because they are so easy to document. Attorneys of record and the organizations for which they work are named in the briefs they file and usually in the decisions rendered by the Supreme Court and lower federal courts. Amicus participation is also briefly noted in the final ruling with organizational names, purpose, and contact information located in the amicus brief itself. Studies that focus only on the groups litigating the case or the amici briefs they file may well miss the degree to which other organizations are involved in the litigation. A far more nebulous strategy than either case selection and sponsorship or filing amicus briefs offers New Christian Right groups an additional opportunity to participate in religious liberty litigation.

This method, referred to here as the legal overseer strategy, alludes to the practice of exercising varying degrees of (usually anonymous) control over the litigation at hand. Constitutional scholar Lee Epstein offers a notable example of this strategy, which is particularly suited to many of the groups in this study:

> It is common knowledge that the NAACP Legal Defense Fund (LDF) sponsored *Brown v. Board of Education of Topeka . . . ,* but nowhere does the brief mention that group. Even more troublesome is that it is virtually impossible to identify groups that might have assisted lead counsel (that is, provided legal expertise and/or funds), but chose to conceal their involvement. So although legal briefs constitute

the primary data sources for those studying group litigation, they are imperfect gauges that tend to underestimate organizational involvement in cases.[37]

Like many legal funding groups, the ADF works quietly in the background of religious liberty litigation. Promotional literature and fund-raising letters provide some insight into the cases in which it is involved, but to the general public the ADF offers few clues as to its funding activities. Thus, although official court reporters will note the attorneys and amici in a particular case, there is usually no indication of the influence, either philosophical or financial, of the ADF.[38]

As mentioned earlier, money from the ADF is not dispensed without conditions. Participating attorneys or firms that seek funding must be willing to litigate their case according to the ADF's ground rules. This may mean pursuing the litigation further or ending it sooner than the attorney actually litigating the religious liberty claim would prefer. It may also mean involving other attorneys in the case whom the ADF believes have more experience in litigating the claim at hand. Just the fact that the ADF can extend or withhold funding to a case gives it a level of control not enjoyed by the other public interest groups in this study. According to Rutherford Institute officials, it is this perceived surrender of control that, in part, precludes them from accepting any ADF funding.[39]

In addition, each attorney who attends the ADF's National Litigation Academy is required to volunteer 450 hours of work on ADF-backed issues in return for the training they receive. Although it is unlikely to ever be named in a brief or other documentation that arises out of these 450 hours of effort per attorney, the ADF clearly controls the direction of litigation in these cases because it chooses how those hours will be repaid.

The CLS Center exercises a much different method of legal overseership. As a membership organization, the CLS has some 4,500 affiliated attorneys, any of whom can tap into the CLS Center's (and ADF-financed) National Legal Resource Center, which offers legal assistance and other resources for litigating religious liberty claims and other issues of concern to the CLS. Beyond this, however, the CLS Center has also been directly involved in cases litigated by CLS member attorneys. Again, it is difficult to determine the extent of CLS Center involvement simply because it is not cited in court reporters unless a member of the CLS Center litigates the claim or writes an amicus brief (or a member attorney acts specifically on behalf of the CLS Center). However, according to former director Steve McFarland, involvement by the CLS Center in religious liberty cases brought by member attorneys has ranged from none to actually ghostwriting all that the attorney named in the briefs files.[40] In instances where the CLS offers considerable assistance, the intellectual flow of the litigation is controlled by the CLS and not the named attorney.

Both the ACLJ and the Rutherford Institute are also capable of acting as legal overseers, although in a considerably different manner than either the ADF or the CLS Center. When litigating as affiliated attorneys of Rutherford or the ACLJ, lawyers are aware that they must act in accordance with the purposes and priority areas of their sponsors. Whatever the nature of their private law practice, these lawyers in their affiliated capacity are named in the briefs as Rutherford Institute and ACLJ attorneys and are expected to carry the banner of their respective organization.

The overseer role of the Rutherford Institute and the ACLJ comes into play when these organizations and their affiliated lawyers set out to decide the litigation strategy of a given case. For example, the Rutherford Institute and one of its affiliated attorneys, Cyrus Zal, struggled over the proper way to frame their legal argument in *Peloza v. Capistrano Unified School District* (1994).[41] In this case, a California high school biology teacher challenged his school district's policy requiring him to teach evolution and banning any discussion of religion, including creationism, from the classroom. Zal wanted to argue that the school district violated the establishment clause by its endorsement and promotion of evolution above all other theories regarding the origins of life.

Rutherford officials, on the other hand, believed that the courts would be sympathetic to free speech arguments that demonstrated how the teacher's academic freedom and religious expression were impinged upon by the school district's policy.[42] In the end, Zal refused to go along with the free speech strategy and the Rutherford Institute withdrew its support from the case, allowing Zal to pursue the case on his own. The school district prevailed in U.S. District Court as well as the Ninth Circuit Court on appeal.[43]

While the overseer type of legal participation is often unobservable directly, the growing network of ACLJ, CLS Center, and Rutherford Institute attorneys demonstrates the appeal of this approach. Not only does the overseeing institution have the advantage of controlling the philosophical flow of the litigation, it also sees its own influence multiplied through the efforts of thousands of affiliated lawyers. Coupled with the funding and training opportunities provided by the ADF, the benefits to the New Christian Right groups that utilize this strategy in their litigation efforts are clear.

Free Speech Clause Strategy

In addition to the above process-oriented strategies New Christian Right attorneys have largely adapted from their liberal counterparts in the courts, there is another, more substance-oriented approach that religious conservatives themselves have perfected, one that shifts their religious liberty efforts from dependence on the religion clauses of the Constitution to the free speech clause.

More than any other constitutional principle, the free speech clause of the First Amendment has come to characterize the religious liberty efforts of the New Christian Right in the courts. The irony in this is obvious. That in certain matters of faith the free exercise or establishment clauses would take a back seat to the free speech clause would seem an especially odd strategy for New Christian Right constitutional lawyers to embrace, given the movement's historic railings against the judiciary for depreciating the value of the religion clauses.[44]

As Liberty Counsel's Mathew Staver describes it, the embrace of the free speech clause was occasioned by "our beating our heads against the wall by arguing most of these [religion] cases as 'establishment clause' and 'free exercise.'"[45] After several years of frustrating losses in the courts arguing the religion clauses, New Christian Right lawyers turned to the free speech clause with a vengeance in the late 1980s. And from at least one perspective, the movement's conversion should have come as no surprise. Writing for the majority in *Capitol Square Review and Advisory Board v. Pinette* (1995), Justice Antonin Scalia declared: "Our precedent establishes that private religious speech, far from being a First Amendment orphan, is as fully protected under the Free Speech Clause as secular private expression. Indeed, in Anglo-American history, at least, government suppression of speech has so commonly been directed precisely at religious speech that a free-speech clause without religion would be Hamlet without the prince."[46]

For obvious reasons this view, which equates religious and secular speech for constitutional purposes and which has been reaffirmed by the Supreme Court several times, is of immense importance to New Christian Right activism in the courts. There are, however, additional reasons why the New Christian Right groups in this study view the free speech clause as central to their religious liberty efforts.

Yale professor Stephen Carter in his acclaimed *Culture of Disbelief* argues that judicial decisions have created a "legal culture that presses the religiously faithful to be other than themselves, to act publicly, and sometimes privately as well, as though their faith does not matter to them."[47] Through an expansive interpretation of the free speech clause, New Christian Right legal organizations are attempting to "level the playing field" by forcing the public square to welcome religious expression on the same terms as it permits secular speech. While the legal arguments in these cases turn on claims of content or viewpoint discrimination by a governmental actor against a religious voice, it is the effect of that discrimination that is of greatest concern to religious conservatives. By denying religious speech rights in one area, the argument goes, it is chilled in others, thereby contributing to the further marginalization of religion.

A second reason for relying on the free speech strategy has little to do with the law. To speak of religion freely is central to the larger mission of evangelical Christianity, which is to spread the gospel. Although the courtroom efforts of these groups serve several different purposes, "keeping the legal door open to evangelization," as Alan Sears of the ADF put it, is a common theme.[48]

This is not to say, of course, as some New Christian Right critics contend, that the ultimate public policy aim of these groups is to obliterate the wall between church and state en route to Christianizing America.[49] The groups in this study have litigated religion cases and performed other legal services for non-Christians. And the precedents their efforts have helped to establish, particularly when grounded in the free speech clause, benefit Christians, non-Christians, and the nonreligious alike. In general, these organizations agree with the sentiments expressed by the Rutherford Institute's John Whitehead: "The religious community must understand that the Constitution protects the rights of everybody. If one religious group loses its rights, then everybody loses their rights. If we want to be strategic, we've got to stand up for the rights of everybody."[50]

Yet the majority of cases these firms pursue are, in fact, brought by

Christians. The reasons for this vary but the extensive use these organizations make of the conservative Christian information infrastructure and its vast network of electronic and print media clearly brings these firms and the causes they champion to the attention of sympathetic audiences.[51] In addition, the unique requirement of the Great Commission itself to actively spread the gospel message raises the possibility of litigation each time the religious expression of a Christian is deemed inappropriate by a school administrator, employer, or municipal law.

The free speech clause strategy discussed throughout the remainder of this study obviously cannot be appealed to in every religion case. Inapplicable because of the facts in some cases, it may also be inappropriate in others from both a constitutional and spiritual standpoint. In his dissenting opinion in *Widmar v. Vincent* (1981), the landmark case on the intersection of religion and speech that was sponsored by the CLS Center, Justice Byron White noted:

> A large part of respondents' argument, accepted by the court below and accepted by the majority, is founded on the proposition that because religious worship uses speech, it is protected by the Free Speech Clause of the First Amendment. Not only is it protected, they argue, but religious worship qua speech is not different from any other variety of protected speech as a matter of constitutional principle. I believe that this proposition is plainly wrong. Were it right, the Religion Clauses would be emptied of any independent meaning in circumstances in which religious practice took the form of speech.[52]

Although New Christian Right lawyers have not completely abandoned their establishment and free exercise clause arguments, the free speech clause, with all of its dangerous appeal as perceived by Justice White, has resulted in several significant religious liberty victories. As a litigation strategy, it will undoubtedly be emphasized by New Christian Right public interest law firms as long as it continues to yield courtroom success.

Faithfulness versus Success

Scholars have noted that organizational maintenance concerns often drive the litigation decisions of interest groups.[53] Although New Christian Right organizations are not exempt from such concerns, they are motivated by additional factors not commonly cited as litigating incentives. In both their promotional literature and interviews with the author, New Christian Right lawyers have been adamant that their goal is faithfulness rather than success. They see a divine hand in the creation of their organizations, the expansion of their donor base, and the spread of their message. And they are the first to admit that being faithful does not require that they win every case.

But in seeking to meet this standard of faithfulness, these groups have shown an affinity for proven strategies of public interest litigation where religion is concerned. Adopting the methods used successfully by interest groups in other areas of law, New Christian Right organizations directly sponsor and fund cases in the federal courts consistent with their litigating priorities. They also participate regularly as amicus curiae. Together with the varying degrees of quiet and even anonymous influence these groups wield over cases litigated directly by others, these strategies reflect the New Christian Right's commitment to maintaining a presence in the courts. And intertwined with its judicial branch efforts on behalf of religion is an emphasis on the free speech clause that stands out in high relief.

It is not surprising that the increased attention paid to the courts by New Christian Right legal organizations has created an atmosphere in which similarly motivated groups (in both a theological and legal sense) must compete with each other for recognition, funding, and ownership rights to the cases in which they are involved—a situation that perhaps makes it difficult to be either completely faithful or successful. Despite this internal competition, New Christian Right lawyers have dramatically increased their participation in federal court religion cases during the last decade. As the following chapters indicate, these groups have not been uniformly successful. But their cumulative efforts in the federal courts coupled with a reliance on the free speech clause have yielded a series of legal precedents that have fundamentally changed the relationship between church and state in America.

5 Scaling the Establishment Wall

Free Speech and the Supreme Court's Religion Cases

[We] are greatly concerned about the Eighth Circuit's usage of the phrase-
ology "religious speech." Is the Eighth Circuit purporting to use a "Super-
Freedom" which melds and encompasses the protections granted to religion, intended to insure the freedom and independence of religion and
religious groups, with the privileges extended to speech by our forefathers?
[We] submit that that the appellate Court was actually attempting to con-
struct and use a "fiberglass pole" with which to ease and assist its efforts
to spring over the Establishment wall. [We] question the use of a semantical artifice such as this to justify a constitutional infringement of this
magnitude.

Petitioners brief, *Widmar v. Vincent,* 1981

In its landmark 1947 decision *Everson v. Board of Education of the Township
of Ewing,*[1] the Supreme Court not only incorporated the establishment
clause of the First Amendment, making it applicable against state government action, it also famously invoked Thomas Jefferson's phrase regarding
a "wall of separation between Church and State."[2] Despite the simplicity of
the wording and the apparent ubiquity of the phrase, there is remarkably
little consensus as to what the "wall of separation" really means. Both secular and religious separationist groups maintain that the wall's demand for a
clear break between religion and government serves to strengthen both institutions.[3] New Christian Right attorneys, on the other hand, interpret the
wall of separation as a restriction on legitimate religious activity, a judicially
imposed "'iron curtain'—preventing each one of us from publicly express-
ing our religious heritage."[4]

The Supreme Court itself has been unable to definitively explain what
Jefferson's metaphor requires of the relationship between church and state,
leading one critic to observe: "The wall has done what walls usually do: it
has obscured the view. It has lent a simplistic air to the discussion of a very
complicated matter. Hence it has caused confusion whenever it has been

invoked. Far from helping to decide cases, it has made opinions and decisions unintelligible. The wall is offered as a reason. It is not a reason; it is a figure of speech."[5]

In a 1995 case set against the backdrop of the university founded by Jefferson, the Supreme Court again took the opportunity to visit the metaphorical wall. The significance of *Rosenberger v. Rector and Visitors of the University of Virginia* lies not only in the Court's landmark decision in this case but also in the manner in which the ruling highlighted the presence and legal arguments of the New Christian Right.[6] *Rosenberger* was but the latest in a remarkable string of religion cases in which the Supreme Court subordinated concerns about the wall of separation while affirming the free speech arguments made by New Christian Right attorneys.

Wide Awake, Free Speech, and the Courts

As evangelical Christian students studying at the University of Virginia in the fall of 1990, Ronald Rosenberger, Greg Mourad, and Robert Prince were increasingly disturbed by the manner in which Christianity was portrayed in several of the university's student magazines and newspapers. To counter these largely negative depictions, as well as fill what they perceived to be a need for a Christian voice at the university, they decided to publish a magazine that would offer a Christian perspective on both religious and secular issues. In November 1990, with the proceeds from donations and the sale of advertisement space, the students were able to print and distribute copies of their first issue of *Wide Awake: A Christian Perspective at the University of Virginia.* In its inaugural issue, editor in chief Rosenberger made it clear that part of *Wide Awake's* mission was "to challenge Christians to live, in word and deed, according to the faith they proclaim and to encourage students to consider what a personal relationship with Jesus Christ means."[7]

Having been formally recognized by the university as a Contracted Independent Organization (CIO), Rosenberger's Wide Awake Productions was permitted access to meeting rooms, computer equipment, and other university resources necessary for the printing of its magazine. More important, CIO status gave student organizations like Wide Awake Productions the opportunity to apply for university funding to help offset the costs of their activities.

The source of the monies available to designated CIO groups was the

University of Virginia's mandatory $14 student activity fee, which was collected from all full-time students and deposited in the university's Student Activity Fund. Organizations wishing to utilize the fund were required to submit vendor bills and receipts to the Student Council's Appropriations Committee for payment of all approved expenses. During the 1990–91 academic year, more than 340 student groups at the University of Virginia attained CIO status. Less than half that number requested reimbursement from the Student Activity Fund, and only 118 groups actually received funding.

In January 1991, Rosenberger applied for $5,862 in Student Activity Fund money to defray the printing costs of publishing *Wide Awake*. The Appropriations Committee denied his request citing university funding guidelines that prohibited the disbursement of funds for religious activities.[8] Contending that *Wide Awake* was not a "religious activity" per se and that his organization had met all the requirements for accessing the Student Activity Fund, Rosenberger appealed the decision to the full Student Council in March 1991 only to have that body affirm the Appropriations Committee's action. Upon appealing the Student Council's ruling to the University of Virginia's Student Activities Committee, his request for funding was again denied. Having no other avenue of appeal within the university, Rosenberger and other members of Wide Awake Productions brought suit against the university's Rector and Board of Visitors in U.S. District Court on 11 July 1991, claiming that the denial of funding unconstitutionally infringed on their rights to free speech and free exercise of religion.

Ten months later, U.S. District Judge James H. Michael Jr. handed down his decision in favor of the University of Virginia. Judge Michael held that the free speech rights of Rosenberger and the other members of Wide Awake Productions had not been violated because the university's Student Activity Fund was technically a "non-public forum" that permitted restricted access so long as such restrictions were reasonable and not imposed to silence a particular viewpoint. The court's decision further stated that because of limited funding considerations as well as the "Federal and State constitutional mandate of state neutrality toward religion," the university's guidelines governing the disbursement of Student Activity Fund monies were reasonable.[9] Judge Michael's passing reference here to the establishment clause is important because it begins to set forth a hierarchical order for the competing free speech, free exercise, and establishment clause claims made by the parties to this case.

Having ruled that the denial of university funding did not violate Rosenberger's free speech rights, Judge Michael considered Rosenberger's free exercise of religion claim: "The heart of the plaintiff's claim is that without SAF [Student Activity Fund] monies WAP [Wide Awake Productions] must devote more time to fund raising and less time to publishing its religious speech. Thus the denial of funding burdens the plaintiff's free exercise of religion by diverting energy away from WAP's main goal: challenging Christians to live according to their faith." Judge Michael went on to state, however, that he failed to see "any burden of constitutional magnitude that ha[d] been imposed on [Rosenberger]," but even if he had, such a burden was justified by the "compelling state interest" of the university in avoiding a violation of the establishment clause.[10]

The court's decision left no doubt as to its sequencing of the rights involved in this case: Ronald Rosenberger's free speech claim was invalid, his free exercise rights had not been unduly infringed upon, and establishment clause concerns had properly guided the university's denial of funding for *Wide Awake*. Disappointed, Rosenberger's lawyers appealed the ruling to the U.S. Court of Appeals for the Fourth Circuit.

Writing for a unanimous three-judge panel in his 14 March 1994 ruling in the case, Judge Sam Ervin III declined to rule on the public forum issue to which much of the district court opinion had been devoted.[11] Instead, he chose to focus on the competing demands of the First Amendment's speech and religion clauses. Ervin noted that because university facilities and resources were still available to Wide Awake Productions for the publication of its magazine, Rosenberger could not legitimately claim that the university had placed a prior restraint, as commonly understood, on his organization's ability to express its views.

However, the circuit court's decision did recognize that a type of prior restraint was inherently a part of the funding guidelines in this case, "because it restrains Wide Awake Productions from gaining access altogether to a funding source generally available to CIOs not engaged in religious expression." As a result, Judge Ervin noted, "[t]his prior restraint ultimately forces the members of Wide Awake Productions—unlike their nonsectarian CIO colleagues—to seek financial sustenance for their speech from coffers outside the University. The Rector and Visitors' funding pro-scription thus creates an uneven playing field on which the advantage is tilted towards CIOs engaged in wholly secular modes of expression."[12]

Acknowledging that the university's funding policy denied religious speech the same access to the Student Activity Fund enjoyed by other stu-dent groups, the Fourth Circuit panel nonetheless concluded that "it would be difficult to view the awarding of SAF monies to Wide Awake as anything but state sponsorship—and therefore advancement—of religious belief."[13] Viewing such sponsorship as a clear violation of the establishment clause's *Lemon* test,[14] the court ruled that the university's compelling state interest justified its placement of "a presumptively unconstitutional condition upon access to government benefits in violation of the Free Speech and Press Clause of the First Amendment."[15]

With this second defeat, Rosenberger's lawyers began to consider whether to appeal the Fourth Circuit's ruling to the Supreme Court. The decision to do so was made easier because of the attention some New Christian Right legal organizations had begun giving the case.

New Christian Right lawyers had initially expressed little interest in *Wide Awake*. As noted earlier, the Charlottesville-based Rutherford Insti-tute was originally approached by Rosenberger for assistance, which it de-clined to offer. By the time the case reached the Fourth Circuit Court of Appeals, however, Rosenberger had renowned church-state scholar, litiga-tor, and CLS member Michael McConnell heading up his legal team and the research support of the CLS Center behind him. In addition, the newly created ADF, organized just two months before the Fourth Circuit handed down its opinion, made getting the Rosenberger case to the Supreme Court one of its top funding priorities.

Having witnessed establishment clause arguments repeatedly triumph over what they believed were legitimate questions of religious expression in previous Supreme Court religion cases, New Christian Right lawyers were eager for a vehicle such as *Rosenberger* to pit the strength of their free speech claims against traditional establishment clause concerns. The Su-preme Court provided just such an opportunity when it granted certiorari to the case on 31 October 1994.

When oral arguments were heard on 1 March 1995, attorneys on both sides lost little time in framing their respective positions in the case. For Michael McConnell, it was a matter of content discrimination against

Rosenberger's religious speech, pure and simple. "Thus," he argued, "if my clients this morning were the SDS [Students for a Democratic Society], if they were vegetarians, if they were members of the Federalist Society, or black separatists, or whatever, there would be no need to be here this morning."[16] For the university's attorney, John C. Jeffries, the case was not about religious speech at all but "funding, and the choices that inevitably must be made in allocating scarce resources."[17] Both positions were well represented when the Court handed down its narrow 5-4 decision in favor of Rosenberger in late June 1995.

Perhaps the most striking feature of Justice Anthony Kennedy's opinion for the majority in *Rosenberger* was its conspicuous reordering of the hierarchy of rights established by the lower federal courts. For a case that had twice been viewed primarily through an establishment clause lens, the majority opinion almost immediately turned to the free speech clause. "Vital First Amendment speech principles are at stake here," Justice Kennedy wrote. "The first danger to liberty lies in granting the State the power to examine publications to determine whether or not they are based on some ultimate idea and if so for the State to classify them. The second, and corollary, danger is to speech from the chilling of individual thought and expression."[18]

Tracing the jurisprudential relationship linking speech, religion, and the state, Justice Kennedy placed particular emphasis on the Court's 1993 *Lamb's Chapel* decision where it ruled that a group wishing to show a Christian film on child-raising in a public school could not be denied access if the school's facilities were made available to other community groups.[19] By way of comparison, the Court in *Rosenberger* noted, "[J]ust as the school district in *Lamb's Chapel* pointed to nothing but the religious views of the group as the rationale for excluding its message, so in this case the University justifies its denial of SAF [Student Activity Fund] participation to WAP [Wide Awake Productions] on the ground that the contents of *Wide Awake* reveal an avowed religious perspective."[20]

In addressing the establishment clause concerns that had proven decisive in the lower federal courts, the majority opinion dispensed with the claim that the wall of separation had been breached by the public funding of a religious magazine. Student Activity Fund reimbursement of third-party creditors rather than student organizations (like Wide Awake Productions) was a far cry, it held, from the direct subsidization of a church or religious activity. Justice Kennedy further stated that both the dissent and the lower courts were wrong to focus on the money expended ("the government usually acts by spending money") and should look instead at the benefit to the recipient. The fact that a program was set up to benefit a number of different secular organizations and happened also to benefit a religious one was really of little consequence, he wrote, since "[a]ny benefit to religion is incidental to the government's provision of secular services for secular purposes on a religion-neutral basis." To scrutinize and try to weed out such incidental benefits from every governmental program, the majority opinion went on to say, would be a far greater violation of the establishment clause under the *Lemon* test than reimbursing printing fees for *Wide Awake* because of the excessive entanglement between government and religion that would result. In short, the Court stated simply, "There is no Establishment Clause violation in the University's honoring its duties under the Free Speech Clause."[21]

The Judicial Pedigree of Rosenberger

The High Court's 5-4 decision to permit public funding of a religious student magazine in *Rosenberger* quickly accorded the case landmark status. But *Rosenberger* is important for other reasons as well. Although the majority opinion appealed to a number of previous Supreme Court rulings to justify its decision, the core issue in *Rosenberger*—the linking of speech, religion, and the state—was grounded in three precedent-setting decisions inextricably tied to the New Christian Right: *Widmar v. Vincent, Board of Education of Westside Community Schools v. Mergens,* and *Lamb's Chapel v. Center Moriches Union Free School District.*

One of the most significant religion cases of the early 1980s, *Widmar v. Vincent* (1981) saw the Supreme Court rule 8-1 that public universities could not deny the use of their facilities to student religious clubs if such facilities were made available to secular student groups. The case centered on an evangelical Christian group at the University of Missouri at Kansas City that had been denied permission to meet in university-owned buildings. While the university had allowed the student religious group Cornerstone to meet on campus for several years, it began to enforce a five-year-old university regulation that specifically barred organizations that might engage in "religious teaching" or "religious worship" from using school property and facilities. The university maintained that such regulations were in keeping with the requirements of the establishment clause.

The student members of the club, represented by James M. Smart Jr., a member of the CLS, argued that such restraints burdened not only their free exercise of religion but also their right to access university facilities where their views might be expressed equally with other groups that enjoyed the university's blessing. The issue of "equal access" for religious speech had been one of the chief areas of concern for the CLS even before *Widmar.* Indeed, securing judicial recognition of the rights of student religious groups to access public facilities as freely as secular noncurricular organizations were permitted to was the primary motivation behind the 1975 creation of the CLS Center.[22]

Although as early as 1943 in *Murdock v. Pennsylvania* the Supreme Court had recognized that some types of religious expression, such as the distribution of religious literature, were protected activities under the free speech clause,[23] the constitutional equating of religious speech with secular speech had not been generally accepted by the lower federal courts. In ruling against the students who brought the *Widmar* suit, for example, U.S. District Court Judge Collinson questioned the students' claim that "the establishment clause must yield to the freedom of speech clause of the first amendment." Citing Supreme Court precedents reaffirming the general free speech rights of students, Judge Collinson noted that religious speech was different from "secular intellectual activities." "In short," he concluded, "speech with religious content cannot be treated the same as any other form of speech. To do so would make a nullity of both the establishment clause and the free exercise clause of the first amendment."[24]

On appeal, the Eighth Circuit Court squarely rejected the lower court's interpretation of the speech and religion clauses of the First Amendment by declaring, "We begin with the proposition that religious speech, like other speech, is protected by the First Amendment." Writing for the court, Circuit Judge Heaney explained that by promoting and recognizing student clubs generally and authorizing their use of campus facilities for club meetings and activities, the university had created a forum for student expression that could not be denied to those who happened to espouse a religious viewpoint. "The University's policy," Judge Heaney wrote, "singles out and stigmatizes certain religious activity and, in consequence, discredits religious groups." In that sense, according to the court, not only had the university infringed on the free speech rights of affected students, but it had also unwittingly violated the establishment clause: "The University's prohibition on worship and religious teaching also hopelessly entangles it in the delicate tasks of defining religion, determining whether a proposed event involves religious worship or teaching, and then monitoring events to ensure that no prohibited activity takes place."[25]

The Eighth Circuit Court's ruling in favor of the Cornerstone club in *Widmar* was subsequently appealed to the Supreme Court by the university. Fearful that the Court would overturn the Eighth Circuit's opinion, the CLS filed an amicus brief urging the Court to deny the university's request for certiorari. The Supreme Court did take the case and in a near unanimous decision affirmed the appellate court's ruling for the club.

Justice Powell's opinion for the 8-1 majority set forth its own hierarchy of rights where religion, speech, and the state intersect:

> On one hand, respondents' [Clark Vincent and other members of Cornerstone] First Amendment rights are entitled to special constitutional solicitude. Our cases have required the most exacting scrutiny in cases in which a State undertakes to regulate speech on the basis of its content. . . . On the other hand, the state interest asserted here—in achieving greater separation of church and State than is already ensured under the Establishment Clause of the Federal Constitution—is limited by the Free Exercise Clause and in this case by the Free Speech Clause as well. In this constitutional context, we are unable to recognize the State's interest as sufficiently "compelling" to justify content-based discrimination against respondents' religious speech.[26]

Throughout the 1980s the free speech argument that triumphed in *Widmar* continued to expand beyond the parameters of the university setting central to that case. In 1986, for example, in a rare instance in which CLS staff attorneys served as counsel of record, a group of Williamsport, Pennsylvania, high school students filed suit against their school district because it denied their religious club permission to meet on school grounds during student activity periods. Declaring the case controlled by *Widmar*, in spite of the difference in academic settings, a U.S. District Court ruled in favor of the students.[27] A year later, however, citing the impressionability of high school students who might take the club's presence as an endorsement by the school, the Third Circuit Court of Appeals rejected the district court's application of *Widmar* to secondary schools and held that the school's ban on religious clubs was constitutional.[28] CLS staff attorneys Samuel Ericcson and Kimberlee Colby, who represented the students at both the district and appellate levels, subsequently appealed the Third Circuit's ruling to the Supreme Court, which granted certiorari.

Before the Court heard oral arguments in *Bender v. Williamsport Area School District* (1986), Congress acted on its own accord to extend the rationale of *Widmar* to student organizations in secondary schools by passing the Equal Access Act of 1984. Officials from the CLS Center who assisted in the drafting of the bill's language realized that *Bender* would serve as the perfect opportunity for the Supreme Court to rule on the constitutionality of the law.[29] But in a narrow 5-4 decision, the Supreme Court declined to consider the constitutionality of the Equal Access Act, ruling that a party to the appellate court suit lacked standing when he challenged the district court's decision, thus negating the need to consider the case on its merits.[30]

In dissent, Chief Justice Burger and Justices White, Rehnquist, and Powell argued that not only did the party have standing but that the case could have been resolved on the merits, as it was clearly controlled by *Widmar*. Chief Justice Burger went on to explain, "[T]he several commands of the First Amendment require vision capable of distinguishing between state establishment of religion, which is prohibited by the Establishment Clause, and individual participation and advocacy of religion which, far from being prohibited by the Establishment Clause, is affirmatively protected by the Free Exercise and Free Speech Clauses of the First Amendment."[31]

Despite the majority's refusal to consider the merits of *Bender*, the CLS Center and other New Christian Right legal organizations were encouraged by the fact that four members of the Court had clearly acknowledged the validity of their argument to extend free speech protection to student religious clubs in secondary schools. The opportunity to formally argue the constitutionality of the Equal Access Act on its merits came to the ACLJ's Jay Sekulow in 1990.

Board of Education of Westside Community Schools v. Mergens (1990) involved a group of students in Omaha, Nebraska, who wanted to form an after-hours Bible club at their high school. The school district denied their request because the club could not properly have a faculty sponsor (a requirement for all student organizations) without the appearance of school endorsement. When informed that its decision violated the Equal Access Act, the school district responded by challenging the constitutionality of the law itself.

The Supreme Court upheld the Equal Access Act by an 8-1 margin. Stating in her plurality opinion that "the logic of *Widmar* applies with equal force to the Equal Access Act," Justice O'Connor attempted to allay the establishment clause concerns of the school district by setting forth what the Court saw as the proper constitutional interaction of speech, religion, and the state: "There is a crucial difference between government speech endorsing religion, which the Establishment Clause forbids and private speech endorsing religion, which the Free Speech and Free Exercise Clauses protect. We think that secondary school students are mature enough and are likely to understand that a school does not endorse or support student speech that it merely permits on a nondiscriminatory basis."[32]

Notwithstanding the near unanimity of the Court on the constitutionality of the Equal Access Act itself, there were clear disagreements among the justices as to the required brightness of that line separating "equal access" from "endorsement" in secondary schools. Writing for himself and Justice Scalia, for example, Justice Kennedy noted that it is "inevitable that a public high school 'endorses' a religious club . . . if the club happens to be one of the many activities that the school permits students to choose." But no violation of the establishment clause could be alleged so long as participation in that club was strictly voluntary.[33]

Justices Marshall and Brennan, on the other hand, called on the school district to vigorously disassociate itself from even the slightest hint of endorsement. Indeed, Justice Marshall suggested that the school could "entirely discontinue encouraging student participation in clubs" generally in order to effectively sever the implied association between the school and its student organizations, including religious clubs.[34]

By 1993 the free speech argument was being applied in cases beyond the realm of college and high school student religious groups. Relying heavily on *Widmar* and *Mergens,* the Supreme Court in *Lamb's Chapel v. Center Moriches Union Free School District* ruled that a public school that opened its doors to community groups for after-school use must equally accommodate religious organizations that desired to use those facilities.

This case involved an evangelical church in New York that sought permission from the local district to use a school building after hours to present a film series on child-rearing produced by the Christian ministry Focus on the Family. The request was denied because school district policy prohibited the use of school property for religious purposes. Writing for a unanimous Court, however, Justice White noted that a secular treatment of parenting would have received different consideration:

> There is no suggestion from the courts below or from the District or State that a lecture or film about child rearing and family values would not be a use for social and civic purposes otherwise permitted by [district policy]. That subject matter is not one that the District has placed off limits to any and all speakers. Nor is there any indication in the record before us that the application to exhibit the particular film series involved here was, or would have been, denied for any reason other than the fact that the presentation would have been from a religious perspective. In our view, denial on that basis was plainly invalid.[35]

Like the others before it, this case further solidified the free speech argument made by New Christian Right attorneys. It also gave Jay Sekulow and the ACLJ, who had argued the case on behalf of Lamb's Chapel, another major legal victory before the High Court.

The coupling of the free speech clause with religious expression, a jurisprudential concept successfully invoked with regularity after *Widmar,* has been the major contribution of the New Christian Right in the Supreme Court. And for the past two decades, that contribution has received solid support from justices from across the ideological spectrum, at least until *Rosenberger,* where the issue of public funding was blended into the already difficult mix of government, religion, and speech.[36]

Referring to *Lamb's Chapel* as "the most recent and most apposite case" for its decision in *Rosenberger,*[37] the majority opinion held that there was little substantive difference between the two cases. By contrast, Justice David Souter in his dissent in *Rosenberger* saw a huge difference because of the funding issue involved in the latter case. Justice Souter commented that in cases like *Widmar, Mergens,* and *Lamb's Chapel,* "[i]t was the preservation of free speech on the model of the street corner that supplied the justification going beyond the requirement of evenhandedness." Funding

Rosenberger's magazine, however, was different: "There is no traditional street corner printing provided by the government on equal terms to all comers, and the forum cases [*Widmar* et al.] cannot be lifted to a higher plane of generalization without admitting that new economic benefits are being extended directly to religion in clear violation of the principle barring direct aid. The argument from economic equivalence thus breaks down on recognizing that the direct state aid it would support is not mitigated by the street corner analogy in the service of free speech."[38] Even though *Rosenberger* was decided by the barest of margins, both the majority and dissenting opinions nevertheless reaffirmed the basic validity of the religion-as-speech argument, at least up to the point that funding becomes an issue.[39]

Rosenberger and the New Christian Right

Few cases reveal the increasing presence of the New Christian Right in the courts quite like *Rosenberger*. First, the case benefited directly from the funding opportunity presented by the timely formation of the ADF. Citing *Rosenberger* as one of his organization's early significant cases, Alan Sears is gratified by the role the ADF played: "The attorneys for Rosenberger couldn't finish the deal without adequate funding. They took the bull by the horns to the High Court but ran out of steam."[40] ADF funding came at a critical time, enabling Rosenberger's attorneys to bring the case to the attention of the Supreme Court.

Second, the CLS Center assisted CLS member and Rosenberger's lead attorney, Michael McConnell, in preparing briefs and arguments for the Supreme Court and filing an amicus brief of its own in the case. Rosenberger himself later gave his personal assessment of the CLS's influence: "I believe that without Douglas Laycock's friend-of-the-court brief, which he wrote for CLS, we may have lost Justice O'Connor's essential fifth vote. Having Michael McConnell . . . join us for the Circuit Court and the Supreme Court was a real coup. He has a brilliant legal mind, and he really supports the rights of Christians in the public square. I think his and Laycock's reputation was important for this case being granted review by the Supreme Court."[41] Although there is no empirical support for Rosenberger's belief that Justice O'Connor was swayed by Laycock's amicus brief for the CLS, there is considerable evidence to suggest that a lawyer's reputation (of the stature enjoyed by both McConnell and Laycock) can positively influence the Court, at least in the granting of certiorari to a case.[42]

Third, the ACLJ also filed an amicus brief in the *Rosenberger* case. Of far greater importance, however, was the Court's reliance on the *Widmar, Lamb's Chapel,* and *Mergens* decisions, the latter two successfully argued by the ACLJ's Jay Sekulow. Demonstrating more than just the power of legal precedent, *Widmar, Mergens, Lamb's Chapel,* and now *Rosenberger* serve as continual reminders to New Christian Right attorneys that they too can prevail in the nation's highest court.

But success there is hardly assured, especially given the tremendous difficulty of balancing the competing claims of the free speech, free exercise, and establishment clauses. Referring to the constitutional conflict among these clauses in her concurring opinion in *Rosenberger,* Justice O'Connor wryly noted, "When bedrock principles collide, they test the limits of categorical obstinacy and expose the flaws and dangers of a Grand Unified Theory that may turn out to be neither grand nor unified"[43]—a verity New Christian Right attorneys learned to their dismay in *Santa Fe Independent School District v. Doe* (2000), which saw the Court consider the religion-as-speech argument for the first time since *Rosenberger.*

The *Santa Fe* case had its origins in a 1992 Fifth Circuit Court decision, *Jones v. Clear Creek Independent School District,* which permitted prayers at graduation ceremonies as long as they were student initiated and student led.[44] Santa Fe Independent School District applied the Fifth Circuit's rationale permitting students to offer prayers from the podium during graduation ceremonies to leading the hometown crowd in prayer from the school's public address system prior to the start of home football games. Although such prayers ostensibly met the "student-initiated, student-led" requirements of *Clear Creek,* representatives of the Texas school district prescreened the texts of the invocation prayers and inspirational messages to be presented for their appropriateness and retained authority to remove speakers or shut off the microphone.

In April 1995 two students and their families filed suit against the school district, claiming that both the graduation and football prayer policies violated the separation of church and state. Eighteen months later, U.S. District Court Judge Samuel Kent ruled that the school district's actions were indeed unconstitutional, as then administered, because they violated the establishment clause.[45] On appeal, a divided Fifth Circuit Court held that graduation prayers were appropriate given the solemn, once-in-a-lifetime nature of such ceremonies as long as those prayers were indeed student initiated and student led. Stating that high school football games could hardly be characterized in the same vein, however, the court held unconstitutional the reciting of prayers over the school's public address system by students prior to athletic contests.[46] The school district appealed the appellate court's ruling on pregame prayers to the Supreme Court, which granted certiorari.

Once again, with financial assistance from the ADF and amicus briefs from the CLS and the Rutherford Institute, New Christian Right legal organizations (led by the ACLJ's Jay Sekulow, who argued the case) laid their free speech arguments before the High Court.

On behalf of the school district, Sekulow argued that Santa Fe had not mandated prayer but had simply made a forum available for private student expression. The fact that the student speech uttered before the football game might be religious in nature or even prayerful was irrelevant, he argued, because it was private. The Court, however, rejected Sekulow's attempt to depict the student invocations as private and protected religious expression. Instead, writing for the 6-3 majority, Justice Stevens viewed the football prayers and the school's apparent endorsement of the practice as a clear violation of the establishment clause:

> Once the student speaker is selected and the message composed, the invocation is then delivered to a large audience assembled as part of a regularly scheduled, school-sponsored function conducted on school property. The message is broadcast over the school's public address system, which remains subject to the control of school officials. The school's name is likely written in large print across the field and on banners and flags. The crowd will certainly include many who display the school colors and insignia on their school T-shirts, jackets, or hats and who may also be waving signs displaying the school name. It is in a setting such as this that "[t]he board has chosen to permit" the elected student to rise and give the "statement or invocation."
>
> In this context the members of the listening audience must perceive the pregame message as a public expression of the views of the majority of the student body delivered with the approval of the school administration.[47]

Although the Court rejected Sekulow's specific religious free speech arguments in *Santa Fe,* it nonetheless cited favorably such precedents as *Mergens* and *Lamb's Chapel* that forbid the "impos[ing of] a prohibition on all religious activity in our public schools." "Thus," the Court went on to say, "nothing in the Constitution as interpreted by this Court prohibits any school student from voluntarily praying at any time before, during, or after the schoolday. But the religious liberty protected by the Constitution is abridged when the State affirmatively sponsors the particular religious practice of prayer."[48]

Beyond Free Speech

In addition to the generally successful free speech strategy adopted by its courtroom defenders, a review of the Supreme Court's religion cases between 1980 and 2000 demonstrates the increasing New Christian Right presence in the High Court. Whether due to financial limitations, strategic considerations, or ignorance, New Christian Right lawyers simply did not participate consistently in Supreme Court religious liberty litigation during the 1980s, passing on several pivotal religion cases.[49] One of the most significant of these was *Employment Division, Department of Human Resources of Oregon v. Smith* (1990), where by a 6-3 margin the Court signaled its unwillingness to exempt religious individuals and groups from generally applicable laws.[50] The Court's decision was castigated by religious conservatives who were particularly upset that the ruling was backed by the conservative wing of the Court, led by Justice Scalia. Since the Court's controversial decision in *Smith,* New Christian Right lawyers have refused to let another religion case reach the High Court without their participation in some manner.

There are several reasons for this, the most obvious being the fact that there were simply more New Christian Right organizations litigating religious liberty claims in the 1990s than in previous decades. However, there are other explanations as well. With ever-increasing budgets, these firms generally have access to greater financial resources now than they did in the past, allowing them to participate more often in Supreme Court religion cases. The levels of financing and participation are important elements in both the cases and the public recognition for which these firms compete. As noted earlier, participation in Supreme Court cases is one way that these organizations can demonstrate to their supporters, their critics, and to each other that they are "players" in the most important judicial arena of all.

Overall, the New Christian Right has been involved in twenty-nine of the Supreme Court's forty-four religion cases decided since the 1980 term. Table 3 lists these cases, the type of New Christian Right participation, details of the Supreme Court's ruling, and the status of the position taken by the New Christian Right lawyers involved in the case.

Several important facets of New Christian Right activism in the courts become apparent on closer examination of these cases. For instance, of the twenty-nine religion cases in which New Christian Right lawyers have participated, 31 percent (n = 9) have been directly funded or sponsored by the New Christian Right (see fig. 1). One hundred percent of these cases have seen New Christian Right participation in the form of amicus briefs.[51] In addition, of the thirteen religion cases decided by the Court since 1990 in which religious conservatives have participated, eleven have seen amicus briefs filed by more than one New Christian Right public interest law firm.[52]

The position taken by New Christian Right organizations in Supreme Court religion cases has enjoyed some success, particularly in cases dealing with unemployment benefits for Sabbatarians,[53] state or federal aid for parochial schools,[54] assistance for students attending religious schools,[55] and counseling services provided by religious organizations.[56] But the movement has also experienced significant defeats on issues dear to religious conservatives such as prayer in schools,[57] creationism,[58] and the free exercise of religion.[59] Although the factual and legal circumstances in each of these cases are unique, the cases listed in table 3 clearly illustrate the mixed record of New Christian Right participation in the Court as financier, counsel, and amicus curiae. But they also demonstrate the movement's consistent success when it has turned to the free speech clause.

With the single exception of *Santa Fe,* the free speech clause arguments advanced by New Christian Right law firms in Supreme Court religion cases since *Widmar* have not only brought victory but have generally received broad approval from justices from across the ideological spectrum. While the New Christian Right has been influential in sponsoring, arguing, and funding the free speech religion cases that have transformed the way religious expression is viewed in America's courts, it has also undoubtedly been the beneficiary of extraordinarily good timing in being able to air these cases before the Burger and Rehnquist Courts, whose blend of religious

Table 3. The New Christian Right in the Supreme Court, 1980–2000

Supreme Court Case	NCR Counsel or Funding	NCR Amicus	Supreme Court's Decision	Status of NCR Position
Mitchell v. Helms 530 US 793 (2000)		ACLJ RI	The Court's 6-3 ruling held that taxpayer money could be used to purchase computer equipment, media materials, and other educational resources for parochial schools without violating the establishment clause.	Prevailed
Santa Fe Independent School District v. Doe 530 US 290 (2000)	ACLJ ADF	CLS LC RI	By a 6-3 margin the Court rejected the argument that student-initiated prayer before football games constituted private, protected speech. Rather, the school's sanctioning of such a practice violated the establishment clause.	Defeated
City of Boerne v. Flores 521 US 507 (1997)	ADF	ACLJ CLS LC RI	In a 6-3 decision the Court ruled that a Texas church could be subjected to historical landmark restrictions because Congress exceeded its powers in passing the Religious Freedom Restoration Act upon which the church's free exercise arguments were founded.	Defeated
Agostini v. Felton 521 US 203 (1997)	ADF	CLS	By a 5-4 margin the Court voted to reverse its 1985 ruling in *Aguilar v. Felton* to allow public school teachers to provide instruction in parochial schools.	Prevailed

Note: ADF = Alliance Defense Fund; ACLJ = American Center for Law and Justice; CLS = Christian Legal Society; LC = Liberty Counsel; RI = Rutherford Institute. Named individuals participated on behalf of organizations other than those listed here.

Table 3. *Continued*

Supreme Court Case	NCR Counsel or Funding	NCR Amicus	Supreme Court's Decision	Status of NCR Position
Rosenberger v. Rector and Visitors of the University of Virginia 515 US 819 (1995)	ADF	ACLJ CLS	The Court held 5-4 allowing a Christian magazine equal access to funding from a public university.	Prevailed
Capitol Square Review and Advisory Board v. Pinette 515 US 753 (1995)		ACLJ CLS LC	Voting 7-2, the Court upheld over establishment clause concerns the right of KKK members to erect a cross in a Columbus, Ohio, public square.	Prevailed
Board of Ed. of Kiryas Joel Village School District v. Grumet 512 US 687 (1994)		ACLJ CLS RI	The Court's 6-3 decision held unconstitutional a special school district created to assist the handicapped children of a Hasidic Jewish community.	Defeated
Zobrest v. Catalina Foothills School District 509 US 1 (1993)		ACLJ CLS	Voting 5-4, the Court upheld public funding for a sign-language interpreter to assist a deaf student at a private religious school.	Prevailed
Church of the Lukumi Babalu Aye v. City of Hialeah 508 US 520 (1993)		CLS RI	The Court unanimously struck down a ban on animal sacrifice that primarily affected only the religious practices of a minority religion.	Prevailed
Lamb's Chapel v. Center Moriches Union Free School District 508 US 385 (1993)	ACLJ	CLS RI	In a 9-0 decision the Court ruled that schools that make their facilities available to secular organizations for after-school use must accommodate religious groups as well.	Prevailed

Case			Description	Result
Lee v. Weisman 505 US 577 (1992)	Sekulow on briefs	CLS LC RI	The Court ruled 5-4 that school-sponsored graduation prayers were unconstitutional.	Defeated
Board of Education of Westside Community Schools v. Mergens 496 US 226 (1990)	Sekulow	CLS RI	The Court held the Equal Access Act to be constitutional by an 8-1 margin.	Prevailed
Jimmy Swaggart Ministries v. Board of Equalization of California 493 US 378 (1990)		CLS	A unanimous Court ruled that religious materials are not exempt from generally applicable sales and use taxes.	Defeated
Frazee v. Illinois Department of Employment Security 489 US 829 (1989)	RI	CLS	In a 9-0 decision the Court held that the denial of unemployment benefits to a man whose personal beliefs (as opposed to those of an established religious sect) forbade him to work on Sunday violated his free exercise rights.	Prevailed
Bowen v. Kendrick 487 US 589 (1988)	CLS	RI	By a 5-4 vote the Court upheld the authorization of federal funds for premarital counseling by public and private groups, including faith-based organizations.	Prevailed
Lyng v. Northwest Indian Cemetery Protective Association 485 US 439 (1988)	CLS	CLS	The Court ruled 5-3 that the Forest Service could harvest timber from and construct roads across land that was considered sacred by Native American groups.	Defeated

Table 3. *Continued*

Supreme Court Case	NCR Counsel or Funding	NCR Amicus	Supreme Court's Decision	Status of NCR Position
Corporation of the Presiding Bishop of the Church of Jesus Christ of Latter-day Saints v. Amos 483 US 327 (1987)		CLS	A unanimous Court held that church employers are not subject to the religious discrimination provisions of the Civil Rights Act of 1964.	Prevailed
Edwards v. Aguillard 482 US 578 (1987)		CLS RI	The Court ruled 7-2 that a Louisiana law requiring the teaching of creationism was unconstitutional.	Defeated
O'Lone v. Estate of Shabazz 482 US 342 (1987)		CLS	Voting 5-4, the Court held that, out of security concerns, prison officials could deny Islamic prisoners permission to attend religious services.	Defeated
Hobbie v. Unemployment Appeals Commission 480 US 136 (1987)		RI	In an 8-1 decision the Court ruled against the denial of unemployment benefits to individuals who refuse to work on Sunday.	Prevailed
Ansonia Board of Education v. Philbrook 479 US 60 (1986)		CLS RI	The Court ruled 9-0 against a school board policy prohibiting more than three days of leave time for religious holidays.	Prevailed
Ohio Civil Rights Commission v. Dayton Christian Schools 477 US 619 (1986)		CLS RI	Ruling 9-0, the Court reversed a lower court ruling that the Ohio Civil Rights Commission could not bring action against a church school for the firing of one of its employees over doctrinal matters.	Defeated

Case		Description	Outcome
Bowen v. Roy 476 US 693 (1986)	RI	In an 8-1 decision the Court denied the free exercise claims of Native Americans who believed the assignment of social security numbers robbed them of control over their spirit.	Defeated
Goldman v. Weinberger 475 US 503 (1986)	CLS RI	The Court held 5-4 that the Air Force was not required to alter its uniform dress code to accommodate the wearing of a yarmulke.	Defeated
Witters v. Washington Department of Services for the Blind 474 US 481 (1986)	CLS RI	The Court held 9-0 that the extension of rehabilitation assistance for study at a Christian school did not violate the establishment clause.	Prevailed
Lynch v. Donnelly 465 US 668 (1984)	RI	By a 5-4 margin the Court ruled that a city-sponsored crèche was permissible since Christmas holiday symbols have largely taken on a secular meaning.	Prevailed
Bob Jones University v. US 461 US 574 (1983)	CLS	In an 8-1 decision the Court upheld IRS policy revoking the tax exempt status of educational institutions, including religious schools, that discriminate on the basis of race.	Defeated
Larson v. Valente 456 US 228 (1982)	CLS	The Court held 5-4 that Minnesota could not impose special registration and reporting requirements on religious organizations that solicit more than 50 percent of their funding from nonmembers.	Prevailed
Widmar v. Vincent 454 US 263 (1981)	CLS Whitehead	The Court ruled 8-1 that universities could not deny the use of their facilities to student religious groups if such facilities were made available to secular organizations.	Prevailed

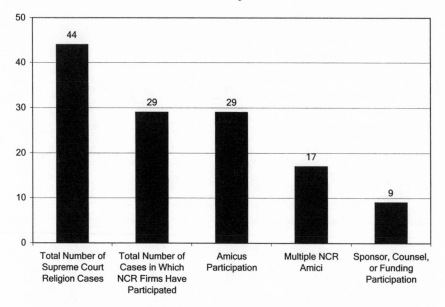

Figure 1. New Christian Right strategies in the Supreme Court, 1980–2000. (Calculated by author. ADF participation based on interviews with ADF officials and information from the ADF's website and promotional materials.)

accommodation and support of the free speech clause has redounded to the advantage of the New Christian Right's free speech strategy.

As the composition of the Court changes, however, New Christian Right lawyers may have to craft their religious liberty arguments without the benefit of conservative ideological allies on the Court who insist on greater accommodation of religious activity or liberal justices who champion the free speech clause.[60]

The New Christian Right and the Wall of Separation

The most important result of New Christian Right activity in the Court has been the highly successful string of precedent-setting cases in which free speech arguments have successfully warded off traditional establishment clause concerns regarding state-sponsored recognition or acknowledgment of religion. No longer can organizations, on the basis of their religious expression or activities alone, be categorically denied access to public facilities that are generally made available to secular groups. Beyond the increasing levels of Supreme Court participation, broad-based attorney networks, and growing financial resources, which are important components of the New Christian Right's presence in the courts, lies the fact that the legal relationship between religion and the state has been fundamentally altered by the free speech arguments made by these groups. Although the New Christian Right's defeat in *Santa Fe* may signal the turning of the free speech tide in the Supreme Court's religion cases, this is unlikely given the unique facts of that case, the majority opinion's acknowledgment that there is no constitutional requirement forbidding religious expression in the public schools, and the weight of precedent from *Widmar* through *Rosenberger.*

The New Christian Right can be expected to continue its efforts in the Supreme Court, but it is important to note that it has never been dependent on that venue alone. New Christian Right attorneys have also actively litigated religious liberty claims in U.S. Courts of Appeal and U.S. District Courts. With the vast majority of all law being decided below the Supreme Court level of the judiciary, a closer analysis of the lower federal court religion cases in which the New Christian Right has participated reveals in sharper detail both the strengths and weaknesses of linking religion to speech.

6 Pathbreakers and Gatekeepers

The Lower Federal Court Response to the New Christian Right

> The Upshur County School Board permitted a group of ministers, politicians, and businessmen to distribute Bibles in all public elementary and secondary schools during regular school hours, when state law compels student attendance. Except as to the very youngest and most impressionable children, the majority concludes that this action did not violate the Establishment Clause. That holding is not only unprecedented; it is also contrary to the spirit and the letter of controlling Supreme Court authority.
>
> Judge Diana Gribbon Motz, U.S. Court of Appeals for the Fourth Circuit, dissenting in *Peck v. Upshur County Board of Education* (1998)

Despite their increased level of activity in Supreme Court religion cases, New Christian Right public interest law firms appreciate the odds of reaching the High Court. Though it has never been easy to get one's case before the justices, the Court's spiraling docket (now close to eight thousand cases a year) coupled with a steady decline in the number of cases granted plenary or full consideration by the Court has made it even more difficult.[1] The efforts of Chief Justice Warren Burger to expand the Court's plenary docket resulted in a record number of cases (184) considered by the Court in both its 1981 and 1983 terms. During the Rehnquist Court years, however, the number of cases reviewed by the Court has declined dramatically, with generally fewer than one hundred cases granted plenary review annually.[2]

Because the Supreme Court grants review to such a small percentage of the cases on its docket each term, organizations that are serious about creating legal change must be prepared to participate in other judicial venues. New Christian Right groups have actively pursued religious liberty claims in both the U.S. District Courts and the U.S. Courts of Appeal. There are several reasons why the firms in this study devote far more time and resources to cases in the lower federal courts than in the higher profile, if infrequent, religion cases that reach the Supreme Court.

First, from a strictly organizational standpoint, several of these firms are well positioned to participate in religious liberty litigation nationwide. The ACLJ draws on a network of some 330 lawyers who voluntarily represent the ACLJ's interests. Rutherford claims to have 1,000 affiliated lawyers through whom it works. The relationship between the CLS Center and the 4,500 members of the Christian Legal Society as well as the informal ties between the ADF and the attorneys to whom it provides training and funding all illustrate the manner in which a handful of New Christian Right legal organizations are capable of multiplying their influence. While each of these groups may focus on a single case in a single courtroom, their large affiliated lawyer networks offer the advantage of being able to track religious liberty disputes and respond quickly to them no matter where they might arise.

Second, the increasing cost of litigation as cases move up through the hierarchy of courts on appeal encourages New Christian Right lawyers to wage their campaigns in the lower courts. Maintaining an active presence in the lower levels of the judiciary is one way for New Christian Right firms to both see their public policy preferences put into law as well as conserve their resources for more expensive litigation.

Third, there are strategic concerns that encourage New Christian Right participation in the lower federal courts. After the Supreme Court upheld a thirty-six-foot buffer zone between an abortion clinic and anti-abortion protestors in *Madsen v. Women's Health Center, Inc.* (1994),[3] Alan Sears of the ADF confessed to his supporters that "we took a hit." Having contributed nearly $40,000 to Mathew Staver's Liberty Counsel, which argued the case, Sears noted that ADF money might have been used more effectively elsewhere: "[*Madsen*] shows us that we may not want to take everything to the Supreme Court."[4] Sears's revealing comment acknowledges that participation in the lower federal courts is not viewed as an inferior alternative to be employed when the Supreme Court option is not available; it is a legal strategy in its own right.

While there are obvious advantages to interest group participation at the Supreme Court level, the U.S. Circuit and District Courts offer organizations the opportunity to participate much more directly than they normally would at the Supreme Court level. And although legal victories in the lower federal courts generally receive far less attention from the media and general public than do Supreme Court decisions, they are nonetheless victories, often with substantial public policy implications of their own. Indeed, as Lee Epstein notes, the lower federal courts "by virtue of the finality of their decisions, [are] important actors in the American judicial system."[5]

By constitutional mandate, recourse to the Supreme Court is possible in "all Cases . . . arising under th[e] Constitution."[6] In reality, however, most cases are disposed of in the lower federal courts. With original jurisdiction in nearly all federal civil, criminal, and bankruptcy cases, the U.S. District Courts decide well over one million cases annually.[7] These decisions may be appealed, but only about 20 percent ever reach the federal appellate courts; and of those, a majority fail. Thus, in most cases, the decisions of the district courts are, in effect, final.

For their part, the U.S. Courts of Appeals are sometimes viewed as "mini Supreme Courts" because of their definitive rulings in approximately 85 percent of all federal cases.[8] One study of three circuit courts pushed the finality percentage even higher, finding that 99.7 percent of the 4,000 rulings handed down were left undisturbed. That is, they either were not appealed, were denied review by the Supreme Court, or the Supreme Court's ruling did not reverse the holding of the lower court.[9]

With most legal decisions being rendered outside the Supreme Court, it comes as no surprise to find New Christian Right lawyers actively litigating religious liberty claims in the lower federal courts. There are several important differences that distinguish their presence in U.S. Circuit and District Courts, however, from their Supreme Court participation, particularly in regard to the free speech strategy, the intensity of their litigation, and the success of their efforts.

Lower Court Expansion of the Free Speech Strategy

At the lower levels of the federal judiciary, New Christian Right public interest law firms participate much more directly than at the Supreme Court level. However, the Supreme Court cases in which these groups have been involved, particularly the free speech line of cases, play an important part in their overall lower court strategy. Once a general precedent is established by the Supreme Court, it falls to the lower federal courts to interpret and apply that decision to cases within their jurisdiction. Although the Court has established "bright-line" rulings in many areas of law (rulings that are clearly and easily applied by the lower courts), its decisions in the area of religion are notable for their bewildering lack of constitutional consistency, which only further complicates the interpretive responsibilities of lower federal court judges.

For example, within months of the Supreme Court's 1992 decision in *Lee v. Weisman,* which declared unconstitutional the practice of school-sponsored prayer at graduation ceremonies,[10] the U.S. Court of Appeals for the Fifth Circuit held that student-initiated, student-led prayers at graduation ceremonies were constitutionally permissible.[11] Like the student-initiated exception to the *Weisman* decision, the lower federal courts may interpret a ruling by the High Court in a way that ultimately minimizes the impact of the Court's initial ruling. Conversely, this same interpretive flexibility also allows the lower federal courts to expand on the Supreme Court's decisions.

Among the religious liberty cases in which the New Christian Right has been involved, there is perhaps no better example of the lower courts' applying and expanding on a Supreme Court ruling than *Hsu v. Roslyn Union Free School District.*[12] The Supreme Court's denial of certiorari to this case in December 1996 sparked considerable controversy because it left in place a lower court decision permitting student organizers to exclude non-Christians from holding leadership positions in their high school Bible club.

The case originated in September 1993 when Emily Hsu approached her principal about forming an after-school Bible club at her New York high school. After several months of debate, the local board of education informed Emily and other prospective club members that it would need to see the proposed club's constitution before it could make a decision to recognize the organization. Accordingly, Emily drafted and submitted to school administrators the bylaws of the Walking on Water Club, which included membership eligibility (open to all Roslyn High School students), the purpose of the organization (to provide fellowship), a listing of club activities (prayer, songs, skits, etc.), and requirements for serving as club officers (limited to professed Christians).

Concerned that this last provision violated the school district's anti-discrimination policy, school officials told Emily that the club could not be recognized unless changes were made to permit non-Christians to serve as officers. She refused and with her younger brother filed suit in U.S. District Court. That court ultimately ruled that the application of the school's non-discrimination policy did not significantly infringe upon the Hsus' free exercise rights.[13]

In November 1995, however, represented by the ACLJ and with the financial support of the ADF, as well as amicus briefs from the CLS Center and Liberty Counsel, the Hsus appealed the district court's ruling. On 15 May 1996 a three-judge panel of the U.S. Court of Appeals for the Second Circuit issued its opinion.

Writing for the unanimous panel, Circuit Judge Dennis Jacobs quickly framed the case in terms of the Equal Access Act. The court held that with the constitutionality of the Equal Access Act clearly established by the Supreme Court's 1990 decision in *Mergens,* it was required to consider how the school district's nondiscrimination policy conformed to the provisions of that act. In particular, the court was concerned about section 407(a) of the Equal Access Act, which prohibited secondary schools from denying "equal access or a fair opportunity to . . . any students who wish to conduct a meeting within that limited open forum on the basis of religious, political, philosophical, or other content of the speech at such meetings."[14]

Rather than seek further guidance from *Mergens* at that time, the appeals court instead turned its attention to a more recent Supreme Court decision, *Hurley v. Irish-American Gay, Lesbian and Bisexual Group of Boston* (1995). In its unanimous ruling in this ADF-financed case, the Supreme Court held that the application of a Massachusetts public accommodations law (which prohibited discrimination based on sexual orientation) to St. Patrick's Day parade organizers who refused to allow a gay pride group to march violated the free speech rights of the *organizers.* The Supreme Court ruled that parade organizers, having the "autonomy to choose the content of their own message,"[15] could decide whom to include or exclude from their parade. The appeals court in *Hsu* subsequently interpreted this decision as recognizing "that the message a group imparts sometimes depends upon its ability to exclude certain people, and that this exclusion may be protected by the First Amendment." In his opinion for the Second Circuit, Judge Jacobs went on to explain the connection between *Hurley* and *Hsu:* "The lesson we draw from *Hurley* is that the principle of 'speaker's autonomy' gives a speaker the right, in some circumstances, to prevent certain groups from contributing to the speaker's speech, if the groups' contribution would alter the speaker's message." While carefully noting that *Hurley* did not control the present case, Judge Jacobs nevertheless saw a fundamental similarity between the parade organizers' exclusion of a gay rights group and the leadership restrictions imposed by the Walking on Water Club: "As in *Hurley*, the Club's decision to exclude is based on its desire to preserve the content of its message. The Hsus claim that having Christian leaders necessarily shapes the content of the religious speech at their meetings, because the nature and quality of the speech at the meetings is dependent upon the religious commitment of the officers. We can accept this claim to the extent that there is an integral connection between the exclusionary leadership policy and the 'religious speech' at their meetings."[16]

Accordingly, the circuit court held that it was permissible for the Walking on Water Club to restrict its president, vice-president, and music coordinator positions to professed Christians "because their duties consist of leading Christian prayers and devotions and safeguarding the 'spiritual content' of the meetings."[17] However, other leadership posts that did not play an integral part in creating and sustaining the "spiritual content" within the club meetings, such as the activities coordinator and club secretary, could not exclude non-Christians, the court stated.

In ruling against the school district, the circuit court explained that it was taking an expansive view of the Equal Access Act as directed by the Supreme Court in *Mergens*. Within that law, the court recognized "the right to associate for the purpose of holding such a meeting [as] a necessary corollary." Thus, although the school district's nondiscrimination policy did not actually prohibit the formation of the Walking on Water Club, its requirement that non-Christians be allowed into club leadership posts denied club members the right to expressive association or the right to associate with (and draw their leadership from) those who have a "shared interest in particular speech." The court concluded its analysis by declaring that the Equal Access Act permitted the Hsus to "preserve the content of the religious speech at their meetings by discriminating in a way that ensures that the Club's leaders will be committed to both its cause and a particular type of expression."[18]

As a case study, *Hsu* is instructive for several reasons. First and most obvious, *Hsu's* combination of funding from the ADF, counsel from the ACLJ, and amicus briefs by the CLS Center and Liberty Counsel again clearly reflects the activity of the New Christian Right in the lower federal courts. Second and more important, *Hsu* illustrates the advantages of the crosscutting arguments embodied in the New Christian Right's free speech strategy. While this study focuses on the religious liberty efforts of New Christian Right public interest law firms, each of these organizations also actively litigates in other areas using arguments that often turn on the free speech clause. As the Second Circuit illustrated by its reference to *Hurley,* New Christian Right lawyers are able to draw on a much larger amount of supportive case law when their religious liberty arguments are not grounded solely in the establishment and free exercise clauses.

Third, *Hsu* underscores the importance of interest group activity in the lower courts, particularly when a group has important Supreme Court precedents to build on. To most observers, *Hsu* probably looked more like a case dealing with exclusion than with free speech. But in obedience to the Supreme Court's directive that the Equal Access Act be "interpreted broadly,"[19] the court of appeals expanded not only on the Supreme Court's analysis of the act but on the very statutory construction of the act itself, finding therein "an implicit right of expressive association"[20] that ostensibly permits discrimination—a significant interpretation (and ironic considering the title) of the Equal Access Act.

In his classic book *Fifty-Eight Lonely Men,* Jack W. Peltason writes, "The Constitution may be what the Supreme Court says it is, but a Supreme Court opinion means, for the moment at least, what the district judge says it means."[21] As a result, the quiet, incremental expansion of a particular right or interest group agenda item within a certain district or circuit is a real possibility. For example, given the Supreme Court's historic decisions on church and state, it may come as a surprise to learn that distribution of Bibles within public schools is not constitutionally impermissible, according to the U.S. Court of Appeals for the Fourth Circuit in *Peck v. Upshur County Board of Education* (1998).[22]

Like many other school boards around the country, the Upshur County West Virginia School Board routinely allowed private organizations to come and make presentations to its students. Representatives from such groups as the Boy Scouts of America, Girl Scouts of America, 4-H, and Little League were permitted to discuss their programs with Upshur County schoolchildren as well as distribute flyers and other written material. Until 1995, the board's written policy specifically prohibited religious and political groups from entering the school to discuss their views with the county's students or to distribute printed matter about their organization to the children.

Responding to criticism that it discriminated against religious and political speech, the board changed its policy in 1995 and set aside a single day each year for private religious groups to enter the school, engage students in conversation, and pass out Bibles and other printed material. The school board did not permit these organizations to enter any classrooms (displays were set up in the halls and library areas) and required that each display be accompanied by a large sign disclaiming any endorsement by the school.

Within two months of the adoption of the modified policy, the board's action was challenged in U.S. District Court as a violation of the establishment clause. That court, however, held that the policy change not only satisfied the demands of the establishment clause but was *required* by the free speech clause, a claim made by the Rutherford Institute attorneys who represented the school board.[23] The Court of Appeals for the Fourth Circuit took the case on appeal.

Writing for the majority, Circuit Judge J. Michael Luttig quickly dispensed with the establishment clause concerns brought by the petitioners. He based his opinion on the line of Supreme Court precedents from *Widmar* to *Rosenberger* that "consistently sustained against Establishment Clause challenge neutral governmental policies that permit[ted] private religious speech . . . on the same terms as private secular speech." By limiting religious speech to a single day each year, requiring large disclaimer signs by the displays, and preventing religious groups from going inside student classrooms, Judge Luttig wrote, the board took sufficient steps to "discourage any mistaken impression that the private speakers are speaking for the Board or the schools."[24]

He then addressed the constitutional necessity of allowing private religious organizations to enter the school. By permitting student access to other nonreligious private organizations, the school board was attempting to fulfill its educational mandate to expose students to a variety of beliefs and opinions. The board's subsequent decision to allow private religious displays on school campuses was nothing more than an acknowledgment that "religious speech is one of many kinds of speech that is consistent with the school's educational mission." For the board to decide otherwise, the court maintained, "would evince the hostility toward religious speech that the Establishment Clause does not require and that the Free Exercise and Free Speech Clauses forbid."[25]

In affirming the lower court's decision, the circuit court relied on Supreme Court case precedents that permitted it to view Bible distribution as primarily a free speech rather than establishment clause issue. In doing so, it again reinforced the importance of the New Christian Right's substantive victories in the Supreme Court to their lower federal court efforts.

Lower Court Contraction of the Free Speech Argument

Of course not all federal judges are sympathetic to the New Christian Right's religion-as-speech arguments, and not all religion cases lend themselves to that approach. In fact, the free speech strategy has been strongly rejected in several lower federal court religion cases, perhaps none more so than a 1993 Seventh Circuit opinion that contrasts sharply with the Fourth Circuit's decision in *Peck*.

Like the Upshur County School Board in West Virginia, the Rensselaer Central School Corporation of Rensselaer, Indiana, had in place a policy that allowed various community groups to distribute literature and other materials to students during school hours as long as permission from the respective school principals and school superintendents was obtained beforehand. Representatives of Gideon International annually sought and received permission to address each fifth-grade class within the Rensselaer school system about their organization and the Bibles they wished to distribute. After a brief introduction, the Gideons opened boxes of small Bibles, and students were allowed to select a copy for their own use. These presentations sometimes took place in the auditorium or gymnasium but often occurred in the fifth-grade classrooms themselves.

Neither Joshua nor Moriah Berger was ever actually present when the Gideons made their Bible presentations in the schools, but their father vigorously petitioned the school board to end the practice as a constitutional violation of the separation of church and state. The board of education considered Mr. Berger's arguments but ultimately resolved to leave its literature distribution policy in place. In 1990, Berger filed suit in U.S. District Court against the school corporation on behalf of his children. His claims were summarily dismissed.[26]

On appeal, the Seventh Circuit Court of Appeals suggested that the district court was "tone deaf to the Constitution's mandate that the government must not establish a state religion" and unanimously reversed the decision of the lower court.[27] The circuit court also strongly condemned the free speech arguments made by Rensselaer's attorneys, which included the ACLJ's Jay Sekulow. After briefly recounting the factual background of the case, Circuit Judge Walter Cummings took direct aim at the free speech strategy:

> Attempting a definitional coup, defendant tells us . . . that this is not, after all, a case about the Establishment Clause but a case about free speech. The issue is said to be the right of Gideons to freely express themselves by handing out Bibles to schoolchildren. Specifically, the Corporation suggests that Rensselaer schools created a designated public forum . . . by issuing an open invitation to speakers in the community to address schoolchildren. Having opened otherwise non-public property to expressive activity, the government is supposedly obliged to treat all speakers equally. To exclude the Gideons, then, would be to discriminate based on the content of their message.[28]

Judge Cummings then opined bluntly: "This approach suffers from two failings: it distorts the facts and misconstrues the law."[29] The unanimous opinion went on to explain that the school district's free speech argument implied that its schools did not participate in the Bible distribution process. This, Judge Cummings wrote, was factually wrong: "The Bibles were distributed by Gideons—it is true—but in public schools, to young children, in classrooms, during instructional time, . . . each year for several decades, in the presence of the teacher and principal, with instructions to return unwanted books not to the Gideons but to teachers. . . . It would be naive in the extreme to draw any conclusion in these circumstances other than that the Corporation was intimately involved if not down-right interested in seeing that each student left at the end of the day with a Gideon Bible in his or her pocket."[30]

The Seventh Circuit Court was particularly troubled by the manner in which the Rensselaer schools were characterized as an open forum—the crux of the New Christian Right's free speech arguments in religious liberty cases. These schools, the court's ruling concluded, did not truly provide an open forum, permitting all speech of which the Gideons were just one form of allowed expression. School officials had previously acknowledged that certain groups were and would continue to be categorically prohibited from addressing their students. Thus, as far as the court was concerned, by disallowing speech that was "offensive to the 'moral being' of children," the school corporation could not then "pretend to be manacled by the dictates of content neutrality" in relation to other speech of which it approved.[31]

The appeals court also expressed its irritation at the school district for manipulating existing case law to support the Gideons' actions. Although Rensselaer Central School Corporation looked to the Supreme Court's decisions in both *Widmar* and *Mergens* for precedent, the court failed to recognize either of these two cases as controlling. According to Judge Cummings, the basic difference between *Berger* and these precedents was the fact that religious groups had sought access to facilities in *Widmar* and *Mergens;* in the present case, the Gideons had sought access to children. As all children are required to go to school, with most enrolled in public schools, Judge Cummings viewed the Gideons' actions as nothing less than taking advantage of a captive audience.[32] "It is all the more odd, then," the court reasoned, "to analyze this case in terms of public forum jurisprudence. A designated public forum is a place. Children, of course, are not."[33]

Finally, the circuit court chided the Rensselaer Central School Corporation for presuming "that the First Amendment interest in free expression automatically trumps the First Amendment prohibition on state-sponsored religious activity." The court acknowledged that in the interest of preserving governmental neutrality toward religion, legitimate religious expression might not always be accommodated. In rejecting entirely Rensselaer's free speech approach to religious liberty in this case, the Seventh Circuit stated simply: "The defendant's attempt to wrench this case out of Establishment Clause jurisprudence must fail."[34]

Free Speech in the Lower Federal Courts

Hsu, Peck, and *Berger* all illustrate the expansive if not always successful free speech strategy of New Christian Right attorneys in the lower courts. As the Seventh Circuit Court in *Berger* correctly noted, the common progenitor of today's free speech–religious liberty cases, *Widmar v. Vincent,* was essentially about accessing physical facilities for religious expression. In the intervening years since that 1981 decision, however, the free speech clause has been successfully invoked by New Christian Right lawyers in the lower federal courts to permit, among other things, college students to challenge the appropriation of their student activity funds for causes or clubs they find offensive[35]; organized prayer by touring groups inside the U.S. Capitol[36]; high school graduation messages with religious content[37]; and the public display of private religious messages in sports stadiums.[38]

In addition to the broadening reach of the free speech clause, the lower federal courts have also seen a dramatic increase in New Christian Right participation in religion cases. With far more of their cases to analyze at this level than in the Supreme Court, distinctive participation patterns of New Christian Right public interest law firms emerge. More important, perhaps, the true strength and inherent limitations of the free speech clause strategy become apparent.

None of the tactics used by New Christian Right public interest law groups in the Supreme Court is abandoned at the lower federal court level. However, the manner in which New Christian Right lawyers wield these tools is considerably different (see fig. 2).

As mentioned earlier, the amicus brief is the favored strategy of New Christian Right public interest law firms at the Supreme Court level. Of the twenty-nine Supreme Court religion cases in which New Christian Right legal organizations participated between 1980 and 2000, all of them were accompanied by an amicus brief submitted by at least one of these firms. And 59 percent of these cases (n = 17) saw multiple New Christian Right amicus briefs submitted. In the lower federal courts, however, New Christian Right attorneys are much less likely to participate as amici. Of the eighty-two religion cases in which these firms participated in the lower courts between 1980 and 2000, just 30 percent (n = 25) were accompanied by at least one New Christian Right amicus brief. Multiple amici submitted by these firms in the lower federal courts were found in only four cases—less than 5 percent of the total.

There is a similar disparity among the more direct participation strategies of New Christian Right firms in the federal courts. At the Supreme Court level, for instance, New Christian Right organizations sponsored or financed only nine cases out of the twenty-nine in which they participated

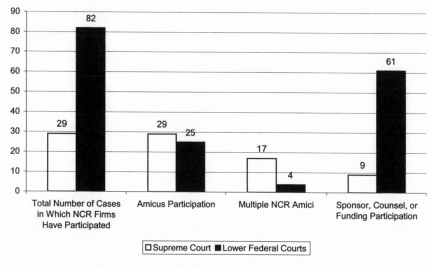

Figure 2. Comparing the Supreme Court and lower federal court strategies of the New Christian Right, 1980–2000.

(31 percent). However, in the lower federal courts these firms directly participated as sponsor or financier in 74 percent of the religious cases in which they took part (n = 61).

There are several important facets to the New Christian Right's direct participation in the lower federal judiciary. First, as discussed in chapter 4, the more direct the participation, the greater degree of control an organization has over the intellectual flow of the litigation process. Figure 3 illustrates that with the exception of the CLS Center which, true to its traditionally "softer" approach to litigation, continues to rely on its third-party privilege as amicus, each of the organizations in this study has sponsored or financed more cases in U.S. Circuit and District Courts than it has participated in as amici.

Much more so than at the Supreme Court level, the activity of the New Christian Right in the lower federal courts reflects its preference for direct participation. At first blush this may appear to contradict earlier statements about the New Christian Right's dependence on the amicus brief. Recall, however, that at the Supreme Court level, the amicus brief was generally the *only* way these firms could participate since few of their cases were granted plenary review by the justices. A more accurate evaluation of these groups

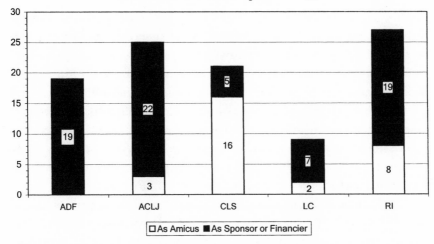

Figure 3. New Christian Right participation in the lower federal courts, 1980–2000. (Calculated by author. ADF participation based on interviews with ADF officials and information from the ADF's website and promotional literature.)

in the courts thus follows from a review of their efforts against the backdrop of the lower federal courts where litigation is less expensive; where no case is subjected to the certiorari lottery for final appellate consideration; and where the adjudicated law (unless it is reversed from above) is just as sound as that which issues forth from the Supreme Court.

New Christian Right litigation in the lower courts is also highlighted by the pronounced presence of the ADF. While providing the financial backing to such high-profile Supreme Court religion cases as *Rosenberger* and *Santa Fe,* the broader influence of the ADF can be seen in the lower courts. The nineteen religion cases it has funded are found in ten separate courts of appeal and several district courts. Since its founding in 1994, it has been involved in more religious liberty cases adjudicated in the lower federal courts than any other New Christian Right legal organization.

The presence of the New Christian Right in the lower courts is also characterized by remarkable individualism. In 82 percent (n = 67) of the litigated cases in the lower federal courts, New Christian Right firms have acted alone. Even the ADF, which was created in part to coordinate the litigation activities of the New Christian Right, utilized the services of the other major New Christian Right groups in just over half of its cases (n = 10). In short, while the collective efforts of New Christian Right organizations in the lower courts indicate a much stronger judicial presence than that observed at the Supreme Court level, there is far greater emphasis on the individual activities of these firms.

The previous chapter noted the commitment of the New Christian Right to participate in *every* Supreme Court case dealing with religion after the 1990 term. Although a similar claim cannot be made with respect to the religious liberty cases litigated in the thirteen U.S. Circuit Courts and ninety-four U.S. District Courts, New Christian Right attorneys have nonetheless dramatically increased the intensity of their efforts in the lower federal judiciary.

Prior to 1990, only the Rutherford Institute and the CLS Center had actively litigated religious liberty claims in the lower federal courts. These two groups, along with Jay Sekulow before he joined the ACLJ, litigated a dozen religious liberty cases between them prior to 1991. Joined by Liberty Counsel and the ACLJ in 1990, the total number of New Christian Right–litigated religious liberty cases between 1991 and 1994 nearly doubled to twenty-two. With the establishment of the ADF in 1994 and its ability to finance conservative legal challenges, New Christian Right litigation took on a level of energy theretofore unknown. From 1994 through mid-2000, New Christian Right public interest law firms have participated in forty-eight religious liberty cases—almost 60 percent of the total number of cases litigated since 1980.

With the shift in litigation strategies away from the amicus brief and the dramatic increase in New Christian Right–litigated cases in the lower federal courts, the question of whether these efforts have made a difference remains. A review of the lower federal court cases in which the New Christian Right has been involved reveals patterns of success similar to that of its Supreme Court activities (see table 4).

Just as in the Supreme Court, New Christian Right lawyers have generally met with only mixed success in the lower courts when making establishment and free exercise clause arguments.[39] Between 1980 and mid-2000, New Christian Right firms participated in seventeen cases in which the establishment clause was the primary constitutional issue at stake. Of these, the position taken by New Christian Right counsel and amici prevailed just six times (35 percent). In those cases in which free exercise considerations predominated (n = 20), the New Christian Right position fared slightly better, prevailing 45 percent of the time (n = 9). Such summary statistics

Table 4. The New Christian Right in lower federal court religion cases, 1980–2000

US Court of Appeals or US District Court Case	NCR Counsel or Funding	NCR Amicus	Federal Court Venue	Federal Court's Decision	Status of NCR Position
Branch Ministries v. Rossotti 211 F3d 137 (2000)	ACLJ		D.C. Circuit	Affirmed lower court ruling that rejected the free exercise and free speech claims of church that lost its tax-exempt status after publishing material critical of President Clinton.	Defeated
Children's Healthcare Is a Legal Duty Inc. v. De Parle 212 F3d 1084 (2000)		CLS	8th Circuit	Affirmed lower court ruling that upheld a provision of the Balanced Budget Act of 1997 that allowed individuals who had religious objections to traditional medical care facilities to receive Medicare and Medicaid assistance for services rendered at religious nonmedical health care institutions.	Prevailed
ACLU of Ohio v. Capitol Square Review and Advisory Board 210 F3d 703 (2000)	ACLJ ADF		6th Circuit	Citing establishment clause concerns, the Court held unconstitutional Ohio's state motto, "With God All Things Are Possible."	Defeated
Gentala v. City of Tucson 213 F3d 1055 (2000)	ACLJ ADF		9th Circuit	Held that Tucson violated the free speech rights of Christian group by denying them reimbursement funding for National Day of Prayer activities in city park.	Prevailed

Note: ADF = Alliance Defense Fund; ACLJ = American Center for Law and Justice; CLS = Christian Legal Society; LC = Liberty Counsel; RI = Rutherford Institute. Named individuals participated independently of the organizations listed here.

Table 4. Continued

US Court of Appeals or US District Court Case	NCR Counsel or Funding	NCR Amicus	Federal Court Venue	Federal Court's Decision	Status of NCR Position
Bynum v. U.S. Capitol Police Board 93 FSupp2d 50 (2000)	ADF		D.D.C.	Held that a U.S. Capitol Police Board rule banning organized demonstrations (including prayer by religious groups touring the building) was vaguely worded, overly broad, and unconstitutional.	Prevailed
Adler v. Duval County School Board 206 F3d 1070 (2000)	LC ADF		11th Circuit	Sitting en banc, the court affirmed a district court ruling that allowed student-selected messages at the beginning or end of high school graduation ceremonies, regardless of whether or not the content of those messages was religious in nature.	Prevailed
Campbell v. St. Tammany's School Board 206 F3d 482 (2000)	ACLJ ADF	CLS LC	5th Circuit	Held that school policy allowing for discussion of religion and religious viewpoints but not outright religious instruction and worship did not violate free speech rights of group that was denied access to school facilities for the purpose of conducting a prayer meeting.	Defeated
Freedom of Religion Foundation v. City of Marshfield 203 F3d 487 (2000)	ACLJ LC		7th Circuit	Upheld transaction in which a portion of city park containing a fifteen-foot-high statue of Jesus was sold to private organization. However, the court also held that the proximity of the statue to city property without any defining boundaries created an unconstitutional perception of endorsement. It then remanded the case for the city to erect a barrier between the two areas.	Prevailed

Case	Organization	Court	Description	Outcome
Pfeifer v. City of West Allis 91 FSupp2d 1253 (2000)	LC	E.D. Wisc	Held that a public library had become a designated public forum because of the array of groups it had previously allowed to use its facilities and thus could not bar the use of a meeting room for a lecture on creationism.	Prevailed
ACLU v. City of Florissant 186 F3d 1095 (1999)	RI	8th Circuit	Reversed lower court ruling that found a city's Christmas holiday display in violation of the establishment clause.	Prevailed
Freiler v. Tangipahoa Parish School Board of Education 185 F3d 337 (1999)	CLS	5th Circuit	Affirmed lower court ruling which held that the establishment clause was violated when the school board mandated that a disclaimer be read before evolution was taught in school biology classes.	Defeated
Altman v. Minnesota Department of Corrections 1999 US Dist. LEXIS 14897 (1999)	ACLJ	D. Minn.	Court upheld the free exercise claims of corrections officials who were reprimanded for reading their Bibles during a mandatory training session on gays and lesbians in the workplace.	Prevailed

Table 4. *Continued*

US Court of Appeals or US District Court Case	NCR Counsel or Funding	NCR Amicus	Federal Court Venue	Federal Court's Decision	Status of NCR Position
Chandler v. James 180 F3d 1254 (1999)	Sekulow		11th Circuit	Reversed lower court ruling that held unconstitutional a school policy permitting nonsectarian, nonproselytizing prayer at graduation ceremonies and other school events.	Prevailed
Strout v. Albanese 178 F3d 57 (1999)	ACLJ		1st Circuit	Rejecting the free speech and free exercise claims of parents whose children attended parochial schools, the court held that Maine's special private school education fund could be restricted to nonsectarian schools.	Defeated
Deboer v. Village of Oak Park 53 FSupp2d 982 (1999)	CLS ADF		N.D. Ill.	Court ordered village to allow the annual meeting of a National Day of Prayer group in a village-owned facility as long as the group's activities were limited to "civic matters," which could include prayer for political leaders.	Prevailed
Bynum v. Fort Worth Independent School District 41 FSupp2d 641 (1999)	ACLJ		N.D. Texas	Held that a Seventh-Day Adventist who lost his position as a Junior ROTC instructor for refusing to work weekends was reasonably accommodated by his employer and thus there was no violation of his religious rights.	Defeated

Case			Court	Description	Outcome
Full Gospel Tabernacle v. Community School District 27 164 F3d 829 (1999)	ACLJ	CLS	2nd Circuit	Court affirmed lower court ruling that rejected viewpoint discrimination claims of group that was denied use of school facilities for religious worship services.	Defeated
ACLU v. City of Stow 29 FSupp2d 845 (1998)	ACLJ		N.D. Ohio	Held that the incorporation of a Christian cross into the city seal violated the establishment clause.	Defeated
Peter v. Wedl 155 F3d 992 (1998)	ADF		8th Circuit	Reversed and remanded lower court decision that held that free speech and free exercise rights were not violated when a Minnesota school district refused to provide a paraprofessional to assist a disabled student enrolled in a parochial school.	Prevailed
Peck v. Upshur County Board of Education 155 F3d 274 (1998)	RI		4th Circuit	Court affirmed lower court decision which held that the dissemination of Bibles by a private group on public school grounds was permissible provided a large disclaimer sign accompanied the display.	Prevailed
Hack v. President and Fellows of Yale College 16 FSupp2d 183 (1998)	RI		D. Conn.	Rejected claims of students that Yale's mandatory residence in coed dormitories requirement violated their religious rights.	Defeated
Christ's Bride Ministries v. Southeastern Pennsylvania Transportation Authority 148 F3d 242 (1998)	LC ADF		3rd Circuit	Reversed lower court in holding that the Transportation Authority had become a designated public forum that impermissibly denied the free speech rights of a religious organization when it removed the group's paid anti-abortion ads from area buses, subways, and railway stations.	Prevailed

Table 4. *Continued*

US Court of Appeals or US District Court Case	NCR Counsel or Funding	NCR Amicus	Federal Court Venue	Federal Court's Decision	Status of NCR Position
Liberty Christian Center, Inc. v. Board of Education of the City School District of the City of Watertown 8 FSupp2d 176 (1998)	ACLJ		N.D. New York	Court held that a school district's denial of permission to use a school cafeteria for after-hours worship services violated the free speech rights of Liberty Christian Center since the cafeteria was opened to other groups, including those presenting a religious message.	Prevailed
In Re Young 141 F3d 854 (1998)		CLS	8th Circuit	Held that the Religious Freedom Restoration Act was still good law as far as federal action was concerned and reversed a lower court ruling that tithes were recoverable under federal bankruptcy law.	Prevailed
In Re Hodge 220 BR 386 (1998)	ACLJ		D. Idaho	Reversed bankruptcy court ruling that allowed trustee to recover tithed offerings as part of bankruptcy proceedings.	Prevailed
Asquith v. City of Beaufort 139 F3d 408 (1998)	CLS		4th Circuit	Upheld the validity of city noise ordinance banning street preachers.	Defeated
Swanson v. Guthrie Independent School District No. 1-L 135 F3d 694 (1998)	RI		10th Circuit	Affirmed lower court ruling that school board policy denying a homeschooled student permission to attend part-time did not violate her free exercise of religion.	Defeated

Case	Organization	Court	Organization	Ruling	Outcome
Waguespack v. Rodriquez 220 BR 31 (1998)	ACLJ	W.D. La.		Upheld bankruptcy court ruling that declared 10 percent tithing as impermissibly high and not allowable as a charitable contribution under the terms of debtor's Chapter 13 bankruptcy plan.	Defeated
Gibson v. Lee County School Board 1 FSupp2d 1426 (1998)	ACLJ	M.D. Fla.		Held that a school district could permissibly incorporate the Old Testament into its Bible History course without running afoul of the establishment clause, but not the New Testament.	Prevailed
Bronx Household of Faith v. Community School District No. 10 127 F3d 207 (1997)	ADF	2nd Circuit	CLS	Court affirmed lower court ruling denying a religious group access to school facilities because the school was a limited public forum.	Defeated
Culbertson v. Oakridge School District, No. 76 119 F3d 5 (1997)	CLS ADF	9th Circuit		Upheld lower court ruling requiring school district to make elementary school facilities available to student religious club.	Prevailed
Lumpkin v. Brown 109 F3d 1498 (1997)	RI	9th Circuit		Held that the dismissal of minister from San Francisco Human Rights Commission for inflammatory comments about homosexuals violated neither his free speech nor free exercise rights.	Defeated
Ceniceros v. Board of Trustees of San Diego Unified School District 106 F3d 1522 (1997)		9th Circuit	ACLJ CLS	Held that school district could not deny high school Bible club the opportunity to meet during lunch hour.	Prevailed

Table 4. *Continued*

US Court of Appeals or US District Court Case	NCR Counsel or Funding	NCR Amicus	Federal Court Venue	Federal Court's Decision	Status of NCR Position
Mockaitis v. Harcleroad 104 F3d 1522 (1997)		CLS	9th Circuit	Held that the secret taping of confession between an inmate and his priest violated the inmate's rights under the Religious Freedom Restoration Act.	Prevailed
Springfield v. San Diego Unified Port District 950 FSupp 1482 (1996)	ADF		S.D. Calif.	Ruled, among other things, that airport restrictions on "expressive activity" including proselytizing improperly infringed upon religious speech.	Prevailed
Chalmers v. Tulon Co. 101 F3d 1012 (1996)	RI		4th Circuit	Court held that religious accommodation in the workplace does not require a company to retain an employee who sends unsolicited letters to coworkers condemning their personal lifestyles and encouraging them to repent.	Defeated
Muller v. Jefferson Lighthouse School 98 F3d 1530 (1996)	LC		7th Circuit	Upheld lower court decision allowing grade-school student to pass out invitations to church-sponsored activity subject to specific school district guidelines.	Prevailed
Living Word Outreach Full Gospel Church v. City of Chicago 1996 US Dist LEXIS 13519 (1996)	ADF		N.D. Ill.	Court dismissed the free exercise claims of a church that had been cited weekly for conducting worship services in a building without a special zoning permit.	Defeated

Case	Organizations	Court	Holding	Outcome
Church on the Rock v. City of Albuquerque 84 F3d 1273 (1996)	ACLJ ADF	10th Circuit	Held that city could not prohibit the showing of a film on the life of Jesus at city-run senior centers or the distribution of New Testaments there because the centers were open to other views.	Prevailed
Hsu v. Roslyn Union Free School District No. 3 85 F3d 839 (1996)	ACLJ ADF CLS LC	2nd Circuit	Ruled that a high school religious club could restrict its leadership positions to Christians.	Prevailed
Rader v. Johnston 924 FSupp. 1540 (1996)	ADF	D. Nebr.	Court held that the University of Nebraska at Kearney could not require freshman students to live in campus housing if students viewed the atmosphere or activities associated with the campus housing as contrary to their religious beliefs.	Prevailed
Rohman v. City of Portland 909 FSupp. 767 (1995)	CLS ADF	D. Oreg.	Court held city policy regulating speech in public square violated the free speech and free exercise rights of street preacher.	Prevailed
Trinity United Methodist Parish v. Board of Education of the City of Newburgh 907 FSupp. 707 (1995)	ACLJ	S.D. New York	Held that school must allow Christian magician the use of its facilities if it was made available for use by other groups.	Prevailed
Brown v. Hot, Sexy, and Safer Productions, Inc. 68 F3d 525 (1995)	ADF	1st Circuit	Upheld lower court ruling that found no free exercise nor free speech violations (upon which relief could be granted) in high school requiring students to attend an AIDS awareness assembly that included graphic depictions of sex.	Defeated

Table 4. *Continued*

US Court of Appeals or US District Court Case	NCR Counsel or Funding	NCR Amicus	Federal Court Venue	Federal Court's Decision	Status of NCR Position
LeBlanc-Sternberg v. Fletcher 67 F3d 412 (1995)	RI		2nd Circuit	Held discriminatory a village zoning ordinance that prohibited the use of private residences as places of worship by Orthodox and Hasidic Jews living in the area.	Prevailed
Daytona Rescue Mission v. Daytona Beach 885 FSupp. 1554 (1995)	LC		M.D. Fla.	Ruled that the free exercise clause was not violated when a city commission denied a homeless ministry permission to locate in areas not zoned for church use.	Defeated
Settle v. Dickson County School Board 53 F3d 152 (1995)	ADF		6th Circuit	Court held that no free speech violations occurred when ninth-grade student was given a zero on a paper she wrote on Jesus (against the specific instructions of her teacher).	Defeated
Peloza v. Capistrano Unified School District 37 F3d 517 (1994)	ADF		9th Circuit	Affirmed lower court ruling that rejected the claims of a high school biology teacher who argued that his free exercise and free speech rights were violated by his school's requirement that he teach evolutionary science.	Defeated
Alpine Christian Fellowship v. County Commissioners of Pitkin 870 FSupp 991 (1994)	RI		D. Colo.	Court ruled that the county violated the free exercise clause when it denied a church a special zoning permit to open a private school on church property.	Prevailed

Case	Party	Court	Holding	Result
Good News/Good Sports Club v. School District of the City of Ladue 28 F3d 1501 (1994)	CLS	8th Circuit	Held unconstitutional a school district policy that restricted all groups except those affiliated with athletics or the Boy and Girl Scouts from using school facilities between 3 and 6 P.M.	Prevailed
Johnston-Loehner v. O'Brien 859 FSupp 575 (1994)	LC	M.D. Fla.	Held that school policy requiring advance approval of school officials for distribution of written material infringed on both the free speech and free exercise rights of student who wanted to hand out fliers regarding a church-sponsored activity.	Prevailed
Pruitt v. Wilder 840 FSupp 414 (1994)	Whitehead	E.D. Va.	Held that the Virginia Department of Motor Vehicles could not ban "GODZGUD" or any other reference to deities on vanity plates without infringing on free speech.	Prevailed
Pope v. East Brunswick Board of Education 12 F3d 1244 (1993)	CLS	3rd Circuit	Upheld lower court ruling that high school must make access to public address system, bulletin boards, and other school resources available to religious clubs if such privileges are extended to other student groups.	Prevailed
Hedges v. Wauconda Community Unit School District No. 118 9 F3d 1295 (1993)	CLS	7th Circuit	Held that school district could not ban outright the distribution of religious literature but could regulate where and how such material was to be disbursed.	Prevailed
Doe v. Duncanville Independent School District 994 F2d 160 (1993)	RI	5th Circuit	Affirmed lower court ruling that team prayers conducted before and after girls basketball games under the direction of the coach violated the establishment clause.	Defeated

Table 4. *Continued*

US Court of Appeals or US District Court Case	NCR Counsel or Funding	NCR Amicus	Federal Court Venue	Federal Court's Decision	Status of NCR Position
Ellis v. City of La Mesa 990 F2d 1518 (1993)		ACLJ	9th Circuit	Held that the display of a cross in a public park violated the no preference clause of the California state constitution.	Defeated
Garnett v. Renton School District 987 F2d 641 (1993)	CLS		9th Circuit	In reversing a lower court ruling that denied students the right to form a high school Bible club, the Court held that the Equal Access Act was not precluded by separation of church and state provisions within the Washington state constitution.	Prevailed
Berger v. Rensselaer Central School Corporation 982 F2d 1160 (1993)	ACLJ		7th Circuit	Court ruled that the distribution of Gideon Bibles in public schools violated the establishment clause. Held that the Gideons had no genuine free speech claim in this case.	Defeated
Washegesic v. Bloomingdale Public Schools 813 FSupp 559 (1993)	RI		W.D. Mich.	Ordered public school to either cover or remove a portrait of Jesus hanging in the school's hallway as it was a violation of the establishment clause.	Defeated
Sease v. the School District of Philadelphia 811 FSupp 183 (1993)	RI		E.D. Penn.	Held that the Equal Access Act did not permit public school faculty sponsors for high school student gospel choir.	Defeated

Case		Court	Description	Outcome
Jews for Jesus, Inc. v. Jewish Community Relations Council of New York 968 F2d 286 (1992)	Sekulow	2nd Circuit	Reversed lower court decision that permitted, on free speech grounds, a threatened economic boycott by an orthodox Jewish group that pressured a New York country club to break its contract with the Messianic Jews for Jesus.	Prevailed
Brody v. Spang 957 F2d 1108 (1992)	RI	3rd Circuit	Remanded case to district court finding it did not have enough information to determine whether religious speech could be included in high school graduation ceremonies.	Defeated
Thate v. D.C. Armory Board 804 FSupp 373 (1992)	RI	D.D.C.	Court ruled that a D.C. Armory policy on signs displayed at RFK Stadium must also allow for religious expression.	Prevailed
DeNooyer v. Livonia Public Schools 799 FSupp 744 (1992)	RI	E.D. Mich.	Court held that school acted out of proper "pedagogical concerns" in refusing to let second-grade student share with her classmates a video of her singing a religious song in church.	Defeated
North Carolina Civil Liberties Union Legal Foundation v. Constangy 947 F2d 1145 (1991)	RI Sekulow	4th Circuit	Affirmed a lower court ruling that declared unconstitutional a state judge's practice of opening his court with prayer.	Defeated
Quappe v. Endry 772 FSupp 1004 (1991)	RI	S.D. Ohio	Upheld elementary school policy requiring student Bible club to meet at 6:30 P.M. rather than 3:45 P.M. to avoid any possible hint of school endorsement.	Defeated

Table 4. Continued

US Court of Appeals or US District Court Case	NCR Counsel or Funding	NCR Amicus	Federal Court Venue	Federal Court's Decision	Status of NCR Position
Grace Bible Fellowship v. Main School Administrative District No. 5 941 F2d 45 (1991)	Sekulow		1st Circuit	Affirmed lower court ruling that school could not ban the use of its facilities for a Christmas dinner put on by a religious group if such were made available to other groups.	Prevailed
Harris v. City of Zion 927 F2d 1401 (1991)	RI		7th Circuit	Ruled that the depiction of a Latin cross and other religious symbols on a municipal seal violated the establishment clause.	Defeated
Slotterback v. Interboro School District 766 FSupp 280 (1991)	RI		E.D. Penn.	Court struck down school ban on distribution of material that promotes a particular religious belief.	Prevailed
Hemry v. School Board of Colorado Springs, School District No. 11 760 FSupp 856 (1991)	Sekulow		D. Colo.	Held as reasonable a school district's policy restricting the distribution of religious literature in its high schools.	Defeated
Gregoire v. Centennial School District 907 F2d 1366 (1990)		CLS	3rd Circuit	Affirmed lower court ruling that barred school officials from denying religious groups access to school facilities made available to other organizations.	Prevailed
Guidry v. Broussard 897 F2d 181 (1990)	Whitehead		5th Circuit	Affirmed lower court ruling that school officials acted constitutionally in rejecting a draft of a valedictory speech for its religious content.	Defeated

Case			Court	Description	Outcome
ACLU of Kentucky v. Wilkinson 895 F2d 1098 (1990)		RI	6th Circuit	Affirmed lower court ruling that permitted the display of a stable scene on the grounds of the state capitol (as part of a larger Christmas display), provided it was accompanied by a large disclaimer.	Prevailed
Smith v. County of Albemarle 895 F2d 953 (1990)		RI	4th Circuit	Held unconstitutional a private crèche display on the grounds of a Virginia county court building.	Defeated
Rivera v. East Otero School District R-1 721 FSupp 1189 (1989)	RI		D. Colo.	Declared unconstitutional a public school policy that required prior approval from school officials for students to distribute material that promoted a religious belief.	Prevailed
New Life Baptist Church Academy v. Town of East Longmeadow 885 F2d 940 (1989)		CLS	1st Circuit	Rejected claim of religious school that subjecting it to oversight by a secular school committee violated the free exercise clause.	Defeated
Smith v. Board of Education, North Babylon Union Free School District 844 F2d 90 (1988)		RI	2nd Circuit	Reversed a lower court decision that required a local high school to change the date of its Saturday commencement ceremonies in order to accommodate the religious beliefs of a graduating senior.	Defeated
Thompson v. Waynesboro Area School District 673 FSupp 1379 (1987)	Whitehead		M.D. Penn.	Upheld right of student to distribute Christian magazine on the grounds of his junior high school.	Prevailed

Table 4. Continued

US Court of Appeals or US District Court Case	NCR Counsel or Funding	NCR Amicus	Federal Court Venue	Federal Court's Decision	Status of NCR Position
Smith v. Board of Education of School Commissioners of Mobile County 827 F2d 684 (1987)		CLS	11th Circuit	Reversed lower court holding that (viewing humanism as a religion) interpreted the public school use of humanist texts as a violation of the establishment clause.	Defeated
Friedman v. Board of County Commissioners of Bernalillo County 781 F2d 777 (1985)		RI	10th Circuit	Sitting en banc, the Court held that a county seal displaying a Latin cross and the motto "With This We Conquer" violated the establishment clause.	Defeated
Bell v. Little Axe Independent School District No. 70 766 F2d 1391 (1985)		CLS	10th Circuit	Upheld lower court ruling that rejected free speech arguments in prohibiting informal religious meeting between students and teachers on public school grounds during school hours.	Defeated
Furr v. Town of Swansea 594 FSupp 1543 (1984)	Whitehead		D.S. Caro.	Held that town ordinance prohibiting street preaching without a permit was a violation of free speech.	Prevailed

admittedly ignore the factual and legal distinctions that accompany individual cases, but even this broad view of the New Christian Right's efforts in the lower federal courts supports the claim made by its attorneys (corroborated by Supreme Court–level religion cases) that the establishment and free exercise clause arguments historically made by these groups were not particularly successful.

Predictably, the free speech strategy that has been so successful in the Supreme Court has also been the catalyst for the majority of the New Christian Right's lower court victories. In analyzing these cases, however, the limitations of the free speech approach to religious liberty begin to appear in a manner that was not evident in the Supreme Court cases that were considered because there were so few of them. In the lower federal courts, New Christian Right groups participated in forty-five religious liberty cases in which free speech arguments were made. Of these, the position taken by these groups as counsel or amicus prevailed twenty-nine times (64 percent). The importance of this line of argumentation to the New Christian Right's religious liberty efforts is obvious: better than half of their total litigated religion cases in the lower courts have looked to the free speech clause. And although the New Christian Right position in *all* lower federal court religion cases has been defeated almost as many times as it has prevailed, the free speech clause is responsible for two-thirds of the movement's total victories (n = 44) in the lower federal courts.

As successful as the free speech argument is, there appear to be inherent boundaries to this strategy that are not easily distinguished by the New Christian Right's record in the Supreme Court. Of the forty-five religion cases categorized as free speech cases in the lower courts, 71 percent (n = 32) concern religious expression in schools. Although there have been many changes in the way the courts view religious expression since *Widmar,* the educational setting central to that case still predominates in its legal progeny.

In the lower courts access to school facilities, recognition of religious school clubs, and school policies on the distribution of religious literature are the most consistently litigated issues of New Christian Right public interest law firms. While Bible clubs and equal access to school facilities have received greater media attention, removing restrictions on student distribution of religious magazines and pamphlets on school grounds has been the most successful area of New Christian Right litigation. Outside the classroom, however, the free speech clause has been successfully invoked in just a handful of disparate cases ranging from license plate lettering to noise and loitering ordinances that restrict speech.

New Christian Right lawyers have succeeded in building on *Widmar*'s foundation and have used that case to free issues of religion from their traditional establishment or free exercise clause bonds. However, as demonstrated by their efforts in the lower federal courts, New Christian Right attorneys are themselves constrained in how far they can stretch that ruling. Court decisions from early 2000 broadened the free speech right to cover religious expression in such areas as city funding for religious activities in city parks[40] and creationism lectures in public libraries,[41] but this represents only an expansion in kind.

The New Christian Right's continued emphasis on the free speech clause and the schools in the federal courts suggests a rather limited opportunity to create change. At present, there appears to be no strategy in place to extend the free speech clause systematically to encase religious expression in other areas. Without a coordinated effort (particularly on the part of the larger firms that have both money and vast networks of lawyers) and a broader application of their litigating strategy, New Christian Right lawyers are limited in their ability to bring about the legal revolution they had hoped would reclaim America.

The Lower Federal Courts: Opportunities and Limitations

Utilization of the lower federal courts is well suited to the organizational design and strategic agenda of New Christian Right groups active in the courts. Given the unlikelihood of a successful appeal, the emphasis these groups place on the lower federal courts is understandable. Since 1990 and particularly since 1994, the organizations that litigate religion from the New Christian Right perspective have dramatically increased their litigation activity in the lower federal courts, much as they have at the Supreme Court level. The actual litigating strategies employed by these groups are not at all different from those they use in their Supreme Court litigation. However, there is much greater direct participation in the lower federal courts.

New Christian Right lawyers are more successful in the lower courts (and the Supreme Court) when they argue religious liberty claims using the free speech clause. Both the free exercise and establishment clauses have been utilized by the New Christian Right in the lower federal courts but neither has provided a consistently successful legal refuge for religious liberty claims. The importance of the free speech clause strategy to the New Christian Right cannot be overstated. It has given life to its litigation efforts, has given it major victories in the federal judiciary, and has helped bring about a genuine transformation in how religion and speech are perceived in the courts. However, just as New Christian Right lawyers have benefited from an expanded interpretation of the free speech clause, they are also limited in the degree to which this strategy can be used.

The success of free speech claims in both Supreme Court and lower federal court religion cases is qualified by the correlation between this strategy and public education. While the New Christian Right has attempted to raise free speech and religious arguments in other areas, it has done so with relatively little success compared to its linking of free speech with religious expression in the schools. At present, there appears to be no strategy in place to extend the free speech clause systematically to protect religious expression in other areas. In short, although the New Christian Right owes much of its rapid growth and reputation in the federal courts to its free speech approach to religion, its efforts may ultimately be constrained by this very same strategy.

7 Money, Media, and (Not So) Gentle Persuasion

New Christian Right Lawyers Outside the Courtroom

We set out the law in these letters . . . and debunk the mystery of separation of church and state. [The demand letters say] "this is what we want and the way we want it resolved. Do it or we'll go to court."
John Stepanovich, former ACLJ deputy chief counsel, 1997

The New Christian Right's embrace of the courts, its adoption of well-established litigation strategies, and its increasing presence in religious liberty cases in the federal courts reflects a deliberate attempt to be actively and anxiously engaged in the often slow process of legal evolution. Although "incremental pragmatism" (the strategy of diligently pursuing many small legal victories en route to more significant gains) has been cited as a means of demonstrating the New Christian Right's commitment to a long-term litigation approach, there is evidence to suggest that patience is not a virtue among New Christian Right public interest law firms.[1] Having historically yielded both the courtroom and the public debate on religious liberty to liberal groups, religious conservatives are simply not inclined to passively await favorable judicial rulings.

Given the importance of political activism in the courts, the impact of judicial rulings, and the accessibility of most federal court decisions, it is understandable that most literature on litigating interest groups and the courts tends to stop just there—at the courts. Though significant, this approach considers only one component of the larger issue of interest groups and the *law*. For example, testifying before the Senate regarding a president's nominee for a position on the federal bench, lobbying for changes in the language of a bill under consideration by Congress, and rallying grassroots support for or against statewide referenda and initiatives represent just a few of the many ways in which interest groups may attempt to exert influence on different facets of the law.

While public interest legal organizations are created to concentrate their resources on the judicial branch, focusing solely on their courtroom activities ignores the considerable lengths to which even these organizations go to influence both the law and the public perception of the law outside the courts. These efforts are not only driven by the same motivation as the outright litigation strategies these groups utilize, they also seek the same basic outcomes in terms of policy change.

There is little more than anecdotal evidence regarding the extra-courtroom activities of litigating interest groups because the information is simply too difficult to assemble. Unlike matters of public record (such as the majority of federal court decisions), there is no easy way to systematically trace the alteration of public policy to the efforts of particular interest groups. This chapter cannot fully explore this topic either. Rather, it seeks to illustrate that New Christian Right groups active in the federal courts are capable of finding fulfillment of their public policy objectives outside the judicial branch.

New Christian Right lawyers spend a considerably greater proportion of their time engaged in extra-courtroom activities than they do in litigation. Part of the reason for this is the fact that religious liberty cases, like most legal disputes generally, are resolved before trial. Rutherford Institute officials estimate that as much as 80 percent of that organization's cases are resolved without setting foot in the courtroom.[2] In assessing the efforts of his ACLJ, Pat Robertson notes that less than 1 percent of the cases in which the ACLJ is involved actually "end up in a court of public record."[3] And the CLS Center's litigation activities have been characterized as a small part of a much larger effort to alter public policy on religious expression.[4]

The extra-courtroom strategies that make up the majority of New Christian Right legal efforts can be broken down into two general areas: internally directed and externally directed. Internally directed strategies are designed to perpetuate the existence of the organization, broaden its financial support base, and increase its capacity to take and resolve cases dealing with religious discrimination. Externally directed strategies, on the other hand, are utilized to directly influence and alter public policies regarding religious liberty. Important in their own right, both of these strategies have a direct impact on the ability of New Christian Right legal groups to perform the litigation services for which they are best known.

Internally Directed Strategies

FUND-RAISING

Like other nonprofit public interest organizations, one of the most important activities in which New Christian Right legal groups must engage is fund-raising. In addition to the money they spend on such administrative necessities as office space and equipment, staff salaries, and bulk mailings to supporters, these firms also bear the considerable cost of litigation, arguing most religious liberty cases pro bono. The expense of public interest law naturally varies according to the individual characteristics of a case, the courtroom strategy utilized (direct sponsorship versus the less expensive amicus brief), and the litigation lifespan of the case.[5]

As might be expected, these organizations utilize conventional methods available to their trade for accessing certain types of funding, such as attorney's fees. After the Supreme Court's landmark decision in *Rosenberger*, for example, the legal team that won that case requested attorney's fees in the amount of $411,874. After adjusting this figure for unwarranted travel expenses, the U.S. District Court judge in Charlottesville ordered the University of Virginia to pay Rosenberger's lawyers $309,518.99.[6]

Attorney's fees, obviously, are not the only way that New Christian Right lawyers raise the funding necessary to litigate religious liberty claims. More commonly, they solicit funds from supporters or potential supporters through the direct mail techniques pioneered by conservative interest groups active in the electoral politics of the early 1980s.[7] The manner in which New Christian Right legal groups solicit funds as well as the pool of donors to whom they address their appeals provide some enlightening insights into this practice.

In order to establish, maintain, and expand access to funding and other resources, New Christian Right groups active in religion cases must make an intriguing appeal. First, they must persuade their donors that they are successfully defending religion from the onslaught of secular humanism and other hostile forces. Staking an ownership claim to a religious liberty case as counsel, financier, or amicus is therefore imperative. These groups must ensure supporters that they are not only active in the courts but that their efforts are successful as well. On the other hand, New Christian Right lawyers must also convincingly argue that there is still much work to be done. They must argue that the courts are still not free from the liberal influence of the past thirty years, that separationist interest groups still prevail too often, and that the rights of religious conservatives still need to be championed.

The twofold nature of this appeal is critical. Failure to make the first point implies that the organization is ineffective, and support (financial and otherwise) for that organization will dwindle. However, for a New Christian Right group not to include the second claim suggests that the secular foes have been vanquished and the battle for religious liberty won. Funding disappears in this instance also as supporters look to other causes in need of their financial backing. Thus, New Christian Right public interest law organizations find that both victories and defeats in the courtroom are vital to maintaining their financial link with supporters.[8]

Raising funds for the defense of religious liberty and other issues is, of course, one of the main purposes of the ADF. As pointed out in previous chapters, with its $9 million budget available to qualified applicants, the ADF is playing an increasingly important role in New Christian Right legal challenges. Initially subsidized by its founding ministries, the ADF's budget is now funded almost entirely by private donations, which requires an ongoing fund-raising effort.

Due to the financial nature of its mission as well as the fact that it is a relatively new organization still in the process of creating a solid donor base, the ADF spends more on fund-raising than any of the other groups active in religious liberty litigation. In 1998, the ADF devoted nearly $1.3 million to fund-raising alone.[9] The growth of its budget from $400,000 in its first year of operation to $9 million in its sixth year testifies to the effectiveness of its fund-raising efforts. Although he realizes that each of these groups largely shares a common donor base, ADF president Alan Sears does not view the success of the ADF's fund-raising efforts as necessarily detrimental to that of other New Christian Right legal organizations.

According to Sears, there are two main views on fund-raising among New Christian Right public interest lawyers: the pie theory and the cattle theory. Those who adhere to the pie theory believe that each time the fund-raising pie is recut (as new groups come to the table), their share decreases.[10] As a proponent of the cattle theory, Sears believes the funding opportunities for New Christian Right organizations are virtually limitless. This theory is based on the biblical proposition in Psalms 50:10 that "my Father owns cattle on a thousand hills." And, as Sears puts it, "We—all believers together—have not yet finished milking the first udder of the first cow."[11]

Sears's optimism aside, squeezing dollars out of people is considerably more difficult than getting milk from a cow. Put simply, a cow does not need a reason to give milk. This is an important consideration in the fundraising efforts of most New Christian Right groups active in the courts, according to the CLS Center. The center gets 65 percent of its funding from annual dues-paying members of its parent organization, the Christian Legal Society: $25 for students and paralegals and $150 for attorneys, judges, law professors, and nonlawyers. CLS Center attorneys believe that reliance on member dues gives them an advantage not enjoyed by other New Christian Right public interest law firms. As Steve McFarland of the CLS Center observed, "Most of our members are attorneys. That gives us more freedom than those groups that rely upon $15 checks. In order to keep those checks coming, they need a 'crisis of the month.' Fear gets people to write checks."[12]

Keeping especially blatant instances of religious liberty infringement before the public eye is one way some New Christian Right organizations motivate those "$15" supporters to donate. A 1997 Rutherford Institute newsletter, for example, listed a number of danger points ("danger" or "danger point" being highlighted fourteen times in red ink) that confront American society. Among these were "the continuing harassment and censorship of [religious] children in the public schools by school officials" and the fear "that the government will increasingly prohibit people from meeting to pray, even in their own homes."[13]

The March 1997 issue of *Casenote,* the newsletter of the ACLJ, listed five cases recently taken by the ACLJ. Of these, one dealt with the distribution of Bibles in a Florida city's visitor center, another with the denial of state-funded educational equipment for a deaf and blind student enrolled in a Christian school, and a third with the exposure of a sixth-grade student in western New York to a teacher's vulgar language and R-rated movies with gratuitous depictions of sex and violence in her public school classes. The two remaining cases involved the perceived endorsement of homosexuality by public high school officials.[14]

With a budget of $9 million, it may seem particularly curious for the ACLJ to resort to the "crisis of the month" tactic. But this approach coupled with the media savvy of the ACLJ's Jay Sekulow is precisely what has enabled that organization to reap the benefits of an ever-growing base of contributors. Like the ACLJ, other New Christian Right public interest law firms appreciate the advantages conferred by mass media exposure. Several of these groups also utilize radio and television to raise their public profile, expand their donor base, and increase their financial reserves.

MEDIA ACCESS

The information infrastructure that originated during the political isolation of religious conservatives grew as the New Christian Right emerged as a full-fledged political movement, and Christian electronic media outlets continued to thrive throughout the 1990s. In 1999, there were 285 television stations (excluding cable) and 1,731 AM, FM, and shortwave radio stations providing Christian programming according to the National Religious Broadcasters (NRB), an organization that tracks Christian media outlets.[15] By comparison, in 1986 there were 1,148 radio and just 67 television stations in the United States that met the NRB's criteria.

The inherent power of the medium coupled with the ongoing growth of Christian media outlets led author and New Christian Right critic Sara Diamond to declare that "religious broadcasting is the single-most-important resource for the Christian Right."[16] The continued expansion of Christian broadcasting has coincided with its use by several New Christian Right litigating groups as a forum for their views on religious liberty, a point of contact with donors, and a means of soliciting additional cases to litigate.

Neither the ADF nor the CLS Center participates extensively in mass media programming. The ADF does advertise on Christian radio stations and officials from both the ADF and the CLS Center are often interviewed in both the religious and secular media. The ADF also indirectly benefits from the considerable media presence of its sponsoring ministries. But neither organization has radio or television programming devoted solely to their courtroom efforts. On the other hand, the ACLJ, Rutherford Institute, and even smallish Liberty Counsel regularly utilize the power of electronic media to offer their assessment of the legal climate of religious liberty as well as tout their own efforts to influence that environment.

Liberty Counsel's Mat Staver, for example, is a frequent presence on the airwaves with two radio programs in limited national distribution. *Freedom's Call,* his two-minute radio commentary that airs five days a week on some one hundred stations nationwide, spotlights religious freedom and free speech controversies throughout the country. He also has a weekday program on the VCY American Radio Network titled *Faith and Freedom*, which takes a more detailed look at many of these same constitutional issues.

On television, Staver can be seen publicizing Liberty Counsel's cases and legal services on some fifty-seven stations nationwide as a monthly commentator on Jerry Falwell's *Listen America* television program.[17] He also hosted *Central Florida Live*, a program that addressed call-in questions and comments about political, religious, and legal issues in central Florida. Because of the broader nature of *Central Florida Live*, Staver did not use it as a forum for Liberty Counsel.[18] However, the twice-weekly broadcast indirectly benefited his organization by gaining Staver a regional reputation as an authority on religious and legal matters.

For nearly a decade John Whitehead of the Rutherford Institute hosted a two-minute syndicated commentary airing five days a week on Christian radio stations worldwide. In March 1998, however, two of the nation's largest Christian radio networks, Moody Broadcasting and VCY/America, cancelled Rutherford's *Freedom under Fire* spots after the institute took up Paula Jones's case against President Clinton. A Rutherford spokesperson at the time predicted that the cancellation would "dampen already sluggish fund-raising."[19]

Hoping to reach a larger listening audience, Rutherford recently replaced the *Freedom under Fire* program with a bimonthly series of public service announcements called *First Liberties*, which are intended to be broadcast over mainstream networks nationwide.[20] Whitehead enjoyed considerable television coverage after Rutherford came to the aid of Paula Jones, but outside of the free publicity generated by that case, the institute has made little use of that medium.

While each of these groups appreciates the opportunities provided by radio and television, the undisputed leader in the use of broadcast media among New Christian Right legal organizations is Jay Sekulow and the ACLJ. Given the relationship between the media and the ACLJ's founder, Pat Robertson, this should come as no surprise. Robertson's media and business acumen saw the Christian Broadcasting Network (CBN) he founded in 1959 grow from an obscure Christian media outlet to a worldwide, multimillion dollar enterprise by the mid-1990s.[21] Along the way, CBN provided Robertson with the national exposure necessary for him to challenge the Republican Party establishment in running for the party's presidential nomination in 1988.

However, it was not Pat Robertson but Paul Crouch Sr., the founder of Trinity Broadcasting Network (TBN), who introduced Sekulow to the power of the media. With over five hundred affiliated stations worldwide, TBN is the largest religious television network in the world with an estimated American audience of twenty-seven million.[22] Sekulow made the first of many appearances on Crouch's network shortly after he argued and won his first Supreme Court case in 1987.[23] Within a year of his initial exposure to TBN's television audience, donations to Sekulow's own public interest law firm Christian Advocates Serving Evangelism quadrupled from $88,000 to $370,000—an increase he attributed solely to his appearances on TBN. Besides giving Sekulow his first media break and providing free air time for his religious liberty television program, Crouch also helped Sekulow become a mini media mogul in his own right by partially subsidizing Sekulow's Sonlight Broadcasting System, a network of television stations in Alabama, Mississippi, and Tennessee.[24]

From 1988 to 1997, Sekulow had his own half-hour television program on TBN where he discussed issues and current litigation related to religious liberty and other areas.[25] He later hosted *Call to Action* and *And Nothing But the Truth,* which were broadcast over the National Empowerment Television network and FamilyNet. In addition to frequent appearances on Robertson's *700 Club* program, Sekulow currently hosts a daily radio show called *Jay Sekulow Live,* which is now broadcast on some 140 stations nationwide.

The substance of both the fund-raising and broadcast media efforts of New Christian Right legal groups tends to focus on their high-profile courtroom efforts. However, they also communicate to their supporters details of their activities on behalf of religious expression outside the courts, where the bulk of their work takes place.

Externally Directed Strategies

Like other public interest lawyers, New Christian Right attorneys are unable or unwilling to litigate every religious liberty claim. There is a financial justification for this, of course, since funding and other resources are limited. But there are other reasons for not litigating a claim of religious discrimination: it may not offer precedent-setting potential (a requirement for involvement by some New Christian Right groups); it too closely resembles another case already in litigation; or it is already covered by existing law.

The fact that a New Christian Right organization whose ostensible purpose is to litigate might decline to file a lawsuit on behalf of a particular claim of religious liberty infringement does not necessarily mean that it is unwilling to seek a resolution to that conflict. New Christian Right legal groups actively seek to influence and change public policy outside the courtroom using public education, prelitigation, and nonlitigation strategies. Although there are important differences among these, their purpose as strategies exterior to the courtroom is really no different than those employed within. It is, simply, to convince policymakers at the local, state, and national level to adopt policies compatible with the New Christian Right's vision of religious liberty.

Public Education

One common extra-courtroom strategy of New Christian Right lawyers focuses on public education. Eager to make as effective use of their resources as possible, these groups attempt to stretch their operating budget by preempting the litigation option. In other words, through their public education efforts, these firms hope to both clarify the finer points of constitutional law relative to religious liberty as well as resolve areas of conflict before the courtroom venue is even considered.

Public education consists of proactively and reactively providing the organization's perspective on a given legal issue to the news media, interested parties, and policymakers. The cost of public education is not insubstantial. In 1998, for example, the ADF provided $1.5 million to qualified cases at various stages of litigation in the courts. During that same period, however, it spent nearly the same amount ($1.4 million) on public education efforts.[26] Rutherford spends about 30 percent of its entire budget on educational services.[27]

The way the information distributed by New Christian Right legal organizations differs from the promotional or propaganda materials sent out by other nonprofit public interest groups is its emphasis on the law. It is a strategy used by both liberal and conservative activists in the courts where ideology is couched in legal precedent invoked to lend credibility to the organization's view of a disputed policy.

Although it is difficult to trace the impact of these efforts, an example of how New Christian Right groups engage in public education can be seen in the actions of the ACLJ in the aftermath of the Supreme Court's ruling in *Lee v. Weisman* (1992), which held impermissible school-sponsored prayers at graduation ceremonies. As mentioned earlier, the Fifth Circuit Court of Appeals soon thereafter upheld the practice of student-initiated, student-led prayers at graduation in its *Clear Creek* decision.[28] The ACLJ immediately sent out a memo to each of the nation's fifteen thousand school superintendents informing them of the *Clear Creek* ruling and explaining the critical "student-led" aspect that distinguished that decision from *Lee*.[29] Outraged, the ACLU and Americans United for Separation of Church and State shot off their own memos to the nation's schools, criticizing the ACLJ's legal analysis and threatening legal action to those schools that followed the ACLJ's recommendations.

The following November the ACLJ again contacted each of the school districts, informing them of a constitutionally appropriate manner for recognizing Christmas and Hanukkah.[30] The ACLU again responded with a clarifying memo. In 1995, the Rutherford Institute engaged in a similar effort by sending out letters of its own to each school district regarding the recognition of religious holidays. Although the ACLU did not take direct issue with the content of that letter, it expressed concern that the letter's true motive appeared to be one that would "dress religion in secular clothing."[31] And, fearing that the Supreme Court's ruling in *Santa Fe* would be misinterpreted to exclude religious viewpoints altogether, the ACLJ announced in 2000 that it would again send a special bulletin to all school districts to clarify what type of religious expression was still permissible in the schools.[32]

Although it is not clear to what extent if any these letters have altered school policy, two conclusions about the public education efforts of New Christian Right legal groups are clear. First, these organizations are taking the initiative to increase public understanding of their interpretation of the law, particularly their free speech approach. Though their detractors maintain that such interpretations are suspect, if not wrong altogether, New Christian Right lawyers view such activity as a way to challenge what they believe is the predominant liberal influence in church-state issues. In doing so, they are also forcing their critics to respond with public education efforts of their own.

Second, the public education efforts of the New Christian Right reflect a desire to utilize the law without resorting to the courts. This distinction is important. If public education alone is successful, then presumably there is no basis for turning to the courts. This calls into question the long-term commitment of the New Christian Right to the judicial branch and whether it is the actual changing of the law itself or the public acceptance of their interpretation of existing law that motivates New Christian Right firms.

PRELITIGATION

Like public education strategies, the New Christian Right's prelitigation efforts also largely take place away from the courtroom. Put simply, prelitigation describes the activities of New Christian Right lawyers from the time a claim of religious discrimination passes the informational phase, becoming a legitimate target for litigation, until the matter is taken up in court. Whereas public education may consist of filling numerous requests for general information or conducting broad-based issue campaigns, prelitigation is much more narrow, focusing on individual disputes and seeking specific remedies.

Very much a matter of degree, prelitigation can range from a simple telephone call or a letter on behalf of a claimant explaining a point of law to the outright threat of an expensive lawsuit if a desired policy change is not forthcoming. In that sense, prelitigation is a no-lose situation for a public interest legal organization because it can simply escalate its demands for change up to the point where the issue goes to court, where it was prepared to fight anyway.

Many of the prelitigation issues that confront New Christian Right public interest law firms may be resolved by a friendly phone call, but others require the appropriately named "demand letter." In general, these letters (directed toward both individual and group policymakers) state the nature of the complaint, the manner in which the New Christian Right group believes the situation should be resolved, and the relevant case law supporting its position.

The organizations in this study all claim to resolve the vast majority of religion-related disputes in the prelitigation stage. Again, outside of their own records, it is practically impossible to comprehensively track their efforts. However, the following examples give some indication of both the type of prelitigation situations in which these groups have been involved and the manner in which they have settled these complaints.

In 1996, a Tennessee woman who applied for a personalized license plate bearing the inscription "God 4 U" contacted the Rutherford Institute after her plate request was denied because computers at the Titling and Registration Division of the Tennessee Department of Safety had been preprogrammed to reject the word "God." The agency reversed itself after the Rutherford Institute intervened. According to the Rutherford attorney who worked on the dispute, "All we had to do was send copies of [district court cases] where the federal court has come down consistently on our side. We pointed out that barring Ms. Wall from receiving a license plate with the word 'God' on it was simply invalid and unconstitutional. We did that on January 21 and we received a ruling on January 31. While that doesn't meet our 5-day response request, it's certainly fast for a state agency."[33]

At a May 1996 meeting with supporters, John Price of the ADF recounted a situation in which a girl was threatened with expulsion by school administrators because of a religious message she left on the school's "free-speech board." The ADF not only contacted the school to explain how this girl's message was constitutionally protected, it also mentioned the substantial legal costs the school would incur if a lawsuit was filed. Price noted that the school then experienced "a marvelous change of heart" that allowed the girl to remain in school and her message posted on the free-speech board.[34]

Liberty Counsel represented a Christian radio station in North Port, Florida, that filed suit against the city for refusing to allow it to post a religious message along a city right of way known during the month of December as "Holiday Card Lane" for the brightly decorated holiday greetings posted by area businesses and schools. During a February 1996 meeting to mediate the suit, Liberty Counsel and city attorney David Levin tentatively agreed on a settlement that would prevent the city from enforcing the ban on posting religious messages as well as have the city pay the attorneys' fees incurred by the radio station manager—approximately $15,000. Levin recommended that the North Port city commissioners approve the settlement because, in his words, "[t]o litigate this issue would obviously cost substantially more than $15,000."[35]

And in the aftermath of the Supreme Court's decision in *Santa Fe,* the ACLJ announced that it would defend any school district in America that was sued for permitting student-led, spontaneous prayer before high school football games. It also promised to bring suit against those schools that "interfere with the First Amendment right of students and community members."[36]

Precisely because these groups can take an individual or organization to court, they have a persuasive ability that may be difficult to counter.[37] John Whitehead of the Rutherford Institute has acknowledged the compelling power associated with litigation threats: "We don't charge our clients . . . but if we sue each school board member, they each have to get a fancy outside law firm to defend themselves."[38] In short, New Christian Right firms fully appreciate that it is both easier and cheaper for policymakers to relent on a given policy affecting religious expression than it is to resist in a court of law.

Like public education, prelitigation allows New Christian Right lawyers to utilize the weight of the law without the costs associated with actual litigation. And although prelitigation is far more difficult to track than the New Christian Right's efforts in the courts, persuading private employers, school boards, state legislatures, and others to alter their policies on religion and religious expression is an important component of its efforts to transform the legal environment surrounding religious liberty.

Nonlitigation

In using nonlitigation strategies, New Christian Right legal groups have much broader ends in mind than they do when using either prelitigation or public education. Directed primarily at elected policymakers, nonlitigation is more pragmatic, less threatening, and rhetorically moderate as New Christian Right organizations seek to build a working political consensus for a particular aspect of religious liberty.[39]

Of the organizations in this study, the CLS Center is the most active in nonlitigation, spending approximately 40 percent of its effort in lobbying and finding points of agreement with policymakers and erstwhile opponents.[40] Playing a key role in the drafting of both the Equal Access Act of 1984 and the Religious Freedom Restoration Act of 1993,[41] the CLS Center has sought congressional support for a number of other religion-related bills including the Religious Freedom Amendment to the Constitution; the Workplace Religious Freedom Act (which would require employers to make a reasonable effort to accommodate employee religious practices and holy days); and a bill to protect tithes and other freewill financial offerings to churches.

The last item grew out of the CLS's desire to extend statutory authority to a decision made by President Clinton in September 1994. At that time the Department of Justice had filed a brief to the Eighth Circuit Court of Appeals in which it agreed that an evangelical church should be forced to turn over to creditors the tithes of a bankrupt couple. The court eventually ruled for the church,[42] but not until after President Clinton told the Justice Department to pull its brief in the case. Unusual in any administration and unprecedented in his own, Clinton's actions were triggered by his deputy counsel's discussions with the CLS and a meeting between the president and the director of the CLS Center, Steve McFarland.[43]

In a March 1997 interview, McFarland stated that the CLS Center had been working closely with other religious organizations and the White House on guidelines for religious expression in federal offices, which he predicted would be released sometime that summer.[44] On 14 August 1997 President Clinton did, in fact, issue an executive memorandum outlining appropriate religious practices and expression in the federal workplace. Affecting some two million federal workers, these guidelines set forth standards for sharing religious literature, religious displays in personal work areas, and other forms of religious expression.[45]

As mentioned earlier, the CLS Center has also joined with other organizations to fashion statements of consensus on such topics as student prayer, distribution of religious literature, and teaching about religion in public schools. Because of the substantive content of these statements as well as the broad coalition that has drafted and/or endorsed them, these guidelines were largely adopted and promulgated by the Department of Education in response to President Clinton's directive to clarify the issue of religious expression in the public schools.[46]

As far as the nonlitigation efforts of the other organizations in this study, both the ACLJ and the Rutherford Institute have endeavored to branch out into this area by opening offices in Washington, D.C., where they can communicate their position on certain issues or provide informational assistance to executive branch agencies and members of Congress. Reflecting its cutbacks in other areas, however, Rutherford closed its Office of Public Affairs in Washington in 1998 after just three years of existence.

In a study of public interest group litigation, these nonlitigation efforts may seem noticeably out of place. They are important, however, because they may decrease the need for future litigation. Speaking of the joint statements on religion the CLS Center helped draft, McFarland acknowledged, "It is hard to prove a negative—like how many lawsuits have been avoided by it."[47] But it would appear that standardizing whole segments of the religious liberty debate via congressional statute, executive order, or joint statements endorsed by liberals and conservatives alike would lead to fewer questions and, ultimately, lawsuits in those areas.

Relying on the Law (But Not the Courts)

As different as public education, prelitigation, and nonlitigation are as strategies used by New Christian Right public interest law firms, they are still bound by the common thread of law. The public education efforts of these groups, for example, seek to instruct others in the requirements of the law, albeit from a distinct perspective. Citing case law favorable to their argument, New Christian Right lawyers frame the issue in question so as to create little doubt as to the legitimacy of the policy change they desire.

Prelitigation goes a step beyond public education by threatening to bring to bear the full force of the law if a particular policy change is not forthcoming. Utilized by both liberal and conservative public interest law groups where religion issues are concerned, the demands for policy change in the prelitigation phase are obviously much more difficult to resist given the costs of litigation.

Finally, nonlitigation also relies on the law by seeking the assistance of policymakers to put into place greater protections for religious expression by statute, executive order, or administrative agency ruling.

The New Christian Right's reliance on these extra-courtroom procedures might be viewed as part of a systematic effort to protect religious expression at every turn. Although these groups monitor and coordinate their efforts in and out of the courts, a more practical interpretation sees the use of these extra-courtroom methods as an acknowledgment of the limitations of a purely judicial approach to policy change. Litigation is expensive as well as time-consuming. Public education, prelitigation and nonlitigation, on the other hand, are just as capable of influencing public policy decisions regarding religious liberty as a courtroom battle and often more quickly and with less expense.

Of course, like the litigation strategies pursued by New Christian Right lawyers, these extra-courtroom efforts do not guarantee success. Public education, for example, is only as effective as it is heeded. Prelitigation pressure is only as good as the promise to litigate behind it. And because of its emphasis on coalition building and political consensus, nonlitigation may yield results far less satisfactory to a group's core supporters.[48]

Not content to let judicial rulings simply filter down to policymakers, New Christian Right public interest law firms are seizing the initiative to introduce favorable court decisions on religious issues to those with policy-making authority. After the long absence of religious conservatives from the public debate on religion, New Christian Right lawyers appear to be leaving little to chance.

8 Legal Right or Gospel Tool?

The Past and Future of the New Christian Right's Free Speech Strategy in the Courts

I have learned that we lose our religious liberties for three primary reasons:
(1) ignorance of the law, (2) hostility toward religion, and (3) apathy. . . .
Most people would rather run than fight and lose their rights rather than
struggle for them. The issue of religious liberty is not simply a legal right—
it is the ability to continue to spread the gospel in a free nation.
                                          Liberty Counsel's Mathew Staver, 1995

During the last two decades New Christian Right lawyers have been active
in religious liberty litigation before the federal courts, using the free speech
clause to make the judiciary take notice of an approach to religion that it
might not have otherwise. Although their Supreme Court efforts are typified by third-party participation as amicus curiae and a decidedly mixed
record where traditional religion clause arguments were made, New Christian Right lawyers have been directly and successfully involved in religion
cases that have appealed to the free speech clause for protection.

In the lower courts, where they participate far more frequently as sponsor
or financier than as amici, New Christian Right public interest law firms
have again had considerable success using the free speech strategy. The limitations of this approach become more evident at this level given the many
more cases available for analysis. The ADF's role as financier in the lower
federal courts has been particularly important. Having never drafted a brief
nor presented an argument before any court under its own name, the existence of the ADF has quickened the pace of religious conservative activism
in the judicial branch.

The presence of the New Christian Right in the courts has also had an
influence on its critics and opponents. By fighting back at what they perceive as a predominating hostile view of religion in the public square, New
Christian Right lawyers have forced "separationist organizations that had
once used the litigation process with great success to pursue constitutional
reform . . . to engage in a more reactive, less aggressive approach to litiga-

tion just to preserve the victories for which they had fought."[1] These groups have also been forced to respond to the efforts of New Christian Right lawyers outside the courtroom.

New Christian Right law firms spend relatively little time in the courtroom compared to the other activities in which they are engaged. This undoubtedly reflects the economic reality associated with litigation. But it also reveals both an honest evaluation of their own status (that is, New Christian Right public interest law firms do not represent a disadvantaged minority whose only recourse is the judicial branch) as well as an unwillingness to yield every religious question to the courts.[2] Although this approach necessarily takes a more limited view of the efficacy of courtroom litigation, it does not demean the law as a tool of political activism. In fact, New Christian Right lawyers are far more dependent on the law than they are the courts for changes in public policy regarding religious liberty.

Although they have largely patterned both their courtroom and extracourtroom efforts after strategies pioneered by the ACLU, NAACP, American Jewish Congress, and other litigating interest groups, the dual and sometimes conflicting nature of the New Christian Right's purpose for turning to the courts to resolve questions of religious liberty sets it apart. Mathew Staver's characterization of religious liberty as both a legal right and a gospel tool concisely summarizes the opportunities and challenges of the New Christian Right's reliance on the free speech clause.

Religious Liberty as a Legal Right

One of the purposes of New Christian Right litigation in this area is to expand the judicial accommodation of religion. In doing so, it benefits from a broad interpretation of religious expression as a legal right, enjoyed by all regardless of denomination. As such, any infringement on that right would presumably draw opposition from other religious organizations that, while theologically disparate, would combine their resources to protect this right that they equally enjoy.

Securing basic rights has been the objective of secular public interest legal organizations such as the NAACP, the ACLU Women's Rights Project, and the Lambda Defense and Education Fund, who have challenged the judicial branch to proclaim Fourteenth Amendment equal protection rights for African-Americans, women, and homosexuals, respectively. They argued that prevailing public opinion and public law notwithstanding, it was incumbent on the judiciary to expand accepted constitutional categories to include the groups they represented.

New Christian Right public interest law firms, on the other hand, are not seeking new, heretofore unarticulated rights to be enunciated by the courts. What they desire is more of a judicial reaffirmation that religion and religious expression are as important now as they were in past eras of American history. But the New Christian Right faces several challenges in its efforts to bring about the type of legal change it envisions.

First, unlike desegregation, restrictive housing covenants, abortion, or physician-assisted suicide, "religious liberty" as a legal right lacks definitional precision. Not only is the term denominationally broad, but it also encompasses a wide range of expression and action that may be linked to almost any secular subject. Does an employee have a right to have his or her Sabbath day off from work? Should medical personnel ignore a patient's religious-based refusal of a lifesaving blood transfusion? Do strict school dress and grooming codes infringe on the rights of those whose clothing, hairstyle, or jewelry is dictated by their religious beliefs? Can municipalities refuse to grant zoning variances to allow individuals to conduct worship services in their homes? The tremendous variety of litigation possibilities in the field of religious liberty makes it very difficult for the New Christian Right to focus strategy and resources on a single policy area.

A significant exception to this, of course, involves the development of the free speech approach to religion and its legislative and judicial progeny that came after many years of consistent, focused effort by New Christian Right legal organizations. Where the claim can plausibly be made, none of these groups fails to argue that the exclusion of the religious from an activity, institution, or facility made available to the secular is a violation of the free speech clause. Yet, in spite of the growing diversity of religion cases in which New Christian Right public interest law firms have participated in the federal courts, no similarly focused strategy has emerged.

The absence of a clear objective to their religious liberty litigation begs the question, how can New Christian Right groups ever attain their legal goals and say the battle is won. Although this may be a healthy situation for a public interest law firm concerned only about the perpetuation of its own existence, genuine concerns about the status of religious liberty in America are not well served by the absence of a guiding purpose to the mass of litigation that purports to defend it.

A second challenge to the legal rights approach to the litigation of religion in the federal courts arises out of the secular consequences of the New Christian Right's dependence on the free speech clause. While their fundraising letters and other promotional materials to supporters tout the free speech strategy as a vehicle for protecting Christian expression, the legal briefs filed by these attorneys are necessarily much broader.

The fact that their message has at times been subject to content restrictions has led some within the New Christian Right to make the ironic free speech link between the religious expression of the 1990s and sexually explicit materials of the 1960s.[3] They take their cue from Justice Scalia who, in his dissenting opinion in *Lee v. Weisman* (1992), declared, "Church and state would not be such a difficult subject if religion were, as the Court apparently thinks it to be, some purely personal avocation that can be indulged entirely in secret, like pornography, in the privacy of one's room."[4] In his later majority opinion in *Capitol Square Review and Advisory Board v. Pinette* (1995), Scalia again addressed the prospect of driving religious expression "underground." Referring to the dissents of Justices Stevens, Souter, and O'Connor, Scalia wrote, "[Their view] exiles private religious speech to a realm of less-protected expression heretofore inhabited only by sexually explicit displays and commercial speech. . . . It will be a sad day when this Court casts piety in with pornography, and finds the First Amendment more hospitable to private expletives than to private prayers."[5]

While the "religion-as-porn" analogy plays well with supporters as a caustic indictment against the Court's view of religion, it also serves as a model legal strategy guiding New Christian Right lawyers. Just as free speech advocates in the 1960s and 1970s maintained that the First Amendment was broad enough to protect sexually explicit materials, New Christian Right lawyers now argue for a similarly expansive reading of the free speech clause to find relief for religious liberty claims.

In doing so, however, they recognize that to swell the free speech clause to accommodate religion necessarily extends the protection of that clause to other viewpoints as well. In this sense, the free speech clause as promoted by New Christian Right lawyers becomes a strange mixture of legal pragmatism and faith. On the one hand, the free speech approach to religion has been consistently upheld by the Supreme Court as a valid legal doctrine that has fundamentally altered the way the law considers religion and religious expression. On the other hand, the judicial recognition of this broad right necessarily protects the views of non-Christian groups, other nonreligious organizations, and some groups that are decidedly in opposition to the principles that New Christian Right lawyers (and their donor base) stand for.

As long as the religious view is heard, maintains the ADF's Alan Sears, such a state is fine: "All we want is the robust exchange of ideas protected by the Constitution. If the gospel can't flourish in a free society then something is wrong."[6] The ACLJ further acknowledges that the "free speech approach allows the KKK, witches, and gay activist groups to do their thing. Our response to that is that we have read the book [the Bible], and we know who wins in the end. We are not afraid."[7]

When these lawyers' free speech arguments in the courts are successful, a legal foundation is created upon which a host of other cases may be predicated, including many that would enjoy the support of religious conservatives. However, legal precedent, especially when broadly defined (as the First Amendment has been by New Christian Right lawyers), may be of use to many other groups, including those whose ideals are opposed by the very firms who helped establish the precedent in the first place. Just as the landmark rulings established by the ACLU's obscenity cases three decades ago paved the way for the current success of the New Christian Right's religion-as-speech arguments, so too have the precedents set forth in the New Christian Right's religion cases laid the basis for the legal successes of groups they strongly oppose.

In the mid-1990s, for example, when students attempted to organize a club for gays and lesbians at East High School in Salt Lake City, Utah, the local school board responded by issuing a policy denying permission to any "non-curriculum" club to organize or meet on school property. The board's 1996 policy decision did not target the gay and lesbian club specifically, but in effectively doing away with all extracurricular clubs within the district's high schools, it was able to keep those students from meeting as well.

The board's actions were immediately challenged by organizers of the student gay and lesbian club. They claimed that the school board's policy change was an unconstitutional attempt to silence the views of gays and lesbians. They further argued that neither the Equal Access Act nor the line of free speech cases from *Widmar* to *Rosenberger* permitted the school board to discriminate against this or any other club on the basis of the ideas it wished to express. On 26 April 2000, using these rulings as the basis for her opinion, U.S. District Judge Tena Campbell ruled for the students and their supporters in holding that the board had inconsistently applied its policy and thereby engaged in unconstitutional viewpoint discrimination.[8]

Religious Liberty as a Gospel Tool

Underlying the courtroom efforts of New Christian Right public interest law firms is their conviction that they are divinely commissioned to use the judicial process to keep the public square open to that message. Religious liberty thus becomes more than a legal right; it becomes a gospel tool. Again, however, the free speech approach to religion creates its own challenges. While leveling the constitutional playing field, it may ultimately threaten the integrity of the very message it seeks to protect.

Carl Esbeck, a one-time interim director of the CLS Center, has written, "Not withstanding the unbroken line of victories for the equal treatment of religion, it must be emphasized that in each case from *Widmar* to *Rosenberger* it was the free speech clause that required nondiscrimination, thereby supplying the victory."[9] Historically New Christian Right supporters had been vocally opposed to what they perceived as a subordination of the religion clauses to other constitutional concerns enunciated by the federal courts.[10] Yet the free speech arguments made by New Christian Right lawyers in religious liberty cases do essentially the same thing. Each of the groups in this study relies on an expanded interpretation of the free speech clause to provide what, as they perceive it, an enervated free exercise or establishment clause cannot.

Granted, not every case can be neatly compartmentalized into the religious liberty/free speech paradigm; some must necessarily be argued using the traditional religion clauses. But in those religious liberty cases where there is a possibility of raising a free speech claim, New Christian Right lawyers appear to turn their back on the religion clauses rather quickly.

When asked during the *Rosenberger* oral arguments of his opinion of the closest legal precedent to the central issue in *Rosenberger,* that of state funding in support of a religious activity, Michael McConnell responded by citing the Supreme Court's 1986 *Witters* decision in which the Court held that the state of Washington could not deny vocational education funding to a student studying for the ministry.[11] When pressed by the justices to explain why he chose that case, McConnell replied, "I'd like to urge you that this is in fact a very close parallel, because . . . there the State was supporting vocational education. Here [in *Rosenberger*], the state is supporting student journalism, and in both cases the State is completely, or should be, completely indifferent as to whether the individuals who benefit or participate in those programs themselves decide to participate, to use those benefits in a way that participates in a religious activity."[12]

Technically speaking, Rosenberger and the other members of Wide Awake Productions were student journalists (they were students and they produced their own magazine), but their purpose in creating *Wide Awake* had nothing to do with improving their writing, typesetting, and publishing skills; it was, as Rosenberger wrote in the inaugural issue, "to challenge Christians to live, in word and deed, according to the faith they proclaim."[13]

McConnell's characterization of *Wide Awake* as a mere student journalistic enterprise whose content under the free speech clause could not be constitutionally repressed by the university's refusal to fund the magazine reinforces the perception that the religion clauses of the Constitution contain little more than second-rate rights, incapable on their own of protecting Rosenberger's religious expression. This is the very attitude that religious conservatives hold responsible for past judicial rulings against religion and it contrasts sharply with the professed desire of New Christian Right attorneys to return to an earlier constitutional era where the religion clauses of the First Amendment meant something.[14]

For all its success in both the Supreme Court and lower federal courts, however, the free speech clause can never be an effective long-term ally of the New Christian Right. Constitutional scholar Mark Tushnet claims that with the free speech emphasis in *Widmar v. Vincent,* "[r]eligion entered the Court's analysis by the back door."[15] He might have phrased it "the school's back door." Without denying the importance of the New Christian Right's free speech victories since *Widmar,* they nevertheless illustrate an expansion only in kind. In the twenty years since the *Widmar* decision, New Christian Right public interest law firms have seen the free speech rationale stretched to include high school Bible clubs, religious literature distribution in elementary and junior high schools, student activity fees in college, and public access to school facilities. Outside the educational setting, however, the free speech argument has yielded little substantive success.

In addition, not every case can be argued using the free speech clause. This innate limitation to the free speech strategy coupled with the seeming inability to transfer its strength outside school boundaries raises serious questions about the ability of New Christian Right law firms to effect lasting changes within both society and the law's view of religion without embracing some additional strategy to protect religious liberty.

There are additional concerns about using the free speech approach to religious liberty litigation. New Christian Right lawyers believe that the judicial application of the free speech clause elevates this aspect of religious liberty to a protected level enjoyed by other types of speech. While separationist detractors see this line of argumentation as little more than an end run around the establishment clause, other critics claim that this approach actually degrades religious expression, removing it from a position of singular importance to become just another form of speech. They question the wisdom of appealing to the secular to protect the sacred. This is an important point because in considering religion and religious practices as a mere viewpoint, it is dislodged from its lofty dwelling with the divine and placed squarely within the baser realm of politics where it is made subject to legislative wrangling, executive caprice, and ultimately adjudication by human judges.

Critics of the New Christian Right's free speech strategy are not unaware of its appeal. As church-state scholar Derek Davis has noted,

> The concept of equal treatment—treating all religious expression the same as other forms of speech—sounds alluringly democratic, pluralistic and fair. To the Christian who, rightly or wrongly, feels increasingly marginalized within American society and disenfranchised by the Supreme Court's many rulings that keep religious exercise out of the public sphere, exercise of the concept may seem like a return to "better" days when Christianity enjoyed an undisputed nationwide hegemony and de facto establishment. But in fact, it may signal the triumph of the post-modern relativist mind, in which every statement is of equal value to any other.[16]

The Fourth Circuit's ruling in *Peck v. Upshur County Board of Education* provides a good example of the legal relativism that can occur when religion is encased in the free speech clause. Although the Rutherford Institute touted this case to its supporters as a victory for Christian expression, the court's actual ruling could be interpreted as coming close to denigrating the Bible.

In upholding the constitutionality of the Upshur County School Board policy allowing religious groups to enter secondary schools and hand out Bibles, the court acknowledged the "unrivaled symbolic power" of that book. But the authority of the Bible in ordering the lives of its believers was immaterial because it was only another form of "speech." Or, as the court put it, "the power of a given religious text must be irrelevant to the constitutional analysis." In short, the opinion concluded, "[T]his case is not about the Bible, but about the principled application of established Supreme Court precedents which hold that the state may no more discriminate against, than it can establish, religion when it opens its facilities to private speech."[17]

This emphasis on free speech is understandable. In terms of substantive victories, the free speech strategy of New Christian Right lawyers has been far more successful than previous arguments that focused on the religion clauses alone. As *Widmar, Mergens, Lamb's Chapel,* and *Rosenberger* demonstrate, free speech considerations have not only guided New Christian Right legal efforts, they have also spawned landmark legal precedents. Indeed, the religious speech approach that was ridiculed by the attorneys for the University of Missouri at Kansas City in *Widmar* two decades ago as a "semantical artifice" is now a recognized constitutional doctrine that commands a clear majority of the Supreme Court.[18] The subsequent ripple effect of these decisions throughout the lower federal courts only amplifies their importance. Few other developments in federal court rulings on religion during the last twenty years can compare in significance to the religion-as-speech argument. But equating religious speech with other forms of protected speech has not come without a price.

One critic of the *Rosenberger* decision wrote of the New Christian Right's free speech–religion nexus: "If religion is understood as just a benign point of view that some people happen to have, then by implication religion is harmless, a meaningless difference. It becomes simply a brand name, or a political party, or a Hallmark card sentiment. . . . [R]eligion is important enough to be treated differently."[19]

For New Christian Right public interest law firms, religion has always been "important enough to be treated differently," so much so that they turned from traditional methods of political activism to the courts, adopted the litigating strategies of their ideological adversaries, and sought religious liberty's refuge not in the religion clauses but the free speech clause. Although it is uncertain whether the New Christian Right will ever create what the nineteenth-century evangelist Jonathan Blanchard described as the "perfect society where the law of God is the law of the land"[20] or return religious expression to a past position of prominence, the federal courts and the free speech clause continue to tempt them with the possibility.

Appendix

Table of Cases

ACLU v. City of Florissant, 186 F3d 1095 (1999)

ACLU v. City of Stow, 29 FSupp2d 845 (1998)

ACLU of Kentucky v. Wilkinson, 895 F2d 1098 (1990)

ACLU of Ohio v. Capitol Square Review and Advisory Board, 210 F3d 703 (2000)

Adler v. Duval County School Board, 206 F3d 1070 (2000)

Agostini v. Felton, 521 US 203 (1997)

Aguilar v. Felton, 473 US 402 (1985)

Alpine Christian Fellowship v. County Commissioners of Pitkin, 870 FSupp 991 (1994)

Altman v. Minnesota Department of Corrections, 1999 US Dist LEXIS 14897 (1999)

Ansonia Board of Education v. Philbrook, 479 US 60 (1986)

Asquith v. City of Beaufort, 139 F3d 408 (1998)

Bell v. Little Axe Independent School District No. 70, 766 F2d 1391 (1985)

Bender v. Williamsport Area School District, 563 FSupp 697 (1983)

Bender v. Williamsport Area School District, 741 F2d 538 (1984)

Bender v. Williamsport Area School District, 475 US 534 (1986)

Berger v. Rensselaer Central School Corporation, 766 FSupp 696 (1991)

Berger v. Rensselaer Central School Corporation, 982 F2d 1160 (1993)

Board of Airport Commissioners of Los Angeles v. Jews for Jesus, 482 US 569 (1987)

Board of Education of Kiryas Joel Village School District v. Grumet, 512 US 687 (1994)

Board of Education of Westside Community Schools v. Mergens, 496 US 226 (1990)

Board of Regents of the University of Wisconsin System v. Southworth, 529 US 217 (2000)

Bob Jones University v. U.S., 461 US 574 (1983)

Bowen v. Kendrick, 487 US 589 (1988)

Bowen v. Roy, 476 US 693 (1986)

Branch Ministries v. Rossotti, 211 F3d 137 (2000)

Bray v. Alexandria Women's Health Clinic, 506 US 263 (1993)

Brody v. Spang, 957 F2d 1108 (1992)

Bronx Household of Faith v. Community School District No. 10, 127 F3d 207 (1997)

Brown v. Hot, Sexy, and Safer Productions, Inc., 68 F3d 525 (1995)

BSA and Monmouth Council v. Dale, 530 US 640 (2000)

Bynum v. Fort Worth Independent School District, 41 FSupp2d 641 (1999)

Bynum v. U.S. Capitol Police Board, 93 FSupp2d 50 (2000)

Campbell v. St. Tammany's School Board, 206 F3d 482 (2000)

Cantwell v. Connecticut, 310 US 296 (1940)

Capitol Square Review and Advisory Board v. Pinette, 515 US 753 (1995)

Ceniceros v. Board of Trustees of San Diego Unified School District, 106 F3d 1522 (1997)

Chalmers v. Tulon Co., 101 F3d 1012 (1996)

Chandler v. James, 180 F3d 1254 (1999)

Chess v. Widmar, 480 FSupp 907 (1979)

Chess v. Widmar, 635 F2d 1310 (1980)

Children's Healthcare Is a Legal Duty, Inc. v. De Parle, 212 F3d 1084 (2000)

Christians v. Crystal Evangelical Free Church, 82 F3d 1407 (1996)

Christ's Bride Ministries v. Southeastern Pennsylvania Transportation Authority, 148 F3d 242 (1998)

Church of the Holy Trinity v. U.S., 143 US 457 (1892)

Church of the Lukumi Babalu Aye v. City of Hialeah, 508 US 520 (1993)

Church on the Rock v. City of Albuquerque, 84 F3d 1273 (1996)

City of Boerne v. Flores, 521 US 507 (1997)

City of Erie, et al. v. Pap's A.M., tdba "Kandyland," 529 US 277 (2000)

Corporation of the Presiding Bishop of the Church of Jesus Christ of Latter-day Saints v. Amos, 483 US 327 (1987)

County of Allegheny v. ACLU, Greater Pittsburgh Chapter, 492 US 573 (1989)

Culbertson v. Oakridge School District, No. 76, 119 F3d 5 (1997)

Daytona Rescue Mission v. Daytona Beach, 885 FSupp 1554 (1995)

Deboer v. Village of Oak Park, 53 FSupp2d 982 (1999)

DeNooyer v. Livonia Public Schools, 799 FSupp 744 (1992)

Doe v. Duncanville Independent School District, 994 F2d 160 (1993)

Doe v. Santa Fe Independent School District, 933 FSupp 647 (1996)

Doe v. Santa Fe Independent School District, 168 F3d 806 (1999)

East High School Prism Club v. Seidel, 95 FSupp2d 1239 (2000)

Edwards v. Aguillard, 482 US 578 (1987)

Ellis v. City of La Mesa, 990 F2d 1518 (1993)

Employment Division, Department of Human Resources of Oregon v. Smith, 494 US 872 (1990)

Engel v. Vitale, 370 US 421 (1962)

Everson v. Board of Education of the Township of Ewing, 330 US 1 (1947)

Frazee v. Illinois Department of Employment Security, 489 US 829 (1989)

Freedom of Religion Foundation v. City of Marshfield, 203 F3d 487 (2000)

Freiler v. Tangipahoa Parish School Board of Education, 185 F3d 337 (1999)

Friedman v. Board of County Commissioners of Bernalillo County, 781 F2d 777 (1985)

Full Gospel Tabernacle v. Community School District 27, 164 F3d 829 (1999)

Furr v. Town of Swansea, 594 FSupp 1543 (1984)

Garnett v. Renton School District, 987 F2d 641 (1993)

Gentala v. City of Tucson, 213 F3d 1055 (2000)

Gibson v. Lee County School Board, 1 FSupp2d 1426 (1998)

Goldman v. Weinberger, 475 US 503 (1986)

Good News/Good Sports Club v. School District, of the City of Ladue, 28 F3d 1501 (1994)

Grace Bible Fellowship v. Main School Administrative District No. 5, 941 F2d 45 (1991)

Grand Rapids v. Ball, 473 US 373 (1985)

Gregoire v. Centennial School District, 907 F2d 1366 (1990)

Guidry v. Broussard, 897 F2d 181 (1990)

Hack v. President and Fellows of Yale College, 16 FSupp2d 183 (1998)

Harris v. City of Zion, 927 F2d 1401 (1991)

Hedges v. Wauconda Community Unit School District No. 118, 9 F3d 1295 (1993)

Hemry v. School Board of Colorado Springs School District No. 11, 760 FSupp 856 (1991)

Hill v. Colorado, 530 US 703 (2000)

Hobbie v. Unemployment Appeals Commission, 480 US 136 (1987)

Hsu v. Roslyn Union Free School District No. 3, 876 FSupp 445 (1995)

Hsu v. Roslyn Union Free School District No. 3, 85 F3d 839 (1996)

Hurley v. Irish-American Gay, Lesbian and Bisexual Group of Boston, 515 US 557 (1995)

In Re Hodge, 220 BR 386 (1998)

In Re Young, 141 F3d 854 (1998)

Jews for Jesus, Inc. v. Jewish Community Relations Council of New York, 968 F2d 286 (1992)

Jimmy Swaggart Ministries v. Board of Equalization of California, 493 US 378 (1990)

Johnston-Loehner v. O'Brien, 859 FSupp 575 (1994)

Jones v. Clear Creek Independent School District, 977 F2d 963 (1992)

Lamb's Chapel v. Center Moriches Union Free School District, 508 US 384 (1993)

Larson v. Valente, 456 US 228 (1982)

LeBlanc-Sternberg v. Fletcher, 67 F3d 412 (1995)

Lee v. International Society for Krishna Consciousness, Inc., 505 US 830 (1992)

Lee v. Weisman, 505 US 577 (1992)

Lemon v. Kurtzman, 403 US 602 (1971)

Liberty Christian Center, Inc. v. Board of Education of the City School District of the City of Watertown, 8 FSupp2d 176 (1998)

Living Word Outreach Full Gospel Church v. City of Chicago, 1996 US Dist LEXIS 13519 (1996)

Lumpkin v. Brown, 109 F3d 1498 (1997)

Lynch v. Donnelly, 465 US 668 (1984)

Lyng v. Northwest Indian Cemetery Protective Association, 485 US 439 (1988)

Madsen v. Women's Health Center, Inc., 512 US 753 (1994)

Marsh v. Chambers, 463 US 783 (1983)

Mitchell v. Helms, 530 US 793 (2000)

Mockaitis v. Harcleroad, 104 F3d 1522 (1997)

Muller v. Jefferson Lighthouse School, 98 F3d 1530 (1996)

Murdock v. Pennsylvania, 319 US 105 (1943)

New Life Baptist Church Academy v. Town of East Longmeadow, 885 F2d 940 (1989)

North Carolina Civil Liberties Union Legal Foundation v. Constangy, 947 F2d 1145 (1991)

Ohio Civil Rights Commission v. Dayton Christian Schools, 477 US 619 (1986)

Oldham v. ACLU Foundation of Tennessee, 849 FSupp 611 (1994)

Notes

Chapter 1

1. Coral Ridge Ministries, "Reclaiming America for Christ," 1996 Conference Brochure.

2. Ibid.

3. Ibid.

4. Other colorful appellations can be found in the literature analyzing the relationship between conservative Christians and politics. See, for example, Thomas J. McIntyre, *The Fear Brokers* (Boston: Beacon Press, 1979); John Charles Cooper, *Religious Pied Pipers: A Critique of Radical Right-Wing Religion* (Valley Forge, PA: Judson Press, 1981); Perry Deane Young, *God's Bullies: Native Reflections on Preachers and Politics* (New York: Holt, Rinehart, and Winston, 1982); Marshall Fishwick and Ray B. Browne, eds., *The God Pumpers* (Bowling Green, OH: Popular Press, 1987); and Clyde Wilcox, *God's Warriors: The Christian Right in 20th Century America* (Baltimore: Johns Hopkins University Press, 1992).

5. According to the Pew Research Center, evangelicals made up 25.4 percent of the total American adult population in 1996. Mainline denominations accounted for 22.1 percent and Catholics 21.8 percent. See Andrew Kohut et al., *The Diminishing Divide: America's Changing Role in American Politics* (Washington, DC: Brookings Institution Press, 2000), 17.

6. Ibid., 18.

7. Ibid., 30–31.

8. James L. Guth et al., "Onward Christian Soldiers: Religious Activist Groups in American Politics," in *Interest Group Politics,* ed. Allan J. Ciglar and Burdett A. Loomis (Washington, DC: Congressional Quarterly Press, 1995), 69. Recent survey research indicates that notwithstanding the difficulty of determining the actual size of the core constituency of the New Christian Right, "a much larger proportion of the citizenry expresses some general sympathy" with the movement. See Kohut et al., *The Diminishing Divide,* 121.

9. Mark J. Rozell and Clyde Wilcox, eds. *God at the Grassroots: The New Christian Right in the 1994 Elections* (Lanham, MD: Rowman and Littlefield, 1995).

10. See Geoffrey Layman, *The Great Divide: Religious and Cultural Conflict in American Party Politics* (New York: Columbia University Press, 2001); and James L. Guth, John C. Green, Corwin E. Smidt, and Lyman A. Kellstedt, "Partisan Religion," *Christian Century,* 21 March 2001, 18–20.

11. See, for example, Steve Bruce, "The Inevitable Failure of the New Christian Right," *Sociology of Religion* 55, no. 3 (Fall 1994): 229–42; Michael D'Antonio, *Fall from Grace: The Failed Crusade of the Christian Right* (New York: Farrar, Straus, and Giroux, 1989); Clyde Wilcox, *Onward Christian Soldiers? The Religious Right in American Politics* (Boulder, CO: Westview, 1996); and Sara Diamond, *Not by Politics Alone: The Enduring Influence of the Christian Right* (New York: Guilford Press, 1998).

12. Kenneth D. Wald, *Religion and Politics in the United States,* 3d ed. (Washington, DC: Congressional Quarterly Press, 1997), 255.

13. John C. Green, "The Christian Right and the 1996 Elections: An Overview," in *God at the Grassroots: The Christian Right in the 1996 Elections,* ed. Mark J. Rozell and Clyde Wilcox (Lanham, MD: Rowman and Littlefield, 1997), 13.

14. Paul Weyrich, "The Moral Minority," *Christianity Today* 43 (6 September 1999): 44.

15. Cal Thomas and Ed Dobson, *Blinded by Might: Can the Religious Right Save America?* (Grand Rapids: Zondervan, 1999), 177.

16. Ibid., 15.

17. Alliance Defense Fund, "Winning Precedent-Setting Cases for You and Your Family," *ADF Briefing* 2 (May 1996): 4.

18. See, for example, Joseph L. Conn, "Courtroom Contender," *Church & State* 45 (June 1992): 4–6; Sara Diamond, "Watch on the Right: The Religious Right Goes to Court," *Humanist* 53 (May–June 1994): 35–37; and Jennifer Bradley, "Fighting the Establishment (Clause)," *American Prospect* 28 (September–October 1996): 57–60. Short general overviews of the New Christian Right in the courts can be found in Gustav Niebuhr, "Conservatives' New Frontier: Religious Liberty Law Firms," *New York Times,* 8 July 1995, 1(N); Julia McCord, "Defending Religious Rights," *Omaha World Herald,* 29 April 1995, 57(SF); Mark Curriden, "Defenders of the Faith," *ABA Journal* 80 (December 1994): 86–89; W. John Moore, "The Lord's Litigators," *National Journal,* 2 July 1994, 1560; and Tim Stafford, "Move Over, ACLU," *Christianity Today* 37 (25 October 1993): 20–24. Information on the individual firms litigating on behalf of the New Christian Right is found in Elizabeth Gleick, "Onward Christian Lawyers," *Time,* 3 March 1995, 57–58, 65; Jim Travisano, "Trying Times: The Rutherford Institute and the Fight for Religious Rights," *Albemarle* 31 (December 1992–January 1993): 62–63, 75–79; "Robertson's Lawyers," *Christian Century,* 21 October 1992, 930; and Hubert Morken, "The Evangelical Legal Response to the ACLU: Religion, Politics, and the First Amendment" (paper prepared for the Annual Meeting of the American Political Science Association, Chicago, 3–6 September 1992).

19. Matthew C. Moen, *The Christian Right and Congress* (Tuscaloosa: University of Alabama Press, 1989), 171–72.

20. See Bruce, "The Inevitable Failure of the New Christian Right."

21. Francis A. Schaeffer, *A Christian Manifesto* (Westchester, IL: Crossway Books, 1981), 46–47.

22. Alliance Defense Fund, "Blessed Is the Nation Whose God Is the Lord," *ADF Briefing* 1 (November 1995): 2.

23. William A. Stanmeyer, *Clear and Present Danger: Church and State in Post-Christian America* (Ann Arbor: Servant Books, 1983), 66.

24. See David Barton, *Original Intent: The Courts, the Constitution, and Religion* (Aledo, TX: Wallbuilder Press, 1996), 241–47.

25. Ibid., 251.

26. Quoted in Melvin I. Urofsky and Martha May, eds., *The New Christian Right: Political and Social Issues* (New York: Garland, 1996), xi.

27. Keith Fournier, *A House United? Evangelicals and Catholics Together* (Colorado Springs: NavPress, 1994), 132.

28. John W. Whitehead, *The Stealing of America* (Westchester, IL: Crossway Books, 1983), 126.

29. See Frank J. Sorauf, *The Wall of Separation: Constitutional Politics of Church and State*

(Princeton: Princeton University Press, 1976); and Gregg Ivers, *To Build a Wall: American Jews and the American Separation of Church and State* (Charlottesville: University Press of Virginia, 1995).

30. For an account of the increased secularization of the New Christian Right's political activities, see Matthew C. Moen, *The Transformation of the Christian Right* (Tuscaloosa: University of Alabama Press, 1992).

31. Winnifred Fallers Sullivan, "The Difference Religion Makes: Reflections on *Rosenberger*," *Christian Century,* 13 March 1996, 292–95.

Chapter 2

1. Alexis de Tocqueville, *Democracy in America,* trans. George Lawrence (New York: Harper and Row, 1988), 295.

2. Ronald Walters, *American Reformers, 1815–1860* (New York: Hill and Wang, 1978), 135.

3. This hegemony was an economic, technological, political, social, and cultural force in America until the beginning of its decline in the late nineteenth century. See James Davison Hunter, *Evangelicalism: The Coming Generation* (Chicago: University of Chicago Press, 1987), 187–202.

4. Winthrop S. Hudson, *Religion in America* (New York: Scribner, 1965), 198.

5. Ian R. Tyrell, *Sobering Up: From Temperance to Prohibition in Antebellum America* (Westport, CT: Greenwood, 1979), 87.

6. Walters, *American Reformers,* 138.

7. Charles C. Cole, *The Social Ideas of the Northern Evangelicals, 1826–1860* (New York: Columbia University Press, 1954), 195.

8. Ibid.

9. Wald, *Religion and Politics in the United States,* 218–19.

10. Paul Kleppner, *Who Voted? The Dynamics of Electoral Turnout, 1870–1980* (New York: Praeger, 1982), 80.

11. Mark de Wolfe Howe, *The Garden and the Wilderness: Religion and Government in American Constitutional History* (Chicago: University of Chicago Press, 1965), 28.

12. Joseph Story, *Commentaries on the Constitution of the United States,* vol. 2, 5th ed. (Boston: Little, Brown, 1891), 628.

13. Quoted in Michael J. Brodhead, *David J. Brewer: The Life of a Supreme Court Justice, 1837–1910* (Carbondale: Southern Illinois University Press, 1994), 128.

14. *Church of the Holy Trinity v. United States,* 143 US 457, 471 (1892).

15. James Davison Hunter, *American Evangelicalism: Conservative Religion and the Quandary of Modernity* (New Brunswick, NJ: Rutgers University Press, 1983), 23–41.

16. See Mark A. Noll, *The Scandal of the Evangelical Mind* (Grand Rapids: Eerdmans, 1995), 110–14.

17. See George M. Marsden, *Fundamentalism and American Culture: The Shaping of Twentieth Century Evangelicalism, 1870–1925* (New York: Oxford University Press, 1980).

18. James Davison Hunter, "The Evangelical Worldview since 1890," in *Piety and Politics: Evangelicals and Fundamentalists Confront the World,* ed. Richard John Neuhaus and Michael Cromartie (Washington, DC: Ethics and Public Policy Center, 1987), 33.

19. See Norris Magnuson, *Salvation in the Slums: Evangelical Social Work, 1865–1920* (Metuchen, NJ: Scarecrow, 1977).

20. In 1908, the Federal Council of Churches of Christ in America was organized to unify and coordinate the social and political efforts of member churches.

21. Wald, *Religion and Politics in the United States,* 220.

22. Ibid., 221.

23. See Lawrence W. Levine, *Defender of the Faith: William Jennings Bryan, the Last Decade, 1915–1925* (New York: Oxford University Press, 1965). Contrary to the opinion of many observers who blame the political disappearance of evangelical Protestants on the public ridicule that followed the 1925 Scopes trial, Mark Noll attributes it to the death of Bryan, the evangelical standard bearer (*Scandal of the Evangelical Mind,* 164–65).

24. Hunter, "Evangelical Worldview," 38.

25. Clyde Wilcox, "Premillennialists at the Millennium," *Sociology of Religion* 55, no. 3 (Fall 1994): 246.

26. For a detailed look at the origins, programming, and influence of evangelical religious broadcasts, see Jeffrey K. Hadden and Charles E. Swann, eds., *Prime Time Preachers: The Rising Power of Televangelism* (Reading, MA: Addison-Wesley, 1981); and Razelle Frankl, *Televangelism: The Marketing of Popular Religion* (Carbondale: Southern Illinois University Press, 1987).

27. Nathan Glazer, "Fundamentalism," in *Christianity and Modern Politics,* ed. Louise S. Hulett (The Netherlands: Walter de Gruyter, 1993), 305.

28. Hunter, *Evangelicalism,* 125.

29. Robert C. Liebman, "Making of the New Christian Right," in *The New Christian Right: Mobilization and Legitimation,* ed. Robert C. Liebman and Robert Wuthnow (New York: Aldine, 1983), 235. The emerging New Christian Right movement was opposed to the Equal Rights Amendment, gay rights initiatives, and textbook and curriculum decisions made by local school districts, among other issues. See Wald, *Religion and Politics in the United States,* 186–93; and Alan Crawford, *Thunder on the Right: The "New Right" and the Politics of Resentment* (New York: Pantheon, 1980), 144–64.

30. *Roe v. Wade,* 410 US 113 (1973).

31. *Engel v. Vitale,* 370 US 421 (1962).

32. *School District of Abington Township v. Schempp,* 374 US 203 (1963).

33. See, for example, Barton, *Original Intent.* Although the Court actually held that public schools may not mandate the recitation of prayers or Bible readings, charges that the justices had "taken God out of the schools" were almost immediately leveled at the Supreme Court. Characteristic of the nationwide reaction to these decisions were the 145 proposed constitutional amendments offered in the U.S. House of Representatives through May 1964 to overturn these rulings.

34. Ralph Reed, *Politically Incorrect: The Emerging Faith Factor in American Politics* (Dallas: Word Publishing, 1994).

35. See John W. Whitehead, *The Second American Revolution* (Wheaton, IL: Crossway Books, 1982), 115–32.

36. Barbara Hinkson Craig and David M. O'Brien, *Abortion and American Politics* (Chatham, NJ: Chatham House, 1993), 39–59.

37. Hunter, *Evangelicalism,* 125.

38. Moen, *The Christian Right and Congress,* 25.

39. Ibid., 26.

40. In an 8-1 decision, the Court rebuffed both the New Christian Right and Ronald

Reagan's Justice Department in holding that the IRS possessed the authority to revoke the tax-exempt status of private schools. *Bob Jones University v. U.S.,* 461 US 574 (1983).

41. Quoted in Moen, *The Christian Right and Congress,* 27.

42. See, for example, Crawford, *Thunder on the Right,* 159–64; Robert C. Liebman and Robert Wuthnow, eds., *The New Christian Right: Mobilization and Legitimation* (New York: Aldine, 1983); Steve Bruce, *The Rise and Fall of the New Christian Right: Conservative Protestant Politics in America, 1978–1988* (New York: Oxford University Press, 1988); Allen D. Hertzke, *Representing God in Washington: The Role of Religious Lobbies in the American Polity* (Knoxville: University of Tennessee Press, 1988); Sara Diamond, *Spiritual Warfare: The Politics of the Christian Right* (London: Pluto Press, 1989); Moen, *The Christian Right and Congress;* Moen, *Transformation of the Christian Right;* Michael Lienesch, *Redeeming America: Piety and Politics in the New Christian Right* (Chapel Hill: University of North Carolina Press, 1993); Sara Diamond, *Roads to Dominion* (New York: Guilford Press, 1995); Wilcox, *Onward Christian Soldiers?;* and Chip Berlet and Matthew H. Lyons, *Right-Wing Populism in America* (New York: Guilford Press, 2000).

43. Moen, *Transformation of the Christian Right,* 92–93.

44. Reagan's attorney general, Edwin Meese III, stated that the appointment of judges was one way to "institutionalize the Reagan revolution so it can't be set aside no matter what happens in future presidential elections." Quoted in David M. O'Brien, "The Reagan Judges: His Most Enduring Legacy?" in *The Reagan Legacy: Promise and Performance,* ed. Charles O. Jones (Chatham, NJ: Chatham House, 1988), 62. Sheldon Goldman graphically illustrates Meese's point in a 1993 article on the judicial legacy of George Bush. Goldman found that as of 3 November 1992, the day Bush was defeated for reelection and some twenty-four years after Lyndon Johnson left office, half of Johnson's judicial appointees to the federal courts were still on the bench. Although primarily in senior rather than active service, Johnson appointees made up nearly 27 percent of total court of appeals senior service judges on election day 1992. At the same time, Eisenhower appointees were almost 13 percent of that total. See Goldman, "Bush's Judicial Legacy: The Final Imprint," *Judicature* 76 (April–May 1993): 295.

45. Although its efforts were generally less pronounced and controversial than its predecessor's (with the notable exception of Clarence Thomas's selection as an associate justice of the Supreme Court), the Bush administration largely continued the tradition of selecting conservatives for the federal bench. See Goldman, "Bush's Judicial Legacy," 285.

46. See Michael McConnell, "Freedom from Religion?" *American Enterprise* 4, no. 1 (January/February 1993): 36.

47. The formation of New Christian Right public interest law firms mirrored the increase in the number of interest groups from across the political spectrum that turned to the courts between the 1970s and 1990s and coincided with the sharp growth in the number of lawyers in America, which nearly tripled during this same period of time. See Lawrence Baum, *American Courts: Process and Policy,* 4th ed. (Boston: Houghton Mifflin, 1998), 64.

48. While the New Christian Right has turned to the courts in earnest only within the past two decades, interest group activity within the judicial branch is not new. Arthur F. Bentley's 1908 classic, *The Process of Government* (ed. Peter H. Odegard [Cambridge, MA: Belknap Press, 1967]), is generally hailed as the first work to recognize the judicial branch as a practical site for interest group activism. In 1959, the groundbreaking study by Clement E. Vose, *Caucasians Only,* focused on the NAACP's judicial strategy to end restrictive housing

covenants (Berkeley: University of California Press, 1959). The NAACP has been the focus of several subsequent studies. See, for example, Michael Meltsner, *Cruel and Unusual: The Supreme Court and Capital Punishment* (New York: Random House, 1973); Richard Kluger, *Simple Justice: The History of Brown v. Board of Education and Black America's Struggle for Equality* (New York: Knopf, 1976); Jack Greenberg, *Race Relations and American Law* (New York: Columbia University Press, 1959); Mark V. Tushnet, *The NAACP's Legal Struggle against Segregated Education, 1925–1950* (Chapel Hill: University of North Carolina Press, 1987); and Stephen L. Wasby, *Race Relations Litigation in an Age of Complexity* (Charlottesville: University Press of Virginia, 1995).

Many scholars followed Vose's suggestion to look beyond the field of racial discrimination for interest group activity in the courts. Significant among these was Richard Cortner's study, which posits the theory that groups disadvantaged in terms of their ability to access and influence the legislative or executive branches would turn to the judiciary to achieve their policy goals ("Strategies and Tactics of Litigants in Constitutional Cases," *Journal of Public Law* 17 [1968]: 287–307). Scholars have found a number of diverse groups to fit the "politically disadvantaged" model including women's organizations (Karen O'Connor, *Women's Organizations' Use of the Courts* [Lexington, MA: Lexington Books, 1980]); Mexican-Americans (Karen O'Connor and Lee Epstein, "A Legal Voice for the Chicano Community: The Activities of the Mexican-American Legal Defense Fund, 1968–1982," in *Latinos and the Political System,* ed. F. Chris Garcia [Notre Dame: University of Notre Dame Press, 1988]); children (Robert H. Mnookin, *In the Interest of Children: Advocacy, Law Reform, and Public Policy* [New York: W. H. Freeman, 1985]); the handicapped (Susan M. Olson, *Clients and Lawyers: Securing the Rights of Disabled Persons* [Westport, CT: Greenwood, 1984]); and the mentally ill (Neal Milner, "The Right to Refuse Treatment: Four Case Studies of Legal Mobilization," *Law and Society Review* 21, no. 3 [1997]: 447–85).

In addition, scholars have found evidence of interest group activity designed to bring about broad policy changes affecting far more than just a particular interest group population. See Sorauf, *Wall of Separation;* Lettie Wenner, *The Environmental Decade in Court* (Bloomington: Indiana University Press, 1984); Eva Rubin, *Abortion, Politics, and the Courts* (New York: Greenwood, 1987); and Joseph F. Kobylka, *The Politics of Obscenity* (New York: Greenwood, 1991).

49. See Sorauf, *Wall of Separation.* The free exercise clause was incorporated in *Cantwell v. Connecticut,* 310 US 296 (1940) and the establishment clause in *Everson v. Board of Education of the Township of Ewing,* 330 US 1 (1947).

50. See Whitehead, *Stealing of America;* and Barton, *Original Intent.*

51. Schaeffer, *A Christian Manifesto,* 47.

52. Sorauf, *Wall of Separation,* 186–90.

53. Ibid., 204.

54. Quoted in Niebuhr, "Conservatives' New Frontier."

Chapter 3

1. Several examples of CLS Center activity outside of the judicial branch are described in chapter 7.

2. See the U.S. Department of Education website at <http://ed.gov/inits/religionandschools>. In addition to information devoted specifically to the issue of religious expression in the public schools, the department's site also references the secretary's previous

directives as well as suggested resources for additional information with links to CLS and other organizations.

3. Quoted in Moore, "The Lord's Litigators." McFarland left the CLS Center in 1999 to become the executive director of the U.S. Commission on International Religious Freedom. He was replaced by Carl H. Esbeck, a professor of law at the University of Missouri School of Law.

4. Roger K. Newman, "Public-Interest Law Firms Crop Up on the Right," *National Law Journal*, 26 August 1996, sec. A, p. 1.

5. Quoted in Curriden, "Defenders of the Faith," 89.

6. Stephen McFarland, interview by the author, Annandale, Virginia, 19 March 1997.

7. See ADF IRS Form 990 (1998).

8. McFarland, interview.

9. Rutherford Institute, year-end financial statements 1999, 9.

10. See Rutherford Institute IRS Form 990 (1998).

11. Whitehead, *Second American Revolution,* 176–77.

12. Quoted in Travisano, "Trying Times," 76.

13. Stafford, "Move Over, ACLU," 24.

14. Quoted in Moore, "The Lord's Litigators." This philosophy, incidentally, does not appear to be shared by Rutherford alumni. Kelly Shackleford and Brad Dacus, who until recently worked as the institute's southwestern and western coordinators, respectively, now head their own public interest law firms, the Liberty Legal Institute in Texas and the Pacific Justice Institute in California, where each serves as president. ADF has extended funding to both and the ACLJ has provided legal assistance. See ADF IRS Form 990 (1998).

15. See Rutherford Institute, year-end financial statements 1998, p. 12 and 1999, p. 13.

16. Megan Rosenfeld, "On the Case for Paula Jones," *Washington Post,* 17 January 1998, sec. B, p. 1.

17. Fournier, *A House United,* 79.

18. Fournier stepped down as executive director on 1 March 1997 to head the Catholic Alliance, an organization created by Robertson's Christian Coalition to promote common political ground between evangelicals and Catholics.

19. Fournier, *A House United,* 93.

20. See Amy Virshup, "A Jew for Jesus," *George* 8, no. 1 (October 1996): 62.

21. Mark I. Pinsky, "Legal Weapon: Jay Alan Sekulow Is the Christian Right's Leading Lion in the Judicial Arena," *Los Angeles Times,* 2 September 1993, sec. E, p. 1.

22. *Board of Airport Commissioners of Los Angeles v. Jews for Jesus,* 482 US 569 (1987).

23. These cases include *Hill v. Colorado,* 530 US 703 (2000); *Santa Fe Independent School District v. Doe,* 530 US 290 (2000); *Schenck v. Pro-Choice Network of Western New York,* 519 US 357 (1997); *Lamb's Chapel v. Center Moriches Union Free School District,* 508 US 384 (1993); *Bray v. Alexandria Women's Health Clinic,* 506 US 263 (1993); *Lee v. International Society for Krishna Consciousness, Inc.,* 505 US 830 (1992); *Lee v. Weisman* (on briefs), 505 US 577 (1992); *U.S. v. Kokinda,* 497 US 720 (1990); *Board of Education of Westside Community Schools v. Mergens,* 496 US 226 (1990); and *Board of Airport Commissioners of Los Angeles v. Jews for Jesus,* 482 US 569 (1987).

24. Fournier, *A House United,* 102.

25. Stafford, "Move Over, ACLU," 24.

26. Transcript of American Civil Liberties Union CenterStage Series, 30 August 1995, <http://www.aclu.org>.

27. Jay Sekulow, ACLJ, 3 June 2000, <http://eclj.org>.

28. Mark I. Pinsky, "Fight for Religious Liberty Brings Lawyer Few 'Amens,'" *Orlando Sentinel,* 9 September 1995, sec. D, p. 5.

29. *Madsen v. Women's Health Center, Inc.,* 512 US 753 (1994).

30. See ADF IRS Form 990 (1998).

31. Liberty Counsel, *The Liberator,* June 2000, 3.

32. Alliance Defense Fund, *ADF Briefing,* September 1995, 4.

33. The founding members of the ADF represent several major evangelical ministries. They include Dr. Bill Bright, president of Campus Crusade for Christ International; Larry Burkett, president of Christian Financial Concepts; Dr. James Dobson, president of Focus on the Family; Dr. D. James Kennedy, president of Coral Ridge Ministries; Marlin Maddoux, president of International Christian Media; and Reverend Donald Wildmon, president of the American Family Association.

34. ADF, letter to donors, February 1996, 4.

35. Wayne Swindler, ADF's chief financial officer, telephone conversation with the author, 12 April 2000.

36. See ADF IRS Form 990 (1998).

37. Ibid.

38. A 1995 *Wall Street Journal* article listed Rutherford's budget at $8 million (Andrea Gerlin, "With Free Help, the Religious Turn Litigious," *Wall Street Journal,* 17 February 1994 sec. B, p. 1). The 1997 budget for Rutherford stood at $4.5 million.

39. See ADF IRS Form 990 (1998).

Chapter 4

1. See Acts 22–28.

2. Alan Sears, interview by the author, Scottsdale, Arizona, 13 January 1997.

3. See ADF Form 990, Statement of Program Service Accomplishments (1998).

4. See, for example, Vose, *Caucasians Only;* Kluger, *Simple Justice;* Sorauf, *Wall of Separation;* Tushnet, *The NAACP's Legal Strategy against Segregated Education;* Karen O'Connor and Lee Epstein, "The Rise of Conservative Interest Group Litigation," *Journal of Politics* 45, no. 2 (May 1983): 479–89; Gregory A. Caldeira and John R. Wright, "Organized Interests and Agenda Setting in the Supreme Court," *American Political Science Review* 82 (December 1988): 1109–27; and Wasby, *Race Relations Litigation.*

5. See Kluger, *Simple Justice;* and Tushnet, *The NAACP's Legal Strategy against Segregated Education.*

6. Alliance Defense Fund, *ADF Briefing,* January 1996, 4.

7. Jay A. Sekulow, *The Christian, the Court, and the Constitution: Your Rights as a Christian Citizen* (Virginia Beach: American Center for Law and Justice, 2000), 3.

8. Christian Legal Society, *The Defender,* no. 1 (1997): 3.

9. Liberty Counsel, *The Liberator,* April 1997, 4.

10. Rutherford Institute, year-end financial statements, 1999, 13.

11. ADF IRS Form 990 (1998).

12. John Stepanovich, interview by the author, Virginia Beach, 25 March 1997.

13. United Press International, "Lawyer Launches Anti-ACLU Group," 23 February 1990, BC Cycle.

14. Steven McFarland, interview by the author, Annandale, Virginia, 19 March 1997.

15. Rutherford Institute IRS Form 990 (1997) Form 990, Program Service Accomplishments, p. 3.

16. Rita Woltz, interview by the author, Charlottesville, Virginia, 29 May 1997.

17. *Widmar v. Vincent*, 454 US 263 (1981).

18. According to the district court ruling at the time attorney's fees were awarded, Rosenberger signed an affidavit "stating that he contacted the Rutherford Institute . . . , hoping to interest it in his case, but to no avail." *Rosenberger v. Rector and Visitors of the University of Virginia,* No. 91–0036-C, 1996 US Dist LEXIS 13799.

19. *Rosenberger v. Rector and Visitors of the University of Virginia,* 515 US 819 (1995).

20. Amicus briefs may be filed to encourage the Supreme Court to grant (or deny) a petition for certiorari as well. In their study of the Supreme Court's 1982 term, Caldeira and Wright found that the presence of three or more briefs at the certiorari stage greatly increased the probability that the Supreme Court would grant certiorari ("Organized Interests and Agenda Setting in the Supreme Court").

21. The Supreme Court has tried to encourage a certain level of quality to the amicus briefs it receives by stating bluntly: "An *amicus curiae* brief which brings relevant matter to the attention of the Court that has not already been brought to its attention by the parties is of considerable help to the Court. An *amicus* brief which does not serve this purpose simply burdens the staff and facilities of the Court and its filing is not favored." Rules of Supreme Court of the United States, Rule 37.1 (revised 1990), quoted in Robert L. Stern et al., *Supreme Court Practice,* 7th ed. (Washington, DC: Bureau of National Affairs, 1993), 562.

22. See Lee Epstein, "Interest Group Litigation during the Rehnquist Era," *Journal of Law and Politics* 9 (Summer 1993): 645. Lee Epstein and Karen O'Connor are largely responsible for the increased scholarly focus on interest group activity in the courts, arising from their reevaluation of Nathan Hakman's research in the mid-1960s. Based on an extensive study of interest group participation in Supreme Court cases between 1928 and 1966, Hakman concluded that the presence and influence of interest groups in the judiciary was practically nonexistent. See Hakman, "Lobbying the Supreme Court—An Appraisal of Political Science Folklore," *Fordham Law Review* 35 (1966): 15–50. Epstein and O'Connor later found that although amicus participation had indeed been slight prior to the 1950s, it had increased dramatically, particularly during the 1960s and 1970s. See Karen O'Connor and Lee Epstein, "*Amicus Curiae* Participation in the United States Supreme Court: An Appraisal of Hakman's Folklore," *Law & Society Review* 16, no. 2 (1982): 311–20.

23. Alexander Wohl, "Friends with Agendas," *ABA Journal* 82 (November 1996): 46.

24. In their study of sample cases from the 1967–87 Supreme Court terms, Donald R. Songer and Reginald S. Sheehan found little difference in the winning percentage between organizations that were supported and not supported by amicus briefs. Songer and Sheehan, "Interest Group Success in the Courts: Amicus Participation in the Supreme Court," *Political Research Quarterly* 46, no. 2 (June 1993): 339–54. In certain other areas, however, scholars have concluded that amici have had an impact. See, for example, Susan Behuniak-Long, "Friendly Fire: Amici Curiae and the *Webster v. Reproductive Health Services,*" *Judicature* 74, no. 5 (February–March 1991): 261; and Lee Epstein and Joseph Kobylka, *The Supreme Court and Legal Change: Abortion and the Death Penalty* (Chapel Hill: University of North Carolina Press, 1993).

25. *Church of the Lukumi Babalu Aye v. Hialeah,* 508 US 502 (1993).

26. Douglas Laycock, "Free Exercise and the Religious Freedom Restoration Act," *Fordham Law Review* 62 (February 1994): 897.

27. *Employment Division, Department of Human Resources of Oregon v. Smith,* 494 US 872 (1990).

28. Laycock, "Free Exercise and the Religious Freedom Restoration Act," 898.

29. Published in 1983, O'Connor and Epstein's "Rise of Conservative Interest Group Litigation" notes the preference conservative interest groups in general seem to have for amicus curiae briefs as a participatory strategy in the courts. As I demonstrate in chapter 6, however, this model does not hold true for religion cases in the lower federal courts.

30. Gregory A. Caldeira and John R. Wright, *"Amicus Curiae* before the Supreme Court: Who Participates, When, and How Much?" *Journal of Politics* 52, no. 3 (August 1990): 802–3.

31. Epstein, "Interest Group Litigation during the Rehnquist Era."

32. Wohl, "Friends with Agendas," 48.

33. Caldeira and Wright, "Organized Interests and Agenda Setting in the U.S. Supreme Court," 1112. Caldeira and Wright learned from several Washington, D.C., law firms that a single amicus brief averaged $15,000 to $20,000 and could cost as much as $60,000.

34. Sears, interview.

35. Woltz, interview.

36. McFarland, interview.

37. Lee Epstein, "Courts and Interest Groups," in *The American Courts: A Critical Assessment,* ed. John B. Gates and Charles A. Johnson (Washington, DC: Congressional Quarterly Press, 1991), 339.

38. Periodically an amicus brief will state that funding from the ADF was used in compiling the brief. See, for example, the brief filed by the National Legal Center for the Medically Dependent and Disabled, Inc., et al., in the physician-assisted suicide cases, *Washington v. Glucksberg,* 521 US 702 (1997) and *Vacco v. Quill,* 521 US 793 (1997).

39. Woltz, interview.

40. McFarland, interview. One source states that the CLS Center provides research support to some three hundred cases annually. See Newman, "Public-Interest Firms."

41. *Peloza v. Capistrano Unified School District,* 37 F3d 517 (1994).

42. Hannah Nordhaus, "Christian Group Crusades in the Courts," *Legal Times,* 27 February 1995, 25.

43. Neither Zal's nor the Rutherford Institute's arguments appeared to garner much sympathy in the federal courts. Addressing the freedom of speech claim, Senior District Judge David Williams wrote: "Simply put the issue I must decide is whether Peloza has a constitutional right to conduct himself as a loose cannon in the classroom" (*Peloza v. Capistrano Unified School District,* 782 FSupp 1412, 1416 [1992]). In its per curiam opinion, the Ninth Circuit Court of Appeals rejected as "patently frivolous" Peloza's claim that the evolution requirement violated the establishment clause (*Peloza v. Capistrano Unified School District,* 37 F3d 517, 520 [1994]). The ACLJ later petitioned the Supreme Court to grant certiorari to the case, which it denied.

44. New Christian Right attorneys do not necessarily believe the free speech strategy is the best alternative in religious liberty cases. In a January 1997 discussion of this issue with the author, the Rutherford Institute's David Melton said, "In an ideal world, I would rather argue using the free exercise or establishment clauses but they are not there and so we use what we can." See also Melton, "The Free Exorcise of Religion" (speech delivered to Students for Individual Liberty and the Liberty Coalition, University of Virginia, 29 January 1997). Appealing to the establishment clause, according to CLS member attorney and eminent church-state legal scholar Michael McConnell, is problematic because of the judicial "inter-

pretation of the Establishment Clause, which is the tendency to use it not as a guarantor of religious liberty, but as an attempt to shut religion out of the public debate." Quoted in Jennifer Howard, "Wide Awake: Holy Constitutional Issues, UVA! Supreme Court Will Hear the Case," *C'ville Weekly,* 31 January 1995, 8.

45. Quoted in Curriden, "Defenders of the Faith," 88.

46. *Capitol Square Review and Advisory Board v. Pinette,* 515 US 753, 760 (1995).

47. Stephen L. Carter, *The Culture of Disbelief* (New York: Basic Books, 1993), 3.

48. Sears, interview.

49. See, for example, Diamond, "Watch on the Right."

50. Quoted in Travisano, "Trying Times," 75.

51. The use of the Christian information infrastructure by New Christian Right public interest law firms is considered in detail in chapter 7.

52. *Widmar v. Vincent,* 454 US 263, 284 (1981).

53. Epstein, "Interest Group Litigation during the Rehnquist Era."

Chapter 5

1. *Everson v. Board of Education of the Township of Ewing,* 330 US 1 (1947).

2. Thomas Jefferson, "Letter to the Danbury Baptist Association, January 1, 1802," in *Writings,* ed. Merrill D. Peterson (New York: Literary Classics of the United States, 1984), 510. The wall metaphor was first referenced by the Supreme Court some seventy years earlier in Chief Justice Waite's majority opinion in *Reynolds v. United States,* 98 US 145, 164 (1878).

3. See Barry Lynn, Marc D. Stern, and Oliver S. Thomas, *The Right to Religious Liberty: The Basic ACLU Guide to Religious Rights,* 2d ed. (Carbondale: Southern Illinois University Press, 1995).

4. Rutherford Institute, letter to donors, March 1997, 4.

5. Robert M. Hutchins, "The Future of the Wall," in *The Wall between Church and State,* ed. Dallin H. Oaks (Chicago: University of Chicago Press, 1963), 19.

6. *Rosenberger v. Rector and Visitors of the University of Virginia,* 515 US 819 (1995).

7. Ronald Rosenberger, "Letter from the Editor," *Wide Awake* (November–December 1990): 2.

8. In 1970, the Rector and Board of Visitors of the University of Virginia adopted formal guidelines for the disbursement of monies from the Student Activity Fund. These guidelines directly prohibited the use of Student Activity Funds by fraternities, sororities, political and religious organizations, and various other groups (although such groups could be granted CIO status). Organizations that did not readily fit into the above categories were prohibited from receiving funding for religious or political activities, social entertainment, honoraria payments, and various other specified activities.

9. *Rosenberger v. Rector and Visitors of the University of Virginia,* 795 FSupp 175, 181 (1992).

10. Ibid., 182, 183.

11. "The long line of public forum cases have taken 'forum' in a fairly literalistic way involving physical space, and we do not see how it advances the jurisprudence to wrench that word out of its accepted form." *Rosenberger v. Rector and Visitors of the University of Virginia,* 18 F3d 269, 287 (1994).

12. Ibid., 281.

13. Ibid., 285.

14. *Lemon v. Kurtzman* (403 US 602, 612–13 ([1971]) set forth a three-pronged test for determining whether a particular governmental policy violates the establishment clause: "First, the [policy] must have a secular legislative purpose; second, its principal or primary effect must be one that neither advances nor inhibits religion . . . ; finally, the [policy] must not foster excessive government entanglement with religion."

15. *Rosenberger v. Rector and Visitors of the University of Virginia,* 18 F3d 269, 287 (1994).

16. Oral argument by Michael W. McConnell, Esq., on behalf of petitioners. *Rosenberger v. Rector and Visitors of the University of Virginia,* 515 US 819 (1995), 1995 US TRANS LEXIS 70, 1–2.

17. Oral argument by John C. Jeffries, Esq., on behalf of respondents. *Rosenberger v. Rector and Visitors of the University of Virginia,* 515 US 819 (1995), 1995 US TRANS LEXIS 70, 24.

18. *Rosenberger v. Rector and Visitors of the University of Virginia,* 515 US 819, 835 (1995).

19. *Lamb's Chapel v. Center Moriches Union Free School District,* 508 US 384 (1993).

20. *Rosenberger v. Rector and Visitors of the University of Virginia,* 515 US 819, 832 (1995).

21. Ibid., 843–44, 846.

22. Steven McFarland, interview by the author, Annandale, Virginia, 19 March 1997.

23. *Murdock v. Pennsylvania,* 319 US 105 (1943).

24. *Chess v. Widmar,* 480 FSupp 907, 918 (1979).

25. *Chess v. Widmar,* 635 F2d 1310, 1315, 1317, 1318 (1980).

26. *Widmar v. Vincent,* 454 US 263, 277 (1981).

27. *Bender v. Williamsport Area School District,* 563 FSupp 697 (1983).

28. *Bender v. Williamsport Area School District,* 741 F2d 538 (1984).

29. Glen Elsasser, "This Time, Will School Prayer Pass Test?" *Chicago Tribune,* 13 October 1985, 1(C).

30. *Bender v. Williamsport Area School District,* 475 US 534 (1986).

31. Ibid., 553.

32. *Board of Education of Westside Community Schools v. Mergens,* 496 US 226, 248, 250 (1990).

33. Ibid., 261 (Kennedy, J., concurring in part and concurring in judgment).

34. Ibid., 270 (Marshall, J., concurring in judgment).

35. *Lamb's Chapel v. Center Moriches Union Free School District,* 508 US 384 (1993).

36. The *Lamb's Chapel* decision in 1993 was supported by a unanimous Court consisting of Chief Justice Rehnquist and Justices White, Blackmun, Stevens, O'Connor, Scalia, Kennedy, Souter, and Thomas. In 1990, *Mergens* saw a divided Court rule 8-1 in favor of the Equal Access Act. Chief Justice Rehnquist was again joined by Justices White, Blackmun, O'Connor, Scalia, and Kennedy as well as Justices Marshall and Brennan. Only Justice Stevens dissented in *Mergens.* The *Widmar* case was likewise decided on an 8-1 vote. Ruling in favor of the student religious club were Chief Justice Burger and Justices Brennan, Marshall, Blackmun, Powell, Rehnquist, Stevens, and O'Connor. Justice White cast the sole dissenting vote.

37. *Rosenberger v. Rector and Visitors of the University of Virginia,* 515 US 819, 830 (1995).

38. Ibid., 888 (Souter, J., dissenting), 889.

39. Justice Kennedy's opinion was joined by Chief Justice Rehnquist and Justices O'Connor, Scalia, and Thomas. Justice Souter's dissent was joined by Justices Stevens, Ginsburg, and Breyer.

40. Alan Sears, interview by the author, Scottsdale, Arizona, 13 January 1997.

41. Quoted in Christian Legal Society, *The Defender,* August 1995, 3.

42. Marc Galanter argues that attorneys who are "repeat players" (lawyers who repeatedly argue before the Court), such as McConnell and Laycock, have the knowledge, experience, and ability to write effective briefs tailored to the individual needs of the justices. Most important, they have credibility in the eyes of the Court. See Galanter, "Why the 'Haves' Come Out Ahead: Speculations on the Limits of Legal Change," *Law and Society Review* 9, no. 1 (Fall 1974): 95–160. See also Caldeira and Wright, "Organized Interests and Agenda Setting in the Supreme Court." In addition, as Kevin McGuire has pointed out, attorneys who have previously worked in the solicitor general's office (as McConnell did in the 1980s) are more likely to air their arguments before the Supreme Court than other lawyers. See McGuire, *The Supreme Court Bar: Legal Elites in the Washington Community* (Charlottesville: University Press of Virginia, 1993), 164–70.

43. *Rosenberger v. Rector and Visitors of the University of Virginia,* 515 US 819, 852 (O'Connor, J., concurring).

44. *Jones v. Clear Creek Independent School District,* 977 F2d 963 (1992).

45. *Doe v. Santa Fe Independent School District,* 933 FSupp 647 (1996).

46. *Doe v. Santa Fe Independent School District,* 168 F3d 806 (1999).

47. *Santa Fe Independent School District v. Doe,* 530 US 290 (2000).

48. Ibid.

49. These included *Marsh v. Chambers* 463 US 783 (1983), which saw the Court uphold the Nebraska legislature's paid chaplaincy program; *Grand Rapids v. Ball* 473 US 373 (1985) and *Aguilar v. Felton* 473 US 402 (1985), where the Court struck down governmental programs providing teachers and other educational resources to students in private schools; and *County of Allegheny v. ACLU, Greater Pittsburgh Chapter* 492 US 573 (1989), where the Court struck down the display of a crèche on the grand staircase leading up to a county courthouse but upheld the display of an eighteen-foot high menorah and a forty-five-foot high Christmas tree outside the building.

50. *Employment Division, Department of Human Resources of Oregon v. Smith,* 494 US 872 (1990).

51. This is consistent with studies that indicate conservative groups participate more frequently in the Supreme Court as amici than as sponsors. See O'Connor and Epstein, "Rise of Conservative Interest Group Litigation"; and Lee Epstein, *Conservatives in Court* (Knoxville: University of Tennessee Press, 1985).

52. This heavy dependence on amicus briefs does not hold true in lower federal court religious liberty cases in which the New Christian Right has participated. Chapter 6 explores the larger role that New Christian Right sponsorship of cases plays in the lower courts.

53. *Frazee v. Illinois Department of Employment Security,* 489 US 829 (1989); and *Hobbie v. Unemployment Appeals Commission,* 480 US 136 (1987).

54. See *Mitchell v. Helms,* 530 US 793 (2000); and *Agostini v. Felton,* 521 US 203 (1997).

55. See *Zobrest v. Catalina Foothills School District,* 509 US 1 (1993); and *Witters v. Washington Department of Services for the Blind,* 474 US 481 (1986).

56. See *Bowen v. Kendrick,* 487 US 589 (1988).

57. *Lee v. Weisman,* 505 US 577 (1992); and *Wallace v. Jaffree,* 472 US 38 (1985).

58. *Edwards v. Aguillard,* 482 US 578 (1987).

59. In addition to *Santa Fe Independent School District v. Doe,* 530 US 290 (2000), other

bitter defeats include *City of Boerne v. Flores,* 521 US 507 (1997); *Lyng v. Northwest Indian Cemetery Protective Association,* 485 US 439 (1988); *O'Lone v. Estate of Shabazz,* 482 US 342 (1987); *Bowen v. Roy,* 476 US 693 (1986); and *Goldman v. Weinberger,* 475 US 503 (1986).

60. Michael McConnell has argued that the very conservatism of the Rehnquist Court alone is cause for concern among religious liberty advocates. According to this view, conservatives on the Court have rightly drawn religion and religious expression back from the margins of society (to which earlier Supreme Court decisions had relegated them) and have encouraged greater public accommodation of religious interests. But these same conservatives have also been more willing to defer questions of religious liberty to elected officials who are not necessarily staunch defenders of the free exercise clause. In other words, this argument contends that in the name of judicial restraint, the Rehnquist Court has abdicated its duty to actively protect the rights of the religious. See McConnell, "Freedom from Religion?" *American Enterprise* 4, no. 2 (January/February 1993): 38.

Chapter 6

1. See David M. O'Brien, "The Rehnquist's Court's Shrinking Plenary Docket," *Judicature* 81 (September–October 1997): 58.

2. William H. Rehnquist, "The 1999 Year-End Report on the Federal Judiciary," *The Third Branch: Newsletter of the Federal Courts* 32 (January 2000): 1–9.

3. *Madsen v. Women's Health Center, Inc.,* 512 US 753 (1994).

4. Alliance Defense Fund, *ADF Quarterly Briefing,* no. 2 (1996): 1.

5. Lee Epstein, ed., *Contemplating Courts* (Washington, DC: Congressional Quarterly Press, 1995), 204.

6. U.S. Constitution, art. 3, sec. 2.

7. Henry J. Abraham, *The Judicial Process,* 7th ed. (New York: Oxford University Press, 1998), 174. In his annual year-end report on the federal judiciary, Chief Justice Rehnquist noted that U.S. District Courts in 1999 saw some 320,194 civil and criminal case filings as well as 1,354,376 filings in U.S. bankruptcy courts ("1999 Year-End Report," 2).

8. See Abraham, *The Judicial Process,* 81; and Christopher P. Banks, *Judicial Politics in the D.C. Circuit Court* (Baltimore: Johns Hopkins University Press, 1999).

9. See Donald R. Songer, "The Circuit Courts of Appeals," in *The American Courts: A Critical Assessment,* ed. John B. Gates and Charles A. Johnson (Washington, DC: Congressional Quarterly Press, 1991), 47.

10. *Lee v. Weisman,* 505 US 577 (1992).

11. *Jones v. Clear Creek Independent School District,* 977 F2d 963 (1992).

12. *Hsu v. Roslyn Union Free School District No. 3,* 85 F3d 839 (1996).

13. *Hsu v. Roslyn Union Free School District No. 3,* 876 FSupp 445 (1995).

14. *Hsu v. Roslyn Union Free School District No. 3,* 85 F3d 839, 854 (1996).

15. *Hurley v. Irish-American Gay, Lesbian and Bisexual Group of Boston,* 515 US 557, 573 (1995).

16. *Hsu v. Roslyn Union Free School District No. 3,* 85 F3d 839, 856, 857 (1996).

17. Ibid., 858.

18. Ibid., 859, 862.

19. *Board of Education of Westside Community Schools v. Mergens,* 496 US 226, 239 (1990).

20. *Hsu v. Roslyn Union Free School District No. 3,* 85 F3d 839, 859 (1996).

21. Jack W. Peltason, *Fifty-Eight Lonely Men: Southern Federal Judges and School Desegregation* (New York: Harcourt, Brace, 1961), 21.

22. *Peck v. Upshur County Board of Education,* 155 F3d 274 (1998).

23. *Peck v. Upshur County Board of Education,* 941 FSupp 1465 (1996).

24. *Peck v. Upshur County Board of Education,* 155 F3d 274, 279, 281 (1998).

25. Ibid., 284.

26. *Berger v. Rensselaer Central School Corporation,* 766 FSupp 696 (1991)

27. *Berger v. Rensselaer Central School Corporation,* 982 F2d 1160, 1171 (1993).

28. Ibid., 1165.

29. Ibid.

30. *Berger v. Rensselaer Central School Corporation,* 982 F2d 1160, 1165–66 (1993).

31. Ibid.

32. Judge Cummings also questioned the basic rationale of this legally impermissible approach in a footnote: "It may be that the Gideons also prefer schools because it gives the Bible distribution an official quality. Some students may be confused and think that Bible reading is a homework assignment (though, given what we know about children of middle school age, it is uncertain whether this would make students more or less likely to read the Scripture[s])." *Berger v. Rensselaer Central School Corporation,* 982 F2d 1160, 1167, note 7.

33. Ibid., 1167.

34. Ibid., 1168.

35. *Southworth v. Grebe,* 151 F3d 717 (1998). On 22 March 2000 the Supreme Court reversed and remanded the lower court's decision by a unanimous vote. See *Board of Regents of the University of Wisconsin System v. Southworth,* 529 US 217 (2000).

36. *Bynum v. U.S. Capitol Police Board,* 013 FSupp2d 50 (2000).

37. *Adler v. Duval County School Board,* 206 F3d 1070 (2000).

38. *Thate v. D.C. Armory Board,* 804 FSupp 373 (1992).

39. Although religion cases often involve crosscutting free exercise, establishment, and free speech clause concerns at the same time, I have summarized and categorized them here as to the central argument in the courts' decisions.

40. *Gentala v. City of Tucson,* 213 F3d 1055 (2000).

41. *Pfeifer v. City of West Allis,* 91 FSupp2d 1253 (2000).

Chapter 7

1. Fournier, *A House United,* 86.

2. Rita Woltz, interview by the author, Charlottesville, Virginia, 29 May 1997.

3. Marion G. (Pat) Robertson, "Religion in the Classroom," *William & Mary Bill of Rights Journal* 4 (Winter 1995): 603.

4. Steven McFarland, interview by the author, Annandale, Virginia, 19 March 1997.

5. Although, as Caldeira and Wright have pointed out, the costs of amicus briefs are far from insignificant ("*Amicus Curiae* before the Court").

6. *Rosenberger v. Rector and Visitors of the University of Virginia,* No. 91–0036-C, 1996 US Dist LEXIS 13799.

7. Guth et al., "Onward Christian Soldiers," 71.

8. As Lee Epstein puts it, "Before a group can seek its specific goals in any arena, . . . it

must first ensure the survival of the organization" ("Interest Group Litigation during the Rehnquist Era," 675).

9. See Alliance Defense Fund IRS Form 990 (1998).

10. As mentioned earlier, at least one of the major New Christian Right firms, the Rutherford Institute, believes its share of the pie has been cut. Its $4.5 million budget is just over half of what it was in 1994, the year the ADF was organized.

11. Alan Sears, interview by the author, Scottsdale, Arizona, 13 January 1997.

12. McFarland, interview.

13. Rutherford Institute, letter to donors, January 1997, 3.

14. American Center for Law and Justice, *Casenote* 6, no. 3 (1997).

15. National Religious Broadcasters, "Christian Broadcasting Grows Again," 1 June 2000, at <http://www.nrb.org>. The NRB considers a radio station "full-time religious" if it carries fifteen or more hours of Christian programming per week. Television stations must carry eighty-four or more hours of Christian programming per week to receive the same designation.

16. Diamond, *Not by Politics Alone,* 24.

17. Listen America, "Listen America Stations," 7 June 2000, at <http://www.listenamerica. net>.

18. *Central Florida Live* is produced by and originates with WTGL TV-52 in Orlando.

19. Ceci Connolly, "Radio Show Dropped for Paula Jones Link," *Washington Post,* 15 March 1998, 20 (A).

20. Rutherford Institute, 7 June 2000, at <http://www.rutherford.org>.

21. CBN is now known as the Family Channel, which is part of International Family Entertainment (IFE), a publicly held company of which Robertson is chairman of the board. Other holdings of IFE include the Ice Capades and the television production company MTM Entertainment.

22. John W. Kennedy, "Redeeming the Wasteland? Christian TV Increasingly Uses Entertainment to Spread Its Message," *Christianity Today,* 2 October 1995, 96.

23. *Board of Airport Commissioners of Los Angeles v. Jews for Jesus,* 482 US 569 (1987).

24. Mark Pinsky, "Attorney Convert Wins Again," *Los Angeles Times,* 8 June 1993, sec. A, p. 18.

25. TBN now features ACLJ attorney Colby Mays in the weekly half-hour program *Battlelines.*

26. ADF, IRS Form 990 (1998).

27. Rutherford Institute, year-end financial statements (1998).

28. *Jones v. Clear Creek Independent School District,* 977 F2d 963 (1992).

29. Kim Lawton, "Do Students Have a Prayer?" *Christianity Today,* 21 June 1993, 45.

30. W. John Moore, "'Tis the Season to be Lobbied," *National Law Journal,* 4 December 1993, 2896.

31. Ryan Szymkowicz, "Letter Starts School-Religion Controversy," *Cavalier Daily* (Charlottesville), 9 November 1995, 4(A).

32. See <http://www.aclj.org>, 19 October 2000.

33. Charlie Appleton, "'God 4 U' No Longer Taboo on State Tags," *Nashville Banner,* 7 February 1997, 1(A).

34. Jim Ashley, "ADF Defends Freedom," *Chattanooga Free Press,* 11 May 1996, 1(B).

35. Tabatha Barham, "City Advised to Settle Suit," *Sarasota Herald-Tribune,* 6 February 1996, 1(B).

36. See "ACLJ Offers to Defend School Districts Sued for Permitting Spontaneous Prayers at High School Football Games," 19 October 2000, at <http://www.aclj.org>.

37. As noted earlier, New Christian Right public interest law firms generally employ methods perfected by other groups. In the 1993 exchange of letters between the ACLJ and the ACLU to the nation's schools, the ACLU inserted the following prelitigation paragraph regarding graduation prayers: "Please understand that if your school system does sponsor prayer at its graduation ceremonies and we are contacted by students and their families, we will most likely pursue litigation." Quoted in *Oldham v. ACLU Foundation of Tennessee,* 849 FSupp 611, 613 (1994).

38. Quoted in Nordhaus, "Christian Group Crusades in the Courts," 2.

39. On a related note, Samuel Walker traces the increasing importance of nonlitigation activities to the ACLU during the Burger court years. Confronted with an increasingly conservative Supreme Court in the 1970s after a remarkable run with the Warren Court (during which time the ACLU won nearly 80 percent of its cases), the "ACLU began to shift its priorities and placed more emphasis on legislative protection of civil liberties. The ACLU Washington office, which had only one staff person in the 1960s, expanded to include over twelve full-time professional lobbyists by the 1980s." Walker, *The American Civil Liberties Union: An Annotated Bibliography* (New York: Garland, 1992), xix.

40. McFarland, interview.

41. See Newman, "Public-Interest Firms."

42. *Christians v. Crystal Evangelical Free Church,* 82 F3d 1407 (1996). Because the court's decision in the case was based on the Religious Freedom Restoration Act (RFRA), which was subsequently held unconstitutional by the Supreme Court, the Eighth Circuit reheard the case in 1997. Holding that RFRA was still good law as far as federal action was concerned, the court ruled that the tithes were not recoverable under federal bankruptcy law. See *In Re Young,* 141 F3d 854 (1998).

43. Sherrie F. Nachman, "Bill Clinton's Divine Intervention," *American Lawyer* (November 1994): 15.

44. McFarland, interview.

45. Peter Baker and Joan Biskupic, "On Workplace Religion Guidelines, Varying Degrees of Faith," *Washington Post,* 15 August 1997, sec. A, p. 23. In drafting these guidelines, the *Washington Post* noted the effort the White House made to enlist "the aid of groups across the political spectrum, including the CLS, the National Council of Churches, the American Jewish Congress, and People for the American Way." See Peter Baker, "Workplace Religion Policy Due," *Washington Post,* 14 August 1997, sec. A, p. 1.

46. Terry Mattingly, "Having to Hide Faith Becomes Issue in 1995," *Knoxville News-Sentinel* (Tennessee), 6 January 1996, 2(B).

47. McFarland, interview.

48. Wilcox, *Onward Christian Soldiers?* 140.

Chapter 8

1. Ivers, *To Build a Wall,* 191.
2. See Cortner, "Strategies and Tactics of Litigants in Constitutional Cases."
3. Melton, "The Free Exorcise of Religion."
4. *Lee v. Weisman,* 505 US 577, 645 (1992).
5. *Capitol Square Review and Advisory Board v. Pinette,* 515 US 753, 767 (1995).

6. Alan Sears, interview by the author, Scottsdale, Arizona, 13 January 1997.

7. John Stepanovich, interview by the author, Virginia Beach, Virginia, 25 March 1997.

8. *East High School Prism Club v. Seidel*, 95 FSupp2d 239 (2000).

9. Carl H. Esbeck, "Equal Treatment: Its Constitutional Status," in *Equal Treatment of Religion in a Pluralistic Society*, ed. Stephen V. Monsma and J. Christopher Soper (Grand Rapids: Eerdmans, 1998), 15.

10. See, for example, Barton, *Original Intent;* Whitehead, *Second American Revolution;* and Mark A. Beliles and Stephen K. McDowell, *America's Providential History* (Charlottesville, VA: Providence Foundation, 1994).

11. *Witters v. Washington Department of Services for the Blind*, 474 US 481 (1986).

12. Oral argument by Michael W. McConnell, Esq., on behalf of petitioners, *Rosenberger v. Rector and Visitors of the University of Virginia*, 515 US 819 (1995), 1995 US TRANS LEXIS 70, 15.

13. Rosenberger, "Letter from the Editor."

14. Pat Robertson referred to this bygone era during a 1995 symposium on religion and the schools at the College of William & Mary: "Now, to the liberal activist judges and their friends and allies, the people of America say very simply: you have violated us long enough. We want our history back. We want our traditions back. We want our Constitution back. And, we want God back in the schools of America." For the full text of his speech, see "Religion in the Classroom," 606.

15. Mark V. Tushnet, "Constitution of Religion," *Review of Politics* 50 (Fall 1998): 652n. 44.

16. Derek Davis, "Equal Treatment: A Christian Separationist View," in *Equal Treatment of Religion in a Pluralistic Society*, ed. Stephen V. Monsma and J. Christopher Soper (Grand Rapids: Eerdmans, 1998), 154.

17. *Peck v. Upshur County Board of Education*, 155 F3d 274, 288 (1998).

18. Petitioner's brief, *Widmar v. Vincent*, 454 US 263 (1981), p. 27.

19. Sullivan, "The Difference Religion Makes," 295.

20. Quoted in Robert E. Webber, *The Secular Saint* (Grand Rapids: Acadamie Books, 1979), 173.

Bibliography

Abraham, Henry J. *The Judicial Process.* 7th ed. New York: Oxford University Press, 1998.
———, and Barbara Perry. *Freedom and the Court: Civil Rights and Liberties in the United States.* 7th ed. New York: Oxford University Press, 1998.
Abramson, Jill. "Conservative Legal Groups Plan Efforts to Keep Bush Administration on Reagan's Judicial Path." *Wall Street Journal,* 21 November 1988, sec. A, p. 18.
Alliance Defense Fund. *ADF Briefing,* May, September, and November 1995, January and May 1996.
———. *ADF Quarterly Briefing,* no. 2, 1996.
———. Letter to Donors. February 1996.
———. IRS Form 990, 1998.
———. <http://www.alliancedefensefund.org>
———. <http://www.adfpray.org>
American Center for Law and Justice. "ACLJ Offers to Defend School Districts Sued for Permitting Spontaneous Prayers at High School Football Games," 19 October 2000, <http://www.aclj.org>.
———. *Casenote,* March 1997.
———. IRS Form 990 (1998).
———. <http://www.aclj.org>.
———. <http://www.eclj.org>.
Appleton, Charlie. "'God 4 U' No Longer Taboo on State Tags." *Nashville Banner,* 7 February 1997, sec. A, p. 1.
Ashley, Jim. "ADF Defends Freedom." *Chattanooga Free Press,* 11 May 1996, sec. B, p. 1.
Baker, Peter. "Workplace Religion Policy Due." *Washington Post,* 14 August 1997, sec. A, p. 1.
———, and Joan Biskupic. "On Workplace Religion Guidelines, Varying Degrees of Faith." *Washington Post,* 15 August 1997, sec. A, p. 23.
Ball, William Bentley. *Mere Creatures of the State? Education, Religion, and the Courts.* Notre Dame: Crisis Books, 1994.
Banks, Christopher P. *Judicial Politics in the D.C. Circuit Court.* Baltimore: Johns Hopkins University Press, 1999.
Barham, Tabatha. "City Advised to Settle Suit." *Sarasota Herald-Tribune,* 6 February 1996, sec. B, p. 1.
Barton, David. *Original Intent: The Courts, the Constitution, and Religion.* Aledo, TX: Wallbuilder Press, 1996.
Baum, Lawrence. *American Courts: Process and Policy.* 4th ed. Boston: Houghton Mifflin, 1998.
Behuniak-Long, Susan. "Friendly Fire: Amici Curiae and the *Webster v. Reproductive Health Services.*" *Judicature* 74, no. 5 (February–March 1991): 261–70.

Beliles, Mark A., and Stephen K. McDowell. *America's Providential History.* Charlottesville, VA: Providence Foundation, 1994.

Bentley, Arthur F. *The Process of Government.* Ed. Peter H. Odegard. Cambridge, MA: Belknap Press, 1967.

Berlet, Chip, and Matthew H. Lyons. *Right-Wing Populism in America.* New York: Guilford Press, 2000.

Bradley, Jennifer. "Fighting the Establishment (Clause)," *American Prospect* 28 (September–October 1996): 57–60.

Brodhead, Michael J. *David J. Brewer: The Life of a Supreme Court Justice, 1837–1910.* Carbondale: Southern Illinois University Press, 1994.

Bruce, Steve. *Firm in the Faith.* Brookfield, VT: Gower Publishing, 1984.

———. "The Inevitable Failure of the New Christian Right." *Sociology of Religion* 55, no. 3 (Fall 1994): 229–42.

———. *The Rise and Fall of the New Christian Right: Conservative Protestant Politics in America, 1978–1988.* New York: Oxford University Press, 1988.

Caldeira, Gregory A., and John R. Wright. "*Amicus Curiae* before the Supreme Court: Who Participates, When, and How Much?" *Journal of Politics* 52, no. 3 (August 1990): 782–806.

———. "Organized Interests and Agenda Setting in the Supreme Court." *American Political Science Review* 82 (December 1988): 1109–27.

Capps, Walter H. *The New Religious Right: Piety, Patriotism, and Politics.* Columbia: University of South Carolina Press, 1990.

Carter, Stephen L. *The Culture of Disbelief.* New York: Basic Books, 1993.

Christian Legal Society. *The Defender,* June and August 1995.

———. *The Defender,* no. 1 (1997).

———. <http://www.christianlegalsociety.org>.

Cohen, Julie. "Doing the Lord's Litigation: Conservative Christians Create Courtroom Fund." *Legal Times,* 28 February 1994, 2.

Cole, Charles C. *The Social Ideas of the Northern Evangelicals, 1826–1860.* New York: Columbia University Press, 1954.

Conn, Joseph L. "Courtroom Contender." *Church & State* 45 (June 1992): 4–6.

Connorly, Ceci. "Radio Show Dropped for Paula Jones Link." *Washington Post,* 15 March 1998, sec. A, p. 20.

Cooper, John Charles. *Religious Pied Pipers: A Critique of Radical Right-Wing Religion.* Valley Forge, PA: Judson Press, 1981.

Coral Ridge Ministries. "Reclaiming America for Christ." Conference Brochure, 1988, 1996.

Cortner, Richard. "Strategies and Tactics of Litigants in Constitutional Cases." *Journal of Public Law* 17 (1968): 287–307.

Craig, Barbara Hinkson, and David M. O'Brien. *Abortion and American Politics.* Chatham, NJ: Chatham House, 1993.

Crawford, Alan. *Thunder on the Right: The "New Right" and the Politics of Resentment.* New York: Pantheon, 1980.

Culver, Virginia. "Lawyer Leading Crusade for Freedom of Religion." *Denver Post,* 26 August 1995, sec. B, p. 6.

Curriden, Mark. "Defenders of the Faith." *ABA Journal* 80 (December 1994): 86–89.

D'Antonio, Michael. *Fall from Grace: The Failed Crusade of the Christian Right.* New York: Farrar, Straus, and Giroux, 1989.

Davis, Derek. "Equal Treatment: A Christian Separationist Perspective." In *Equal Treatment of Religion in a Pluralistic Society,* ed. Stephen V. Monsma and J. Christopher Soper, 136–57. Grand Rapids: Eerdmans, 1998.

Denniston, Lyle. "Airport Speech Ban: Foiled by the Facts?" *American Lawyer* 9, no. 4 (May 1987): 119.

Diamond, Sara. *Not by Politics Alone: The Enduring Influence of the Christian Right.* New York: Guilford Press, 1998.

———. *Roads to Dominion.* New York: Guilford Press, 1995.

———. *Spiritual Warfare: The Politics of the Christian Right.* London: Pluto Press, 1989.

———. "Watch on the Right: The Religious Right Goes to Court." *Humanist* 53 (May–June 1994): 35–37.

Edel, Wilbur. *Defenders of the Faith: Religion and Politics from the Pilgrim Fathers to Ronald Reagan.* New York: Praeger, 1987.

Elsasser, Glen. "This Time, Will School Prayer Pass Test?" *Chicago Tribune,* 13 October 1985, sec. C, p. 1.

Epstein, Lee. *Conservatives in Court.* Knoxville: University of Tennessee Press, 1985.

———, ed. *Contemplating Courts.* Washington, DC: Congressional Quarterly Press, 1995.

———. "Courts and Interest Groups." In *The American Courts: A Critical Assessment,* ed. John B. Gates and Charles A. Johnson, 335–71. Washington, DC: Congressional Quarterly Press, 1991.

———. "Interest Group Litigation during the Rehnquist Era." *Journal of Law and Politics* 9 (Summer 1993): 639–717.

———, and Joseph Kobylka. *The Supreme Court and Legal Change: Abortion and the Death Penalty.* Chapel Hill: University of North Carolina Press, 1993.

Esbeck, Carl H. "Equal Treatment: Its Constitutional Status." In *Equal Treatment of Religion in a Pluralistic Society,* ed. Stephen V. Monsma and J. Christopher Soper, 9–29. Grand Rapids: Eerdmans, 1998.

Finkelman, Paul, ed. *Religion and American Law: An Encyclopedia.* New York: Garland, 2000.

Fisher, Marc. "Unlikely Crusaders; Jay Sekulow." *Washington Post,* 21 October 1997, sec. D, p. 1.

Fishwick, Marshall, and Ray B. Browne, eds. *The God Pumpers.* Bowling Green, OH: Popular Press, 1987.

Flowers, Ronald B. *That Godless Court? Supreme Court Decisions on Church-State Relationships.* Louisville, KY: Westminister John Knox Press, 1994.

Foskett, Ken. "Religion to the Rescue." *Atlanta Journal and Constitution,* 5 November 1991, sec. D, p. 1.

Fournier, Keith. *A House United? Evangelicals and Catholics Together.* Colorado Springs: NavPress, 1994.

Frank, Douglas. *Less Than Conquerors: How Evangelicals Entered the Twentieth Century.* Grand Rapids: Eerdmans, 1986.

Frankl, Razelle. *Televangelism: The Marketing of Popular Religion.* Carbondale: Southern Illinois University Press, 1987.

Galanter, Marc. "Why the 'Haves' Come Out Ahead: Speculations on the Limits of Legal Change." *Law and Society Review* 9, no. 1 (Fall 1974): 95–160.

Gerlin, Andrea. "With Free Help, the Religious Turn Litigious." *Wall Street Journal,* 17 February 1994, sec. B, p. 1.

Glazer, Nathan. "Fundamentalism." In *Christianity and Modern Politics,* ed. Louise S. Hulett, 299–307. The Netherlands: Walter de Gruyter, 1993.

Gleick, Elizabeth. "Onward Christian Lawyers." *Time,* 3 March 1995, 57–65.

Goldman, Sheldon. "Bush's Judicial Legacy: The Final Imprint." *Judicature* 76 (April–May 1993): 282–97.

———. "Reagan's Judicial Legacy: Completing the Puzzle and Summing Up." *Judicature* 72 (April–May 1989): 318–30.

Green, John C. "The Christian Right and the 1996 Elections: An Overview." In *God at the Grassroots: The Christian Right in the 1996 Elections,* ed. Mark J. Rozell and Clyde Wilcox, 1–14. Lanham, MD: Rowman and Littlefield, 1997.

Greenberg, Jack. *Race Relations and American Law.* New York: Columbia University Press, 1959.

"Groups Take Church-State Fights to Classrooms." *National Law Journal,* 13 December 1993, 5.

Guth, James L., John C. Green, Lyman A. Kellstedt, and Corwin E. Smidt. "Onward Christian Soldiers: Religious Activist Groups in American Politics." In *Interest Group Politics,* ed. Allan J. Ciglar and Burdett A. Loomis, 55–76. Washington, DC: Congressional Quarterly Press, 1995.

Guth, James L., John C. Green, Corwin E. Smidt, and Lyman A. Kellstedt. "Partisan Religion." *Christian Century,* 21 March 2001, 18–20.

Hadden, Jeffrey K., and Charles E. Swann, eds. *Prime Time Preachers: The Rising Power of Televangelism.* Reading, MA: Addison-Wesley, 1981.

———. *Secularization and Fundamentalism Reconsidered.* New York: Paragon House, 1989.

Hakman, Nathan. "Lobbying the Supreme Court—An Appraisal of Political Science Folklore." *Fordham Law Review* 35 (1966): 15–50.

Hertzke, Allen D. *Echoes of Discontent: Jesse Jackson, Pat Robertson, and the Resurgence of Populism.* Washington, DC: Congressional Quarterly Press, 1993.

———. *Representing God in Washington: The Role of Religious Lobbies in the American Polity.* Knoxville: University of Tennessee Press, 1988.

Howard, A. E. Dick. "The Supreme Court and the Serpentine Wall." In *The Virginia Statute for Religious Freedom,* ed. Merrill D. Peterson and Robert C. Vaughan, 313–49. Cambridge: Cambridge University Press, 1988.

Howard, Jennifer. "Wide Awake: Holy Constitutional Issues, UVA! Supreme Court Will Hear the Case." *C'ville Weekly,* 31 January 1995, 8–9.

Howe, Mark de Wolfe. *The Garden and the Wilderness: Religion and Government in American Constitutional History.* Chicago: University of Chicago Press, 1965.

Hudson, Winthrop S. *Religion in America.* New York: Scribner, 1965.

Hunter, James Davison. *American Evangelicalism: Conservative Religion and the Quandary of Modernity.* New Brunswick, NJ: Rutgers University Press, 1983.

———. "The Evangelical Worldview since 1890." In *Piety and Politics: Evangelicals and Fundamentalists Confront the World,* ed. Richard John Neuhaus and Michael Cromartie, 19–53. Washington, DC: Ethics and Public Policy Center, 1987.

———. *Evangelicalism: The Coming Generation.* Chicago: University of Chicago Press, 1987.

Hutcheson, Richard G. *Mainline Churches and the Evangelicals.* Atlanta: John Knox Press, 1981.

Hutchins, Robert M. "The Future of the Wall." In *The Wall between Church and State,* ed. Dallin H. Oaks, 17–25. Chicago: University of Chicago Press, 1963.

Ivers, Gregg. "Organized Religion and the Supreme Court." *Journal of Church and State* 32 (Autumn 1990): 775–93.

———. "Religious Organizations as Constitutional Litigants." *Polity* 25 (Winter 1992): 243–66.

———. *To Build a Wall: American Jews and the American Separation of Church and State.* Charlottesville: University Press of Virginia, 1995.

Jefferson, Thomas. *Writings.* Ed. Merrill D. Peterson. New York: Literary Classics of the United States, 1984.

Jelen, Ted. *The Political Mobilization of Religious Beliefs.* New York: Praeger, 1991.

Jorstad, Erling. *The New Christian Right, 1981–1988.* Lewiston, NY: Edwin Mellon Press, 1987.

———. *The Politics of Moralism: The New Christian Right in American Life.* Minneapolis: Augsburg, 1981.

Kaminer, Debbie N. "2d Circuit Chose Poor Precedent in 'Hsu.'" *National Law Journal,* 20 January 1997, sec. A, p. 15.

Kennedy, John W. "Redeeming the Wasteland? Christian TV Increasingly Uses Entertainment to Spread Its Message." *Christianity Today,* 2 October 1995, 92–102.

Kleppner, Paul. *The Third Electoral System, 1853–1892.* Chapel Hill: University of North Carolina Press, 1979.

———. *Who Voted? The Dynamics of Electoral Turnout, 1870–1980.* New York: Praeger, 1982.

Kluger, Richard. *Simple Justice: The History of Brown v. Board of Education and Black America's Struggle for Equality.* New York: Knopf, 1976.

Kobylka, Joseph F. *The Politics of Obscenity: Group Litigation in a Time of Change.* New York: Greenwood, 1991.

Kohut, Andrew, John C. Green, Scott Keeter, and Robert C. Toth. *The Diminishing Divide: America's Changing Role in American Politics.* Washington, DC: Brookings Institution Press, 2000.

Lawton, Kim. "Do Students Have a Prayer?" *Christianity Today,* 21 June 1993, 45.

Laycock, Douglas. "Free Exercise and the Religious Freedom Restoration Act." *Fordham Law Review* 62 (February 1994): 883–904.

Layman, Geoffrey. *The Great Divide: Religious and Cultural Conflict in American Party Politics.* New York: Columbia University Press, 2001.

Levine, Lawrence W. *Defender of the Faith: William Jennings Bryan, the Last Decade, 1915–1925.* New York: Oxford University Press, 1965.

Liberty Counsel. *The Liberator,* April 1997, June and July 2000.

———. <http://www.lc.org>.

Liebman, Robert C. "Making of the New Christian Right." In *The New Christian Right: Mobilization and Legitimation,* ed. Robert C. Liebman and Robert Wuthnow, 227–38. New York: Aldine, 1983.

———, and Robert Wuthnow, eds. *The New Christian Right: Mobilization and Legitimation.* New York: Aldine, 1983.

Lienesch, Michael. *Redeeming America: Piety and Politics in the New Christian Right.* Chapel Hill: University of North Carolina Press, 1993.

Listen America. "Listen America Stations." 7 June 2000. <http://www.listenamerica.net>.

Lynn, Barry, Marc D. Stern, and Oliver S. Thomas. *The Right to Religious Liberty: The Basic ACLU Guide to Religious Rights.* 2d ed. Carbondale: Southern Illinois University Press, 1995.

Magnuson, Norris. *Salvation in the Slums: Evangelical Social Work, 1865–1920.* Metuchen, NJ: Scarecrow, 1977.

Marsden, George M. *Fundamentalism and American Culture: The Shaping of Twentieth Century Evangelicalism, 1870–1925*. New York: Oxford University Press, 1980.

———. *Understanding Fundamentalism and Evangelicalism*. Grand Rapids: Eerdmans, 1991.

Martin, William. *With God on Our Side: The Rise of the Religious Right in America*. New York: Broadway Books, 1996.

Marty, Martin E. *Religion and Republic: The American Circumstance*. Boston: Beacon Press, 1987.

Mattingly, Terry. "Having to Hide Faith Becomes Issue in 1995." *Knoxville News-Sentinel*, 6 January 1996, sec. B, p. 2.

McClellan, James. *Joseph Story and the American Constitution*. Norman: University of Oklahoma Press, 1971.

McConnell, Michael. "Freedom from Religion?" *American Enterprise* 4, no. 1 (January/February 1993): 34–43.

McCord, Julia. "Defending Religious Rights." *Omaha World Herald*, 29 April 1995, 57(SF).

McGuire, Kevin T. *The Supreme Court Bar: Legal Elites in the Washington Community*. Charlottesville: University Press of Virginia, 1993.

McIntyre, Thomas J. *The Fear Brokers*. Boston: Beacon Press, 1979.

McLellan, Vern. *Christians in the Political Arena*. Charlotte, NC: Associates Press, 1984.

McLoughlin, William. *The American Evangelicals, 1800–1900*. New York: Harper and Row, 1968.

Melton, David. "The Free Exorcise of Religion." Speech delivered to Students for Individual Liberty and the Liberty Coalition, University of Virginia, 29 January 1997.

Meltsner, Michael. *Cruel and Unusual: The Supreme Court and Capital Punishment*. New York: Random House, 1973.

Milner, Neal. "The Right to Refuse Treatment: Four Case Studies of Legal Mobilization." *Law and Society Review* 21, no. 3 (1987): 447–85.

Mnookin, Robert H. *In the Interest of Children: Advocacy, Law Reform, and Public Policy*. New York: W. H. Freeman, 1985.

Moe, Terry M. *The Organization of Interests*. Chicago: University of Chicago Press, 1980.

Moen, Matthew C. *The Christian Right and Congress*. Tuscaloosa: University of Alabama Press, 1989.

———. *The Transformation of the Christian Right*. Tuscaloosa: University of Alabama Press, 1992.

Moore, W. John. "The Lord's Litigators." *National Journal*, 2 July 1994, 1560.

———. " 'Tis the Season to be Lobbied." *National Law Journal*, 4 December 1993, 2896.

Morken, Hubert. "The Evangelical Legal Response to the ACLU: Religion, Politics, and the First Amendment." Paper prepared for the Annual Meeting of the American Political Science Association, Chicago, 3–6 September 1992.

Nachman, Sherrie F. "Bill Clinton's Divine Intervention." *American Lawyer* (November 1994): 15.

Nash, Ronald H. *Evangelicals in America: Who They Are, What They Believe*. Nashville: Abingdon Press, 1987.

National Legal Resource Center. "What Is an Intranet?" 18 June 1997. <http://www.nlrc.org>.

National Religious Broadcasters. "Christian Broadcasting Grows Again." 1 June 2000. <http://www.nrb.org>.

Neuhaus, Richard John. *The Naked Public Square.* Grand Rapids: Eerdmans, 1984.

———, and Michael Cromartie, eds. *Piety and Politics: Evangelicals and Fundamentalists Confront the World.* Washington, DC: Ethics and Public Policy Center, 1987.

Newman, Roger K. "Public-Interest Law Firms Crop Up on the Right." *National Law Journal,* 26 August 1996, sec. A, p. 1.

Niebuhr, Gustav. "Conservatives' New Frontier: Religious Liberty Law Firms." *New York Times,* 8 July 1995, 1(N), 3(N).

Noll, Mark A. *The Scandal of the Evangelical Mind.* Grand Rapids: Eerdmans, 1995.

———, David W. Bebbington, and George A. Rawlyk, eds. *Evangelicalism.* New York: Oxford University Press, 1994.

Nordhaus, Hannah. "Christian Group Crusades in the Courts." *Legal Times,* 27 February 1995, 2, 25.

Oaks, Dallin H., ed. *The Wall between Church and State.* Chicago: University of Chicago Press, 1963.

O'Brien, David M. "The Reagan Judges: His Most Enduring Legacy?" In *The Reagan Legacy: Promise and Performance,* ed. Charles O. Jones, 60–101. Chatham, NJ: Chatham House, 1988.

———. "The Rehnquist's Court's Shrinking Plenary Docket." *Judicature* 81 (September–October 1997): 58–65.

O'Connor, Karen. *Women's Organizations' Use of the Courts.* Lexington, MA: Lexington Books, 1980.

O'Connor, Karen, and Lee Epstein. "*Amicus Curiae* Participation in the United States Supreme Court: An Appraisal of Hakman's Folklore." *Law & Society Review* 16, no. 2 (1982): 311–20.

———. "A Legal Voice for the Chicano Community: The Activities of the Mexican American Legal Defense Fund, 1968–1982." In *Latinos and the Political System,* ed. F. Chris Garcia, 255–68. Notre Dame: University of Notre Dame Press, 1988.

———. "The Rise of Conservative Interest Group Litigation." *Journal of Politics* 45, no. 2 (May 1983): 479–89.

Olson, Susan M. *Clients and Lawyers: Securing the Rights of Disabled Persons.* Westport, CT: Greenwood, 1984.

———. "Interest Group Litigation in Federal District Court: Beyond the Political Disadvantage Theory." *Journal of Politics* 52, no. 3 (August 1990): 854–82.

Peltason, Jack W. *Fifty-Eight Lonely Men: Southern Federal Judges and School Desegregation.* New York: Harcourt, Brace, 1961.

Pierard, Richard A. "Religion and the New Right in the 1980s." In *Religion and the State,* ed. James E. Wood Jr., 393–17. Waco, TX: Baylor University Press, 1985.

———. *The Unequal Yoke: Evangelical Christianity and Political Conservatism.* Philadelphia: J. B. Lippincott, 1970.

Pinsky, Mark I. "Attorney Convert Wins Again." *Los Angeles Times,* 8 June 1993, sec. A, p. 18.

———. "Fight for Religious Liberty Brings Lawyer Few 'Amens.'" *Orlando Sentinel,* 9 September 1995, sec. D, p. 5.

———. "Legal Weapon: Jay Alan Sekulow Is the Christian Right's Leading Lion in the Judicial Arena." *Los Angeles Times,* 2 September 1993, sec. E, p. 1.

Reed, Ralph. *Politically Incorrect: The Emerging Faith Factor in American Politics.* Dallas: Word Publishing, 1994.

Rehnquist, William H. "The 1999 Year-End Report on the Federal Judiciary." *The Third Branch: Newsletter of the Federal Courts* 32 (January 2000): 1–8.

Reichley, A. James. "Pietist Politics." In *Christianity and Modern Politics,* ed. Louisa S. Hulett, 253–67. Berlin: Walter de Gruyter, 1993.

Ribuffo, Leo P. *The Old Christian Right.* Philadelphia: Temple University Press, 1983.

Robbins, Thomas, and Dick Anthony, eds. *In Gods We Trust: New Patterns of Religious Pluralism in America.* 2d ed. New Brunswick, NJ: Transaction Publishers, 1990.

Robertson, Marion G. (Pat). "Religion in the Classroom." *William & Mary Bill of Rights Journal* 4 (Winter 1995): 595–606.

"Robertson's Lawyers." *Christian Century,* 21 October 1992, 930.

Rosenberger, Ronald. "Letter from the Editor." *Wide Awake* (November–December 1990): 2.

Rosenfeld, Megan. "On the Case for Paula Jones." *Washington Post,* 17 January 1998, sec. B, p. 1.

Rowland, C. K. "The Federal District Courts." In *The American Courts: A Critical Assessment,* ed. John B. Gates and Charles A. Johnson, 61–85. Washington, DC: Congressional Quarterly Press, 1991.

Rozell, Mark J., and Clyde Wilcox, eds. *God at the Grassroots: The New Christian Right in the 1994 Elections.* Lanham, MD: Rowman and Littlefield, 1995.

Rubin, Eva. *Abortion, Politics, and the Courts.* New York: Greenwood, 1987.

Rutherford Institute. *Action Newsletter,* April 1997.

———. IRS Form 990 and Year-End Financial Statements, 1997, 1998, 1999.

———. Letter to Donors. January 1997, March 1997.

———. <http://www.rutherford.org>.

Savage, David G. "School Prayer Just a Start for Some Christian Activists." *Los Angeles Times,* 25 December 1994, sec. A, p. 1.

Schaeffer, Francis A. *A Christian Manifesto.* Westchester, IL: Crossway Books, 1981.

Scheppele, Kim Lane, and Jack L. Walker Jr. "The Litigation Strategies of Interest Groups." In *Mobilizing Interest Groups in America,* ed. Jack L. Walker Jr., 157–83. Ann Arbor: University of Michigan Press, 1991.

Sekulow, Jay A. America Online-American Civil Liberties Union Center Stage Series Transcript. 7 October 1997. <http://www.aclu.org>.

———. *The Christian, the Court, and the Constitution: Your Rights as a Christian Citizen.* Virginia Beach: American Center for Law and Justice, 2000.

Songer, Donald R. "The Circuit Courts of Appeals." In *The American Courts: A Critical Assessment,* ed. John B. Gates and Charles A. Johnson, 35–59. Washington, DC: Congressional Quarterly Press, 1991.

———, and Reginald S. Sheehan. "Interest Group Success in the Courts: Amicus Participation in the Supreme Court." *Political Research Quarterly* 46, no. 2 (June 1993): 339–54.

Sorauf, Frank J. *The Wall of Separation: Constitutional Politics of Church and State.* Princeton: Princeton University Press, 1976.

Stafford, Tim. "Move Over, ACLU." *Christianity Today* 37 (25 October 1993): 20–24.

Stanmeyer, William A. *Clear and Present Danger: Church and State in Post-Christian America.* Ann Arbor: Servant Books, 1983.

Staver, Mathew D. *Faith and Freedom.* Wheaton, IL: Crossway Books, 1995.

Stern, Robert L., Eugene Gressman, Stephen M. Shapiro, and Kenneth S. Geller. *Supreme Court Practice.* 7th ed. Washington, DC: Bureau of National Affairs, 1993.

Story, Joseph. *Commentaries on the Constitution of the United States*. Vol. 2. 5th ed. Boston: Little, Brown, 1891.

Strossen, Nadine. "How Much God in the Schools? A Discussion of Religion's Role in the Classroom." *William & Mary Bill of Rights Journal* 4 (Winter 1995): 607–38.

Sullivan, Winnifred Fallers. "The Difference Religion Makes: Reflections on *Rosenberger*." *Christian Century*, 13 March 1996, 292–95.

———. *Paying the Words Extra: Religious Discourse in the Supreme Court of the United States*. Cambridge, MA: Harvard University Press, 1994.

Szymkowicz, Ryan. "Letter Starts School-Religion Controversy." *Cavalier Daily* (Charlottesville), 9 November 1995, sec. A, p. 4.

Thomas, Cal, and Ed Dobson. *Blinded by Might: Can the Religious Right Save America?* Grand Rapids: Zondervan, 1999.

Tidball, Derek J. *Who Are the Evangelicals? Tracing the Roots of the Modern Movements*. London: Marshall Pickering, 1994.

Tocqueville, Alexis de. *Democracy in America*. Trans. George Lawrence. New York: Harper and Row, 1988.

Travisano, Jim. "Trying Times: The Rutherford Institute and the Fight for Religious Rights." *Albemarle* 31 (December 1992–January 1993): 62–79.

Truman, David B. *The Governmental Process*. New York: Knopf, 1951.

Tushnet, Mark V. "Constitution of Religion." *Review of Politics* 50 (Fall 1988): 652.

———. *The NAACP's Legal Struggle against Segregated Education, 1925–1950*. Chapel Hill: University of North Carolina Press, 1987.

Tyrell, Ian R. *Sobering Up: From Temperance to Prohibition in Antebellum America*. Westport, CT: Greenwood, 1979.

United Press International. "Lawyer Launches Anti-ACLU Group." 23 February 1990, BC Cycle.

United States Department of Education. <http://www.ed.gov/inits/ religionandschools>.

Urofsky, Melvin I., and Martha May, eds. *The New Christian Right: Political and Social Issues*. New York: Garland, 1996.

Utter, Glenn L., and John H. Storey. *The Religious Right: A Reference Handbook*. Santa Barbara, CA: ABC-CLIO, 1995.

Virshup, Amy. "A Jew for Jesus." *George* 8, no. 1 (October 1996): 62–66.

Vose, Clement E. *Caucasians Only*. Berkeley: University of California Press, 1959.

Wald, Kenneth D. *Religion and Politics in the United States*. 3d ed. Washington, DC: Congressional Quarterly Press, 1997.

Walker, Jack L. *Mobilizing Interest Groups in America*. Ann Arbor: University of Michigan Press, 1991.

Walker, Samuel. *The American Civil Liberties Union: An Annotated Bibliography*. New York: Garland, 1992.

Walsh, Edward, and Bill Miller. "School Prayer Is Dealt a Blow." *Washington Post*, 20 June 2000, sec. A, p. 1.

Walters, Ronald. *American Reformers, 1815–1860*. New York: Hill and Wang, 1978.

Wasby, Stephen L. *Race Relations Litigation in an Age of Complexity*. Charlottesville: University Press of Virginia, 1995.

Watt, David Harrington. *A Transforming Faith: Explorations of Twentieth-Century American Evangelicalism*. New Brunswick, NJ: Rutgers University Press, 1991.

Webber, Robert E. *The Secular Saint*. Grand Rapids: Acadamie Books, 1979.

Wells, David F., and John D. Woodbridge, eds. *The Evangelicals*. Nashville: Abingdon Press, 1975.

Wenner, Lettie. *The Environmental Decade in Court*. Bloomington: Indiana University Press, 1984.

Weyrich, Paul. "The Moral Minority." *Christianity Today*, 6 September 1999, 44–45.

Whitehead, John W. *The Second American Revolution*. Wheaton, IL: Crossway Books, 1982.

———. *The Stealing of America*. Westchester, IL: Crossway Books, 1983.

Wilcox, Clyde. *God's Warriors: The Christian Right in 20th Century America*. Baltimore: Johns Hopkins University Press, 1992.

———. *Onward Christian Soldiers? The Religious Right in American Politics*. Boulder, CO: Westview, 1996.

———. "Premillennialists at the Millennium." *Sociology of Religion* 55, no. 3 (Fall 1994): 243–61.

Wohl, Alexander. "Friends with Agendas." *ABA Journal* 82 (November 1996): 46–48.

Wood, James E., ed. *Religion and Politics*. Waco, TX: Baylor University Press, 1983.

Woodbridge, John D., Mark A. Noll, and Nathan O. Hatch. *The Gospel in America: Themes in the Story of America's Evangelicals*. Grand Rapids: Zondervan, 1979.

Young, Perry Deane. *God's Bullies: Native Reflections on Preachers and Politics*. New York: Holt, Rinehart, and Winston, 1982.

Index

ACLJ. *See* American Center for Law and Justice

ACLU. *See* American Civil Liberties Union

ADF. *See* Alliance Defense Fund

Alliance Defense Fund, 4–5, 8, 11, 27, 28, 29, 30, 40, 46–47, 136; and Blackstone Legal Fellowship, 44; budget, 42; case selection criteria, 42, 49; and the Center for Law and Religious Freedom, 33; founding, 41–42; fundraising, 123–24; Grants Review Committee, 43; and *Hsu v. Roslyn Union Free School District,* 90–91; and *Hurley v. Irish-American Gay, Lesbian, and Bisexual Group of Boston,* 90; influence of, 44, 99; interlocking relationship with other New Christian Right litigating organizations, 42–43, 87; Legal Advisory Group, 43; as legal overseer, 56; and Liberty Council, 40; and media access, 125; mission statement, 41; and National Legal Resources Center, 33; and National Litigation Academy, 40, 43, 56; obligation of ADF-trained lawyers, 44, 56; and prelitigation, 131; and public education, 128; and *Rosenberger v. Rector and Visitors of the University of Virginia,* 51, 66, 74; and Rutherford Institute, 35, 36; and *Santa Fe Independent School District v. Doe,* 76; training resources for affiliated attorneys, 43. *See also* Sears, Alan

American Anti-Slavery Society, 15

American Bible Society, 16

American Center for Law and Justice, 1, 11, 28, 29, 30, 36, 40–41, 100, 120, 140; and ADF, 43; and aggressive litigation, 39; attorney network, 87; and *Berger v. Rensselaer Central School Corporation,* 95; case selection criteria, 49; creation of, 36– 37; efforts outside the courtroom, 121; and European Centre for Law and Justice, 39; and fundraising, 124–25; and *Hsu v. Roslyn Union Free School District,* 90–91; institutionalization of, 39; and *Lamb's Chapel v. Center Moriches Union Free School District,* 73; as legal overseer, 57; and media access, 38, 125, 126; and nonlitigation efforts, 133; and public education efforts, 129; and *Rosenberger v. Rector and Visitors of the University of Virginia,* 75; and *Santa Fe Independent School District v. Doe,* 76, 129, 131; and Slavic Centre for Law and Justice, 39; source of funding, 38. *See also* Fournier, Keith; Robertson, Marion G. (Pat); Sekulow, Jay Alan

American Civil Liberties Union, 169n. 39; and Center for Law and Religious Freedom, 32; as model for New Christian Right activism, 11, 47, 137, 140; challenges governmental aid to religion, 25; New Christian Right criticism of, 8–9; reaction to New Christian Right public education efforts, 129, 169n. 37; and Rutherford Institute, 35

American Council of Christian Churches, 19

American Family Association, 3, 5–6, 27

American Jewish Congress, 8, 11, 25, 32, 47, 137

Americans United for the Separation of Church and State, 8, 25, 32, 129

American Temperance Society, 14

American Temperance Union, 14

Anti-Saloon League, 15

Apostle Paul, 39, 46

Attorney General's Commission on Pornography, 42

About the Author

Steven P. Brown holds a Ph.D. from the University of Virginia and is an assistant professor of political science at Auburn University.